ONCE UPON
A TIME IN MAKKAH

ONCE UPON
A TIME IN MAKKAH

THE STORY OF
SALEH KAMEL
VISIONARY, ENTREPRENEUR, PHILANTHROPIST

With best wishes,
Patricia Lancaster

Best wishes
Sir William Patey

PATRICIA LANCASTER & SIR WILLIAM PATEY

NOMAD
PUBLISHING

ONCE UPON A TIME IN MAKKAH

The Story of Saleh Kamel, Visionary, Entrepreneur & Philanthtropist
Patricia Lancaster & Sir William Patey KCMG

© Dar Saleh Limited 2024

Note:
Nomad Publishing is also issuing a twin Arabic edition to this biography
of Saleh Kamel, with many similarities to this English edition, but
separately authored in its own original Arabic edition,
under ISBN 9781914325960 as

من مكة وإليها - سيرة صالح عبدالله كامل

Published by Nomad Publishing in 2024
Email: info@nomad-publishing.com
www.nomad-publishing.com

ISBN 978-1-914325-77-9

Contents

AUTHOR FOREWORD

Having worked in Middle East journalism for more than 40 years, I had heard the name Saleh Kamel many times in a variety of business contexts. I remember reading an obituary when Saleh Kamel died in 2020 and thinking the world had lost one of the great Saudis, one of a generation instrumental in making the kingdom the global powerhouse it is today.

My co-writer on this book, Sir William Patey, who has enjoyed a long and distinguished career in the British Foreign Service, acting as the British Ambassador to a number of countries in the region, including Saudi Arabia, had met Saleh Kamel a number of times but was on little more than nodding terms. It was therefore, with an open mind that we approached writing Saleh Kamel's story. Both of us were intrigued by this boy from the sandy alleys of Makkah who grew up to develop a multibillion-dollar business empire, growing in step with the meteoric rise of the once humble desert kingdom of Saudi Arabia to major international prominence. Who doesn't want to know more about starting out with little and turning it into a very great deal?

However, during the course of our research – interviewing family, friends, business associates and employees, in Saudi Arabia, Egypt, Tunisia and London – we were to learn that there was much, much more to the remarkable Saleh Kamel than his billionaire status.

We would discover a human being with insight and vision who believed that serving God, his country, the needs of his family and of mankind as a whole, were paramount to his continued success, wellbeing and happiness; a man with deep religious beliefs and huge integrity who 'played fair' and yet who was listed by Forbes as a leading global millionaire while still in his early forties.

I personally have been deeply moved by some of the accounts of Saleh Kamel's family, friends and associates. The stories of his business acumen are legion but those who knew him well shared accounts of his quick humour, his generosity, his deep empathy with people of all creeds, colours and social strata, and his many random acts of kindness.

As we neared completion of this book – which I hope you will enjoy – I was aware that I would miss Saleh Kamel. I have thoroughly enjoyed meeting his family and those who knew and loved him. Being part of telling the story of this remarkable man has been a privilege and, even though to my great sadness I was never able to meet him in person, I know I shall carry a part of Saleh Kamel – his wit and his wisdom –in my heart, wherever I go.

Patricia Lancaster, with William Patey
March 2024

CHAPTER ONE

THE EARLY YEARS

A tall, though slightly stooped man, dressed in an immaculate white *thobe*[1] and *ghutra*[2] , walked slowly but purposefully along the 200m stretch of Corniche in Jeddah at dusk. His madas sandals were hand tooled in leather and artfully embroidered in the traditional style. He leaned somewhat heavily on a carved ebony stick, topped by an elegantly fashioned bone handle.

Most of the families enjoying the balmy sea air on the Corniche that evening would have recognised Saleh Kamel, the billionaire entrepreneur, media mogul, banker and businessman they had watched on television and been reading about in newspapers and magazines for most of their lives.

Walking was not a pastime Saleh Kamel – despite the best advice of his doctors – engaged in overmuch, but it was during a recent family to Cannes, the charming Mediterranean riviera town on the south coast of France, that he rediscovered how very pleasant a walk by the sea can be on a gentle, temperate evening. Today had been a trying one. Business presented myriad challenges that usually he delighted in meeting but today he was in need of a little time for reflection.

This evening, the Corniche in Jeddah, Saleh Kamel observed, did not feel as if it was three thousand and more miles from the Croisette

1   Traditional white gown worn by men in Saudi Arabia
2   Traditional cloth head covering

in Cannes. Around him families strolled together – walking, talking, laughing and quietly but determinedly disagreeing. Fathers pushing prams while at the same time chastising their sons; mothers wiping away tears when an ice cream suddenly bit the dust, leaving only a sad and empty cone behind; skateboarding teenagers annoying everyone else on the pedestrianised walkway, despite their obvious and impressive skills. People were not so different, wherever in the world you found them.

Although a gregarious man Saleh Kamel sometimes enjoyed solitary times such as these. He thought again of Cannes and how he would enjoy being there again with the family in August. Between now and then there would be many thousands of air miles racked up, to cities around the world, but these would be mainly business trips and, although there was usually an element of business in all his journeys, Cannes held a special place in his heart.

Some wonderful, relaxing times had been spent there, watching his own children, and now his grandchildren, grow up.

Across the wide, pink asphalt, pedestrian walkway, a dark coloured limousine, kept pace with Saleh Kamel's slow but steady perambulation. The waves of the Red Sea pounded relentlessly against the concrete piers below and the elderly gentleman wondered, not for the first time, why he did not take this route home from the office more often. It was not the fastest course between the two points but it was, beyond doubt, the most beautiful.

Sitting on the various benches strategically placed for those enjoying the sea air, Saleh Kamel noticed children of all ages – oblivious to the activity around them – tapping away on their mobile phones, their thumbs doing a frenzied jig across individual keyboards. He smiled. This is progress, like it or not, he thought.

As he watched some of the young faces, seemingly enthralled by what they were viewing, his mind was transported back over more than six or seven decades to his childhood home in Makkah when, as a young boy, he would be equally engrossed in childhood pursuits.

He recalled one particular game - kuboosh -played with sheep bones – at which he had excelled. A large circle would be drawn in the dust of the alley behind his home with a bare heel. Each young player would then place a selection of small sheep bones – of similar sizes – within the circle. The other players would seek to remove the bones by hurling stones at them. The winner would be the boy whose bone remained in situ to the last.

Hours had been spent in that dusty Makkah alley. He could almost hear the triumphant cries of the young victor as a particularly difficult bone was sent packing.

There was a definite skill to dislodging the bones; some boys did it with aplomb, others were hopeless. A heavy bone was a definite advantage – some of the lighter ones would skitter right out of the circle with little more than a strong breath on them.

Saleh Kamel laughed to himself as he recalled how the game and the sheep bones had provided him not only with hours of fun, but also with an early opportunity to explore his resourcefulness. Aged about eight or nine, he realised that by filling the bones with metal, thus adding to their weight, he could greatly increase their potential for remaining in the circle. He filled a few with lead and, when they had registered considerable success, sold them on to his playmates. Soon he was inundated with orders. Those lead-filled bones became very popular with local boys, he recalled with an inward chuckle.

The night sky around him was filled with high-rise buildings, each of them lit up in a different colour. This was a very different Jeddah from the city of his youth. Throughout its long history Jeddah, which Saleh Kamel first grew to know and love in his early teens, has always been an important city. Sometimes referred to as the Bride of the Red Sea, its success owes much to its geographical location as the gateway for Muslims travelling from across the globe to visit Islam's holy cities of Makkah and Madinah.[3]

---

3 Makkah and Madinah are the official Saudi spellings of the holy cities, often also known internationally as Mecca and Medina respectively.

Jeddah's pilgrimage trade, together with its flourishing seaport, had made it the centre of economic activity in the Kingdom of Saudi Arabia for many decades. The second largest conurbation in the country after Riyadh, it had been the diplomatic capital of the country and the location of the Saudi Ministry of Foreign Affairs, as well as the embassies and missions of foreign governments until the 1980s, when these were transferred to Riyadh.

The historic centre of the city, known as the Al Balad district, was established around 646 CE, although there is evidence of human habitation there as long ago as 250 BCE. In the early years of the 16th century, the city was frequently the target of attacks by itinerant Bedouin tribes and also by marauding Portuguese troops seeking to enrich their European empire.

At the instigation of Mamluk Sultan Al-Ghori, the penultimate Mamluk sultan, a fortified wall was constructed around the city in 1509. Six strong gates allowed the free flow of people and horse-drawn transport during the hours of daylight, and safety and security from pillage and plunder, when they were closed against all comers every evening at dusk. By 1947, with the growth in popularity of the automobile, the city walls were demolished and economic expansion swiftly followed. New buildings were erected, the harbour was deepened and enlarged to accommodate bigger vessels, and a desalination plant – the world's largest at the time – was constructed in the early 1970s. The city's economy, once dependent on pilgrim expenditures and fishing, diversified to include steel-rolling mills, oil refineries, and the manufacture of cement and pottery.

Though different from the Jeddah of his youth, it was the city in which he had chosen to make his home for the last few decades, and this evening, with the people, the lights, and the sound of the sea, there was nowhere else in the world Saleh Kamel would rather be, he reflected before signalling to his driver and walking towards his car for the short drive home along the seafront.

Saleh Kamel was regarded as something of a legend, both in Saudi

Arabia and internationally, yet most of his nine children insist that for much of their childhoods they were completely unaware of the lofty position their father held in the world of international business. While the outside world saw him as a powerhouse of innovation, ingenuity, and achievement, to his children, at least in their early years, he was just "Baba" – the popular Arabic term for "Dad" – a regular, easygoing, fun-to-be-with father who always had time to listen and, when necessary, provide emotional support.

Saleh Kamel would have strongly disagreed with wider public opinion that everything he touched turned to gold. Far from claiming to have the Midas touch, he readily admitted to his failures. He once told his daughter Aseel[4] that if he ever wrote a book, it would not be about his successes, because they were well documented, but about his failures, which, as he wryly observed, nobody knew very much about.

"The important thing is not winning or losing but being ready to grasp the opportunities as they arise. That was what my father firmly believed," added Aseel.

Saleh Kamel was born on August 7, 1941, in the beautiful mountain town of Taif, an hour's drive east of Makkah. His family, like so many others, left their Makkan home during the summer months to escape the intense heat of the holy city. In the case of Saleh Kamel's father, the move was instigated at the command of his employers, the Royal Court, which would decamp to Taif for the hot season.

At this time Saudi Arabia as we know it today was barely ten years old. Its founder, King Abdul Aziz bin Abdulrahman Al Saud, known as Ibn Saud, was in the twilight of his life. The history of modern Saudi Arabia began in 1902 when the young Ibn Saud, then in exile

---

4 The name Aseel, with a root meaning of "smooth and silky" is completely different in Arabic from the name of her sister, Asseel, with a root meaning of dusk or sunset, who also appears in this book. In English the names transliterate to be almost the same. This note is added to try to pre-empt any natural confusion between the two when written in English.

in Kuwait, led a group of warriors to recapture Riyadh. It was to take another ten years to drive the Turkish garrisons from Al Hasa on the Gulf, only leaving the western kingdom of Hijaz under the control of the Hashemites supported by the Turks. By 1925, Ibn Saud had taken control of the Hijaz, which contained the two holy cities of Makkah and Madinah, as well as Jeddah. Makkah was captured in 1924, and a year later Jeddah was taken. Ibn Saud was declared the King of Nejd and Hijaz, which united the west and east of the peninsula of Saudi Arabia.

This status was recognised by Britain in 1927 with the Treaty of Jeddah, although the Russians had got in first with diplomatic recognition a few months earlier. Within a few years, Ibn Saud faced a rebellion by members of the Ikhwan (the followers of Muhammad Ibn Abd Al-Wahhab, not to be confused with the outlawed Akhwan Al-Muslimineen in Egypt), who had helped in his military conquest of the Hijaz. With the crushing of the rebellion, Ibn Saud reached the zenith of his power.

Prior to the rise of the House of Ibn Saud, the Hijaz, including Makkah, Taif, and Jeddah, was governed by the Hashemite Sharif Hussein Ibn Ali under the authority of the Ottoman Sultan. By the time Saleh Kamel was born in 1941, the Hashemite and Turkish garrisons had been expelled from the Hijaz by Ibn Saud, and the Kingdom of the Nejd and Hijaz had been renamed the Kingdom of Saudi Arabia in 1932 to reflect the fact it had been conquered by Ibn Saud.

Saleh Kamel's father Abdullah was just a young boy when Ibn Saud made his entry into Makkah, in 1924. As an old man, Abdullah would fascinate his grandchildren by recounting, almost in the style of an exciting and exotic fairy tale, how "the Brothers Army" entered the holy city, dressed in *ihram* (the Islamic dress for performing Umrah or pilgrimage) and on horseback. "It was very exciting for us," Abdullah told them. "We were just boys, almost lost in the crowd, being jostled and carried along, our feet barely touching the ground. Everyone was headed in the same direction – to see the Brothers galloping around the Kaaba on their beautiful horses, shouting loudly that Makkah was now protected by the peace of Allah and the peace of Ibn Saud."

Saleh Kamel was always a dutiful son who took his responsibilities to his parents very seriously from an early age. His family noted that after the death of his parents, and even during their lifetime, when he could not be with them, Saleh Kamel would begin every day by listening to a tape recording made by his mother and father, asking God to bless his efforts in the day ahead.

To fully understand this devotion, it is important to know a little of the Kamel family history.

Over recent decades, the Kamel family has worked hard to achieve its success, but its labours were not always so well rewarded. The family has known hard times financially – indeed, when asked if he was born with a silver spoon in his mouth, Saleh Kamel once quipped that even to own a spoon was an advantage that should never be underestimated.

By the time Saleh Kamel's father, Abdullah, was born in 1910, his grandfather Mohammad Ibrahim Kamel, the President of the Scholars at the Holy Haram in Makkah, was already elderly and infirm. When poor health forced Mohammad to reduce his working hours, the family's income decreased accordingly.

Mohammad had hoped Abdullah would follow in his footsteps and become a religious scholar, but his son, although he showed great promise at school, was forced to leave full time education when the family could not afford to buy the necessary books to equip him for the final year of study leading up to his exams.

In desperation, Mohammad took the young Abdullah to the cloth shop of his cousin Issa, and asked for a small loan to cover the shortfall between his savings and the price of the necessary books. Issa angrily refused to grant the loan but said if the family really was in such dire financial straits, he would offer Abdullah a full-time job in his shop.

Abdullah did not hesitate. In the absence of a living wage from his father's labour, it was clear that the burden of keeping the proverbial "wolf from the door" would now require his own financial input. Accordingly, he quit school and started work at Issa's cloth shop early the next morning. In his later years, he sometimes recalled how, although he did not resent going out to work to help support his family, he was desperately unhappy at the way his father had been humiliated by having insufficient funds to pay for his continued education.

Even though Abdullah worked long hours selling cloth, in the evenings the boy would attempt to keep up with his studies by reading the books and homework of his former classmates. His hard work paid off when his teacher, impressed by his former pupil's diligence, allowed Abdullah to take the final examination, even though he was no longer officially a student at the school. Abdullah rewarded his teacher's confidence by passing with flying colours.

Having proved himself a loyal and trustworthy employee in the cloth shop for just less than two years, Abdullah, now aged 17, was able to apply for a position as a clerk in the Ministry of Foreign Affairs. In later life, he would recall an episode when he was called upon to clear his Uncle Issa's overflowing sewage well; the task reinforced his decision to make the move from his uncle's shop and join the civil service. It was an action that would change the Kamel family fortunes forever.

Abdullah's career in government would take him from a position as lowly clerk to becoming Director-General of the Prime Minister's Office. He was a well-loved and trusted employee of Prince (later King) Faisal, whom he worked alongside for some 44 years.

Those who knew him well believe Abdullah never forgot his father's early humiliation and say he strived to ensure that none of his own children should ever be put in a similar position. In addition to his impressive career in government, he ran a successful business as a *mutawif* – an individual appointed by the Ministry of Hajj to act as a guide for pilgrims, providing a variety of essential supports and services. Abdullah first began the job as a young boy, running errands and performing other small tasks for pilgrims. Later he would be granted a license to operate as an Umrah & Hajj company – often referred to by Saleh Kamel and his colleagues as the Tawafa Company. It was expensive to procure this permission, but it meant Abdullah was officially licensed to travel abroad to recruit potential pilgrims from their native lands, thus greatly increasing his earning potential.

On the dusty streets of his beloved Makkah, Saleh Kamel continued to reveal an entrepreneurial flair rare in one so young. Following his earliest exploit as a seller of sheep bones, he saw the potential in one of his mother's most delicious recipes – a traditional concoction of boiled chickpeas, spices, and sour pickles known locally as *baleela*. The young Saleh Kamel persuaded his mother to make a large quantity of the dish, and within minutes he managed to sell all his stock, while it was still warm and at a considerable profit, to a group of friends playing in the alley outside his home.

On a television programme more than six decades later, Saleh Kamel noted: "I like to work ... Even as a child I would enjoy making toys and trinkets that I would sell to my friends." This zeal for identifying a need and transforming it into a business opportunity would remain strong throughout his life.

A childhood friend, Ahmed Al Hamdan, remembered another example of how Saleh Kamel employed his entrepreneurial acumen and zeal when, as young as just nine or ten years old, Saleh Kamel and his primary-school classmates were attempting to put on an end-of-year concert for staff and students:

"We had ambitions to put on a small play and decided the performance would be much enhanced by wearing costumes and perhaps producing a few programmes. However, we were just schoolboys, little kids. There was no money available for such things. Most of us shrugged our shoulders and thought no more of it. The show would go on without costumes and programmes, as far as we were concerned. But Saleh Kamel could not let it rest. He thought about it for maybe 24 hours and came back to us with a plan.

"He decided that we would visit local dignitaries and business-men to plead our case. We would describe our dilemma and explain how their sponsorship could solve the problem. I'm not sure we were all on the same page. I still remember feeling rather overawed to meet some of the local big-shots of the time. But Sheikh Saleh was unfazed and, of course, he was proved right. For the most part, they admired our courage in approaching them and rewarded us with enough cash for us to fulfil our ambition to buy simple costumes and produce a few programmes. The school play that year was a big success."

Drawing on that early experience, Ahmed Hamdan went on to note:

"Later in life, Sheikh Saleh was to succeed in bringing a range of entertainment to millions of people through his media enterprises. I like to think that I played a small part in his first triumph in that arena."

A one-time colleague in his media enterprises and a professor of media studies, Cairo-based Dr. Sami Abdul Aziz, would describe Saleh Kamel as a "fisherman of opportunities. Saleh Kamel was always good at catching them, regardless of their location!"

His children would agree with this description but confirm that making money was not the be-all and end-all for their father. His daughter Haneen explained:

"We might be sitting at the dinner table with him, having a conversation, when suddenly he would become silent and gaze into thin air. It happened a lot. I came to realize he was consid-ering some new scheme or business idea that had popped into his mind, probably triggered by the conversation we had been having minutes earlier.

"It wasn't simply about making money with my father; it was

part of who he was. It was in his blood, you might say. He was constantly thinking about ways of making or improving things, right up until the end of his life. If his ideas made money that was, of course, a bonus, but it was not the driving force."

Saleh Kamel's beginnings were humble, but he was not alone in this. These were humble times in the Kingdom of Saudi Arabia as the country sought to find its place on the world stage. Today, for those who do not know the country, the first thing that comes to mind about Saudi Arabia is the immense oil wealth that began to dominate global energy markets during the 1970s. But the images most commonly associated with Saudi Arabia during its early oil age are a million miles from day-to-day life in the desert Kingdom less than a generation before.

During Saleh Kamel's early childhood, it would have been impossible to envisage the modernized oil-rich state Saudi Arabia has become today. Oil had only been discovered in 1938, and although the Kingdom would eventually account for 20% of the world's oil known oil reserves, back in the 1940s the economy of the Hijaz region was based exclusively on trade and religious tourism largely controlled by a handful of leading merchant families. The Saudi Arabia of the final decade of Ibn Saud's life was unrecognisable from the world of Saleh Kamel's childhood years.

"We had no supermarkets or refrigerators back then," Saleh Kamel would tell his children. "Shopping was done every day – the bakers for bread, the butchers for meat, and so on. There was no electricity available in Makkah, except in the Holy Mosque, where electricity was provided courtesy of a special generator installed by an Indian man called Kindiwani. Most students in Makkah would study at the Holy Mosque because it was the only place lit with electricity, my brother Hassan and I among them.

"I remember the first night I saw our town lit with electricity. My brother Hassan and I arrived from Taif to find all the streets of Makkah glowing brightly, which was something entirely new to us. It looked beautiful. Before that, there were small power stations, like that in the Holy Mosque, while in the alleys we had power generators, installed to power the grain mills that produced our flour. These same generators also charged radio and car batteries, although in those days, cars in Makkah were few and far between. Indeed, car owners were regarded as local celebrities.

"As boys, if we saw numerous radio batteries on charge as we walked through the alleys, we knew that a concert broadcast by the Egyptian singer Umm Kulthoum[5] was imminent.

"People gathered in each other's houses to listen to her concerts. Crowds would gather together at all sorts of places to listen to Umm Kulthoum; those lucky enough to have a radio would open their shutters wide to allow their neighbours to hear her voice. Her voice was regarded as something wonderful to be enjoyed by the whole community.

"Years later, the Commission for the Promotion of Virtue and the Prevention of Vice considered this act sinful and chased people who did that across the desert."

Saleh Kamel marvelled at the change. "It's amazing how religious beliefs, which one would imagine should always remain constant, alter and change with changes in social attitudes and peoples' beliefs."

For most of Ibn Saud's reign he ruled over a feudal pre-industrial society. By the time the founding King of the country died – in Taif on November 2, 1953 – oil revenues were beginning to flow. Between 1938 and 1958 the Saudi government's annual revenues rose from $7 million to peak above $180 million. During this period there was no central government service to speak of. The civil service barely existed beyond a handful of the King's advisers and secretaries. These were the earliest days of the modernisation of the Kingdom, when nearly

---

5 Umm Kulthoum was an Egyptian singer and film actress active from the 1920s to the 1970s. For many years she was the leading singer of the Arab world, and her songs to this day are classics well known by all.

every new innovation was opposed by conservative theologians. In one instance Ibn Saud overcame religious objections to the wireless and radio by convincing theologians that any instrument capable of conveying the words of the Holy Quran could not possibly be the work of the devil.

Before his death, Ibn Saud had made provision for the succession to pass down the line of his sons. Saleh Kamel lived long enough to see that succession pass through six kings: Saud, Faisal, Khalid, Fahd, Abdullah, and Salman, the last of the sons of Abdul Aziz to ascend to the throne of Saudi Arabia.

During these seminal years, Saleh Kamel's father, Abdullah Mohammad Kamel, was a government employee, based in Jeddah. Honest and conscientious, Abdullah's strongly developed work ethic would bring him to the attention of Prince Faisal bin Abdul Aziz, the third of Ibn Saud's sons, who would reign as king from 1964 to 1975.

In the beginning however, although Abdullah held a respectable position, remuneration was far from lavish and he, like many government employees, sought other employment to boost the family income.

The young Saleh Kamel showed an awareness of his family's circumstances, which were generally mirrored in those of his friends. As old friend Ahmed Al Hamdan noted:

"Nobody was rich in those days. We were all in the same boat. We were well cared for, but there was no money for what we would have regarded as luxuries. In fact, I'm not sure we would even have understood the concept of luxuries. Our mothers would cook a family meal, which included meat maybe once a week. That was probably the closest to luxury we got back then."

With his father away in Jeddah working to help build a secure base for his wife and children, the young Saleh Kamel worked hard to be supportive towards his mother and to help keep his younger siblings in check. His parents had high hopes of his oldest brother Hassan going to university, and he was always encouraged to study. Hassan would repay their confidence by becoming a doctor, specialising in paediatrics, once he had completed his studies in Cairo. Saleh Kamel would later recall:

"I was very attached to my elder brother Hassan. They let me go to school with him when I was far too young to understand anything much that was being taught; I just wanted Hassan's company. I sat next to him during his first primary year and when he moved on to the second grade, I continued to attend school with him. This went on throughout Hassan's second and third grades until he joined the fourth grade, when I was old enough to attend first-grade classes myself.

"Because I was always with Hassan, his friends and classmates were also mine; they became my peers. Consequently, the difference in age and interests that would normally apply were overlooked. They saw me as being among their peers. This may have given me an extra maturity.

"As for my life outside the school, I was naughtier and more mischievous than Hassan. He was the first-born, so my parents practiced their parenting skills on him and based their rules for the rest of us on Hassan's personality. When I came along, I broke many of those rules.

"Hassan was calm and did not participate in dangerous games with the other kids in the alley, whereas I was something of a daredevil. There were two types of children in the alley: the naughty ones and the well-behaved ones. Hassan was of the latter. I was not".

"Putting lead in the *kuboosh* bones was probably my first 'work'. I was then between seven and eight years old – I do not remember exactly. Another source of capital came from tips from our father's customers – pilgrims coming to Makkah from Turkey, Iraq, and Libya.

"Hassan and I would do small jobs for them, running errands or perhaps bringing them tea. As a reward they would leave us a small tip for our services before they left for their respective homelands. When we received this cash, Hassan would spend his – often, at my insistence, on me – but I would always save mine. In this way I began accumulating money in a capital fund." For many years, the Kamel family enjoyed a strong association with the Hajj and pilgrims from across the world. One of the five tenets of Islam demands that every Muslim who is able must make the pilgrimage, known as the Hajj, at least once in their lifetime.

The Hajj is always made in the twelfth and final month of the Islamic calendar (Dhu al-Hijjah), when the population of Makkah has been known to triple. Meanwhile, those making the Umrah, or lesser pilgrimage, are a feature throughout the year, ensuring a steady stream of income, particularly welcome in the days before the commercial exploitation of Saudi Arabia's oil wealth, making it the obvious place for Abdullah to channel his energies when he looked for a means of increasing the family coffers. Saleh Kamel recalled:

"I believe I learned to respect the work ethic from my father, who was with the late King Faisal for forty-four years. There were two things my late father, God rest his soul, loved – his work and his family. He always wanted the best for us, so in addition to his employment as a government official, and later with King Faisal, he supplemented his income by working as a guide – a *mutawif*[6] – in Makkah."

"His own father, my grandfather Mohamed Kamel, was a man of great knowledge and was President of Scholars at the Holy Mosque in Makkah for some years, during the time of the Ottomans. All pilgrimage guides at that time had to be certified by my grandfather. When the time came, it was an obvious way for my father to earn a little extra money to help his family."

Later, Saleh Kamel would also work as a mutawif for pilgrims visiting Makkah. Having spent his youth and childhood in the city, he

---

6 A *mutawif* was much more than a mere guide. A *mutawif* would often travel far afield to recruit pilgrims to the Hajj and, on their arrival was expected to host, house, feed and take care of them – as a guest of God – in every way.

knew every street and alley, as well as many of the people involved in hospitality. He was well versed and practiced on transportation methods and other essential services. His work as a guide also gave him a particular knack for problem solving and organization that continued throughout his life.

"Logistics held a lifelong fascination for Sheikh Saleh," a childhood friend explained. "He was in his element as a guide, dealing with problems. When a particular bus did not arrive, or when a scheduled delivery of a hundred tents was found to be five or six tents short, for him it was never a disaster but just another of life's challenges."

Abdullah Kamel, Saleh Kamel's father, was keen that all his children should have a good education. However, it is unlikely he ever imagined that the second born of his nine offspring would demonstrate the extraordinary vision and flair required to become one of the Kingdom's wealthiest self-made men, valued by the Forbes Rich List as a billionaire as early as the 1990s.

"My father certainly passed on his work ethic to his children," Sheikh Saleh noted. "He also demanded absolute honesty in all things, and he encouraged us to be supportive and caring of each other. I took my responsibilities to him, my mother, and all my siblings very seriously from an early age.

"My father would often speak about his own father, who is mentioned in several books on the history of Makkah, because of his role as President of the Scholars; he was something of a legend to us all. As far as we knew, the family had lived in Makkah for over 700 years. The Kamel family like to think of themselves as part of the fabric of the Holy City. It plays an important role in our history."

Over the centuries, much has been written about the holy city of Makkah and its people. In ancient times it lay on the old caravan route that linked the countries of the Mediterranean with Southern Arabia, East Africa and South Asia. It was an important trading post, a place where merchants of all races met together to exchange goods, money and ideas. Its cosmopolitan ambience – then and now – is reinforced by the constant flow of visiting pilgrims from around the globe, particularly during the annual Hajj season when the population of the city increases dramatically.

Makkah holds a special allure for all Muslims – it was the birthplace of the Prophet Muhammad and a destination to which followers of Islam are required to make pilgrimage at least once in their lives, if they can afford to do so. The city is also the home of the Holy Kaaba, which stands at the heart of the of the Sacred Mosque and marks the direction to which Muslims turn in prayer five times a day.

During the early years of Abdullah Kamel, the economy of the holy city was dependent on the sale of dates, animal hides, and pilgrim revenues. The city is among the world's most ancient entrepôts and, with its rich cultural heritage, probably the most diverse in the Muslim world. Camel caravans once formed a vital part of the city's bustling economy. Nomadic tribes would bring their wares, including locally mined metals such as gold, silver, copper, tin, and lead, plus their livestock and leather products, to be sold or traded for goods from as far away as Africa, India and China. The famous scholar and traveller Ibn Battuta first visited the city in the first half of the 14th century and remained there for three years. He recorded daily events, including the Hajj, the camel caravans and day-to-day life in the city at that time, in detail. Ibn Battuta was particularly complimentary about the people of Makkah, whom he praised for being clean, humble, and kind. Makkans were also willing to share everything they had to help someone who had nothing, the scholar observed.

In his early years, the young Saleh Kamel would see the centuries-old, trader mentality in operation all around him – buying, selling, exchanging one range of goods for another. Such vibrant trade was commonplace not only in shops and offices, but also in the market and even on street corners.

Traditionally, those who are able travel to from Makkah to Taif to escape the intense heat of the summer months – which regularly rise to more than 49 °C (121°F). The popular mountain resort lies some 65km (40 miles) to the south, at an altitude of 1,500m (about 5,000 feet) above Makkah. Every summer, Saleh Kamel and his family would relocate to this mountain retreat, known and loved for its rich bounty of grapes, pomegranates, figs, roses, and honey. After the searing heat of Makkah, Taif's cool mountains, deep wadis, and lush fruit groves provided a welcome retreat Saleh Kamel would speak fondly of throughout his life.

He would recall the distinctive smell of the roses grown in the region, famous for their unique 30-petal bloom and the distinctive oil (or *attar*), it produced. Taif roses continue to be harvested to provide some of the world's most expensive rose oil, sometimes referred to by the international perfume trade as the "Essence of Arabia". Saleh Kamel would insist that this smell, wherever in the world he came across it, would instantly transport him to his childhood and summers in the cool, green mountains of Taif.

Clearly, the young Saleh Kamel had a great appetite for life. A contemporary of the time remembers how his natural leadership qualities always made him a popular figure to be around. Saleh Kamel's eldest son, Abdullah, recalls how his father would frequently recount tales of his childhood:

"He would tell us, his children, tales from those days, of his childhood enterprises selling boiled chickpeas and bones filled with lead on many, many occasions. He did not feel ashamed of this, in fact, he was rather proud of it."

And why wouldn't he be? It was clear even then that with his lucrative foray into *baleela* selling and the opportunities offered by his leaded sheep bone sales, the young Saleh Kamel was well and truly on his way.

CHAPTER TWO

THE MAKKAN WAY

S aleh Kamel would often speak of being highly driven in his business dealings, but his compulsion to succeed was not spurred by financial motives alone. It may have started that way, but it was the challenge – the thrill of the chase and the quest for victory – that energised him the most.

A school friend who would go on to become a trusted colleague as VP of Internal Audit and supervision at Saleh Kamel's Dallah company, as well as his general confidante and brother-in-law, Dr Naji Nazer, recalls how Saleh Kamel was always dynamic in his thinking. Referring to the end-of-year play at school, earlier recalled by another friend, for which Saleh Kamel organised groups of students to petition local businessmen and dignitaries for their support, Dr Naji says this vitality stayed with Saleh Kamel all his life.

"Of course, in the eyes of the local big-shots, we were just little boys, but they could see we were enthusiastic and prepared to work towards achieving our goal. People liked our courage and initiative. It encouraged them to be generous.

"Even 50 or 60 years later, Sheikh Saleh had the same sort of charisma. He encouraged people with his energy, his enthusiasm and the belief that with God's help, all things are possible.

"Of course, Sheikh Saleh liked to make money – we all like to see our labour rewarded – but he liked the feeling of satisfaction that came when an idea or a project came to fruition much more. For him that was more important than the cash rewards that accompanied success," added Dr Naji.

In an interview with a leading international business magazine, Saleh Kamel himself outlined how, for him, the thrill of the chase was paramount.

"When I have an idea, I become totally focused on breathing life into it and to getting it off the ground. When it is established, the challenge then is to find the right people to manage it. This is sometimes the most defying aspect of all. A good manager is invaluable in establishing a successful enterprise, while a bad one will destroy any hope of success.

"It is rewarding to see things fall into place and poised for success, but I have noticed that that is also when my focus changes and I begin to look for new opportunities."

Ahmed Al Hamdan recalled with affection how being around Sheikh Saleh was always eventful:

"He was full of good ideas, it made him an entertaining boy to be friends with. Life was always more exciting when Saleh Kamel was leading the game or the task. His attitude encouraged us all to be just a little bit more adventurous, just a little braver."

It was the young Saleh Kamel's courage and initiative, along with his propensity for taking the lead, that had already marked him out as 'one to watch' by the time he had reached his teens. "He showed a great aptitude for zoning in on an opportunity, but more often than not, the opening he identified was to the benefit of all of us, not just to himself," remembers former school friend Siraj Ghurab.

"For example, Sheikh Saleh – like many of us boys – was an enthusiastic member of the scouting movement. He loved the challenges being a part of the organisation presented, as well as the rewards his efforts produced."

The Boy Scout movement was founded in Britain in 1908 by cavalry officer Robert Baden-Powell. It soon became popular around the world and was widely embraced. Baden-Powell's idea was that boys should organize themselves into small groups, or "packs" of six or seven under a boy leader, chosen from their ranks. Their pursuits would include tracking and reconnaissance, mapping, signalling, first aid, and all the skills that arise from camping and general outdoor activities. To become a scout, a boy would promise to be loyal to his country, help other people around him and, in general, obey the scout law, a simple code of chivalrous behaviour. The boys in Saleh Kamel's pack embraced the scouting ethos with enthusiasm.

"However," Siraj Ghurab continued, "there was something sadly lacking in our pack. To become a bona fide part of the international scouting fraternity, we had to have the official Boy Scout uniform and we didn't. "It was Sheikh Saleh who first drew our attention to it. Nobody else had thought to address the question. Life in Saudi Arabia in the 1940s and 50s was not as it is today. There were certain things that were simply not available to us and we accepted that. But not Sheikh Saleh.

He began researching how to import scouting supplies from overseas. Eventually, with the help of his father, he was able to secure a commercial licence – he was probably the youngest Saudi ever to do so – which allowed him to import uniforms, badges, and other types of equipment, to sell to his fellow scouts.

"Very soon, our dusty thobes discarded, we were marching around in full regalia, extremely proud Boy Scouts, running through the alleys of Jeddah wearing our green shirts and shorts, with whistles hanging on our chests."[7]

Saleh Kamel would later describe this process as "identifying a need and utilising the resources available to meet it." It would become his modus operandi and one that would, eventually, lead him to

7   Saleh Kamel maintained a good relationship with both local and regional scout associations, but was never far from the World Scout Foundation which, in recognition of his generous support to the Foundation, awarded him a certificate of Baden-Powell Fellowship on November 3rd 1986.

international billionaire status and the global entrepreneurial halls of fame.

There was no shortage of willing helpers when Saleh Kamel began his first foray into the media at high school. As he explained to a journalist:

"A passion for the media was instilled into me by my school-teachers. Of course, I had no notion of what the media was back in those days, but I knew that I enjoyed my responsibilities organising the school assembly and my position as head of the debating society.

"I was also an avid reader. My father's brother – Abdulsalam who was unmarried, had a great passion for reading, particularly magazines. With no children of his own, he tried to encourage us all – but especially my brother Hassan and I – to become more educated and cultured.

"Both my parents were keen that we should have a good traditional education, but I think they believed some of the things Uncle Abdulsalam encouraged were rather frivolous and might detract from the more serious business of formal schooling.

"Abdulsalam was aware of this, but he knew he was giving us something special by opening up our minds to things that were not available on the school syllabus. He would sneak books out of literature and a variety of magazines into our home, hidden under his clothes and we loved him for it.

"Looking back, I believe he did us a great favour. His 'mischief' sowed the seeds of our cultural development and reading is a passion that has stayed with me all my life."

Saleh Kamel's daughter Haneen remembers many hours spent in bookshops with her father.

"Wherever we went my father would have a favourite bookshop and we would have to spend hours there with him while he chose what seemed, at the time, like dozens of books. I remember there was a shop in London's Westbourne Grove where he could easily spend a whole afternoon – and sometimes did – or so it seemed to us. As children, we just wanted to be out enjoying the excitement of London and all it had to offer, but my father took such pleasure from browsing in a bookshop. Such a simple act. Nobody would ever refuse to accompany him, if invited." Saleh Kamel believed his early love of the written word played a significant part in his later experiences in the media. In a television interview he explained how:

"My first magazine was produced with the help of a group of friends in my second year of secondary school. We had a wall where people could post messages, poems, and short stories, as well as notices requesting items and offering things for sale. I saw immediately how popular it was, everyone congregating there to read anything new that was posted. It occurred to me that this concept might be developed. I decided my best option would be to expand the concept by starting a magazine for my fellow students; I suppose I would have been about 13 years old.

"At that time the Preparatory Scholarship Programme was the only secondary school in the Kingdom, so – in honour of the school – I named the new magazine 'The Mirror of Scholarship'. "I loved reading and it was a real thrill to produce a publication that was immediately successful. I loved seeing it being read by so many students on campus.

"Of course, at that time, I had no comprehension of the importance of the media, nor even the meaning of the word. Later, I would come to realize its vital role in society. I would embark on many media-related projects during my life, but at that time I only knew it made me popular with my friends and, I felt, gained me the respect of my teachers.

"I enjoyed the admiration of those around me, but I was not setting myself any goals. I was simply enjoying the moment. However, over a period of time I realised how what was written in the magazine could influence its readers and make a real difference but this didn't come to me all at once. Each step took time."

In addition to making his mark on the media and journalism, Saleh Kamel was also beginning to develop his diplomatic skills. In an eloquent dedication in the first edition of 'Mirror', he profusely thanked the parents of all the students who had put their energies into producing the publication and dedicated their collective achievement to "His Majesty King Saud", as "an expression of love, loyalty and thanks for a secondary school established by Royal Decree. The dedication added that the students – led by Saleh Kamel – were convinced, as a result of the royal largesse, that they would go on to "record educational progress in the Kingdom in the brightest ink in the pages of Saudi Arabia's history."

Beyond the school gates, others were not slow to recognize the young Saleh Kamel's emerging skills and early triumphs. Some time after the launch of his school magazine, he would become the first Saudi student in Jeddah to be officially honoured for his achievements by the late King Fahd, then the country's Minister of Education.

His old friend from the alleys, Ahmed Al Hamdan, believes that growing up in Makkah made Saleh Kamel look at life in a particular way. He explains his logic carefully:

"Makkah is quite unique. From our earliest years, we were surrounded by people with a gift for spotting commercial opportunities. Some have referred to it as the 'Makkah mentality'. The city is arid and landlocked, its earning capacity is generated almost exclusively by the pilgrims who pass through the city. Each pilgrim presents a window of opportunity, consequently the whole economic ethos of Makkah revolves around serving those religious visitors.

"Any attempt to exploit them would be very much frowned upon by the local community, but that same community must remain focused on the pilgrims' wants and needs and try, wherever possible, to make them happy in order to earn themselves a living.

"If someone comes back to their accommodation after a long

day, they want to relax, drink a cup of tea or coffee, and reflect on all the things they have seen. When you have served ten thousand pilgrims, you realise this and you are prepared, ready with their tea or coffee, when they return home.

"Sheikh Saleh took this 'Makkah mentality' with him through life. He was ever alert to what was required in a particular situation and would put his mind to how he might best fulfil that need."

There is likely much truth in what Ahmad Al Hamdan says, and he is not the first to make the observation. Historians have described Makkah as the Venice of the Middle East, in the sense that as far back as the 14th century, it served as a hub for traders and salesmen from around the region and as a bridge between Europe and Asia.

Makkah occupied a prime location on the ancient trading routes. Its merchants dealt in a wide variety of trade goods, including sugar, salt, textiles, spices, slaves, gold, frankincense, incense, pearls, copper, and horses, and were known far afield for their commercial talent.

With the arrival of Islam in the Arabian Peninsula in the 7th century, trade expanded further towards eastern regions building and developing commercial routes. This greater reach of their territory allowed Makkans to meet diverse people along the routes, including some who, naturally enough, would influence their thinking and beliefs. The famous Islamic scholar and traveller Ibn Battuta who, as previously mentioned, spent two years (1325-1327) in Makkah, living piously in the company of religious scholars, observed:

"The life I lead is one of the most agreeable; I was always part of the processions around the Kaaba, in the service of God, and in the closeness of the Holy sites."

With, or without the commercial influence of his esteemed forefathers, the young Saleh Kamel was a bright boy with a real flair for business who, wisely, never allowed his schoolwork to suffer as a result of his entrepreneurial enthusiasm. Indeed, there are instances of how, bringing the two streams together would sometimes pay dividends, as became apparent during his university years.

Saleh Kamel thrilled his parents by winning a scholarship to study in Cairo, where his elder brother Hassan was already at medical school. In those days it was commonplace for young Saudi men to travel abroad to complete their education, with Cairo and Beirut being popular choices.

However, following the inauguration of Riyadh University (later renamed King Saud University), Saleh Kamel returned to Saudi Arabia.

"There were many reasons,' he explained later. "Hassan was studying medicine, which consumes a lot of time and effort, so we were not able to spend as much time together as I had hoped and I felt I could be more helpful to my family from Riyadh. I was working to increase the Tuwafah business, which was best done from the Kingdom and, when there was a university in my own country, why should I go to a foreign land?"

Ahmed Al Hamdan puts it simply:

"Sheikh Saleh did not find 'his' people in Egypt at that time. Many of his friends from Makkah and Jeddah were already enrolled at Riyadh University (later King Saud University) and, as I have said, Sheikh Saleh was an extremely popular person, so we all tried hard to persuade him to join us there."

Saleh Kamel's student years at the Riyadh University Faculty of Commerce were described by him as being "fertile ones". His friends recall that he was in his element discovering new opportunities.

It did not take Saleh Kamel long to settle down in Riyadh. He moved into a shared villa with a number of friends from Makkah and Jeddah, among them Ahmed Al Hamdan and Siraj Ghurab. Both of them recall how, after the housemates had shared an evening meal, Saleh Kamel would often occupy the communal kitchen for several hours, preparing some savoury dish or sweetmeat to sell at university the following day.

"All the jobs where Allah has best helped me succeed were based on a need of mine or the community", Sheikh Saleh noted in an

interview. His gift, of course, was identifying that need.
Still involved in securing supplies for the burgeoning Scouting movement in the Kingdom, he had managed to locate a competitively priced supplier in Lebanon.

"I travelled to Lebanon and brought back with me Scout suits: belts, knives, whistles, and some books. By this time, I had managed to buy a car, so I would load it up and go around the schools selling items out of the back of the car.

"I had also been made Secretary of the Student Union, and I spent a great deal of time attending to union-related matters. Being a fairly new institution, the university was working hard to develop close links with the local community. We would host symposia, sporting events, and cultural events, to which we would invite a great number of officials, artists, and scholars. It was a successful way of drawing local residents and dignitaries into the life of the university, but it was intensive and required continuous effort. It was a whole new exciting world for most of us, but it also resulted in the problem of keeping up with our studies.

"In order to keep up with my course work, I would borrow lecture notes from other students and copy them at night, which was tiring, especially since the house we shared was often full of distractions."

Ahmed Al Hamdan recounts how Saleh Kamel would often take himself off to a coffee house in the evening. Here he could sit outside, sip coffee, and concentrate on writing up his notes in relative peace and quiet. On more than one occasion he would fall asleep there, only to be woken up, perhaps hours later, by the coffee house owner, anxious to close up his premises."

Ahmed Al Hamdan recalls: "Sheikh Saleh gathered people to him by the sheer force of his personality; that's what made him such an obvious leader. But knowing he would be disturbed at home, he regularly took himself off to find a quiet space where he could write up his notes."

On one such evening, Saleh Kamel decided that he was probably not the only student in the same situation.

"I knew there must be others like me who, for whatever reason, were not always able to be at a particular lecture at a specific time. I needed a means of copying the lecture notes and making them widely available but unfortunately, at that time, photocopying was not yet available.

"I looked into the problem and decided that if I invested in a stencil machine, I could produce multiple copies of the notes I was transcribing and sell them to students in the same position as myself. Before too many days had passed, I became the proud new owner of the machine I hoped would be the answer to my problem. Right from the beginning, I had a strong feeling that, correctly handled, this idea would be one to pay dividends, and it did.

"The stencil machine was expensive and the work had to be turned around quickly. Lecture notes were typed up on special silk paper from which multiple copies could be run off. Of course, with the development of modern technology this would now be a very simple process, but back then it was quite laborious.

"At the beginning, I was concentrating on producing printed notes only for my year, but it soon became clear that there was a much wider market and the enterprise grew.

"However, I knew I had to be careful. There was great suspicion of any sort of printed pamphlet or publication in Saudi Arabia at that time and I did not want to find myself on the wrong side of the law. I knew my work was innocuous but, to be sure, I went to the head of the intelligence service at the time, a gentleman called Umar Shams. I told him what I had in mind and explained my concerns; I said I did not want to find myself accused of distributing publications without permission."

Saleh Kamel was right to be cautious, Saudi Arabia was approaching the end of a difficult period in its history and if there was a mild paranoia in the air around this time, it was not surprising. Throughout his life, Saleh Kamel was careful to adhere to the law wherever he invested and do all possible to ensure that his investments remained safe from any civil disturbances or illegitimate official interference – not always straightforward, as he frequently operated in areas which witnessed more than their fair share of revolutions and political upheaval.

The Kingdom had already been facing financial problems as King Saud took the throne in 1953 on the death of his father, King Abdul Aziz, the founder of modern Saudi Arabia. By the late 1950s Saudi Arabia was facing bankruptcy and was forced to seek a loan from the International Monetary Fund (IMF).

Around the same time, the influence of Egypt's leader, Gamal Abdul Nasser, was on the rise across the Arab world. Following his nationalisation of the Suez Canal in 1956, he promoted a new and intoxicating brand of Arab nationalism in which there was no place for Arab kings. Nasser was seen as a direct threat to the Al Saud. Following claims in Egyptian newspapers that King Saud was behind a plot to assassinate Nasser, numerous Arab newspapers denounced the Saudi monarch. Meanwhile, in Cairo, Nasser called for the overthrow of the Al Saud family and sent Egyptian troops to Yemen.

In response to both internal and regional challenges – such as the threat from Nasser, the war in Yemen, and economic difficulties – Crown Prince Faisal took the helm and started his programme of reform. Within a few years, Faisal's skilful economic management and strict programme of austerity had reduced the national debt and set the country on a new path. He also tightened control of various administrative reforms and greatly improved the country's education system, particularly in regard to women.

With the death of Imam Ahmed ibn Yahya, the warrior monarch who drove the Turks out of Yemen and was murdered in an attempted coup in the country in 1962, Saudi Arabia soon found itself involved in a proxy war with Nasser's Egypt, with over 60,000 Egyptian troops on Saudi Arabia's southern border. In such a climate, Saleh Kamel's desire to have total transparency in his dealings showed a keen appreciation of the pervading political situation.

> "At the time, it was risky for an individual to own a printing machine or anything similar because of the possibility such a contraption might be used to produce political publications. I was well aware of this so I asked Umer Shams if he would send a typist from the intelligence service to work with me. In this way, I reasoned, the intelligence service could ensure that everything was above board, keep an eye on me, and be sure my work was no threat to anyone.

> "He laughed at my worries but, nevertheless, he appointed not one but three typists from the intelligence service to work for me part-time. Thereafter, I had three excellent typists and also avoided scrutiny from the security services, or any of the related problems that might result from their suspicions.

> "I made a good profit from student notes produced from that stencil machine. Suddenly, business was booming. Eventually, I couldn't handle all the business from home so I leased a shop in the Al-Malaz district of the city."

Once he had completed his studies at King Saud University, Saleh Kamel took up a position at the Ministry of Labour and Social Affairs for a short time. His next career stop was the Ministry of Finance, where he was part of a team supervising the spending and overlooking the expenses of a number of government ministries. He acquitted himself well at the Ministry of Finance, being promoted many times and receiving numerous letters of appreciation – including one from the Minister of Health – thanking him for plans he had mapped out and control systems he had put in place for the Ministry. He was a hardworking employee, and in 1968 was sent for a six-month training seminar on planning and development held at the Saudi General Management Institute.

It was during his time at the Finance Ministry, according to friends and former colleagues, that Saleh Kamel fine-tuned his financial skills. As one explained:

"Sheikh Saleh was never short of ideas. He always had one or two projects on the go and one or two more waiting in the wings. He was blessed with an imagination for these things. However, his years with the Ministry of Finance gave him the necessary expertise to be able to develop and expand as a businessman. During his years there, he refined and polished his financial acumen to the point where, along with the idea for a new business venture, he also possessed the proficiency to cost it and to anticipate any hiccups – in short, make a much more informed decision than he might have been capable of previously."

As students living together in the villa in Riyadh, the young friends had often discussed their hopes and ambitions. Saleh Kamel had high regard for family life and made no secret of his ambition to become a husband and father sooner rather than later.

In the Riyadh of the late 1950s and early 1960s, marriages – while not strictly "arranged" – were often encouraged and even engineered by families. If a suitable partner could not be found within the extended family – cousins or second cousins – the net would be cast a little wider to include family friends or close associates. As with most things, Saleh Kamel was rather more independent than most when it came to choosing a bride.

Still elegantly beautiful and surrounded by her children and a variety of nephews, nieces, and grandchildren in the Jeddah family home she shared with Saleh Kamel for many years, his wife Mayda takes up the story:

"Sheikh Saleh was a friend of my brothers, Abdulfattah and Naji Nazer. He knew them both well but it was my cousin Ibrahim who first showed him my photograph. Sheikh Saleh must have liked what he saw because he began driving to my school and watching me as I left at the end of the day. I would have been about sixteen years old. Sheikh Saleh was twenty-four.

"We never exchanged words, but it was brought to my attention that he would like to meet me. Everything was handled in the traditional way – in those days it was traditional or nothing – so he respectfully approached Abdulfattah, who talked to my father, and a meeting was arranged. I had nothing to do with it, everything was handled by the men."

For the young Mayda, the sophisticated and worldly young Saleh Kamel must have been an unusual and impressive person to meet. Clearly, he made a good impression: "He was tall – tall and handsome with great charisma," Mayda remembers. "These were attributes my husband would continue to possess until the last day of his life," she added.

Just four months later, on October 3, 1965, Saleh Kamel and Mayda were married in Jeddah and the following October, they welcomed the arrival of their firstborn child, Abdullah.

The newlyweds made their home in Riyadh, where Saleh Kamel was working for the Ministry of Finance. Within a few months, his parents would join them in their large home, where, two years later, they celebrated the birth of a daughter and named her Ghadeer.

Mayda recalls how Saleh Kamel was thrilled when his children were born and especially proud to name his son Abdullah, after his father.

He was very much a "hands-on" father and would happily tend to the every need of his young son and daughter, including feeding and, if necessary, changing diapers, Mayda recalled. Because he was a government employee, keeping regular office hours, he was around a lot in those first two or three years and able to enjoy the early, memorable moments with his two babies. However, thoughts of branching out were already gaining traction. Saleh Kamel had a few irons in the fire, and Mayda was not in the least surprised when he announced his intention to leave the Ministry of Finance and to branch out on his own.

Mayda knew her husband had nurtured business ambitions from a very early age. He had already come a long way from the days when he earned SR40 a year from the Tuwafah business in Makkah, and she didn't doubt for a moment that he would achieve success in whatever he set his mind to.

"I cannot claim to have been directly involved in Sheikh Saleh's attempts to develop his business, but I was always supportive of his work. He was determined and I never doubted he would fulfil his dreams. He would often practice his speeches on me, reading them out and asking for advice on one point or another but, in truth, only rarely could I make a suggestion that would improve on what he had already composed. He really was an excellent public speaker. He didn't need much help."

Saleh Kamel was always an eloquent orator by all accounts. Years later, this proficiency, coupled with his unique skill-set, would make him a popular television show guest, who was frequently asked for – and enthusiastically gave – his opinions on a wide variety of subjects.

Arabic is a rich language, which can be spoken at many levels. Saleh Kamel was, it seems, able to transmit his message to all sections of society without ever being out of his depth.

"He had the gift of being able to transmit his message to every-one. Whether he spoke in 'street' Arabic or classical Arabic, he could grab peoples' attention and hold it until his point was made," explained a business colleague. "I heard him speak at many conferences and it was always a pleasure. He could inject humour and irony into a speech to 500 people in a way that made each of them feel he was speaking directly to them."

In the early years of his marriage Saleh Kamel, then in his late twenties, began to recognise his abilities and realise the possibilities a change of direction might open up for him. His position with the Ministry of Finance had served him well, but it was time to spread his wings. With this in mind, he resigned from government service.

"I had seen first-hand the rewards of government service," he observed. "Maybe that was only back then, but my father worked for 44 years with Prince Faisal (who later became King) and didn't end up a millionaire or even well off.

"When we were in Makkah, his salary frequently ran out before the end of the month and we would be obliged to borrow small amounts of money from a neighbour who ran a firewood business.

"I decided at an early age that that life was not for me. I have always been fascinated by the science of business and the nature of how it works. When I joined the Ministry of Finance, I hoped it would help me develop the skills I learned at the university's Faculty of Business. Before that my idea of business was limited and somewhat primitive. I knew university would help me combine my sense of direction with the more scientific aspects of business development, and it did. Almost immediately, I began applying rules and theories I was learning in the classroom into the family's Tuwafah [pilgrim guide] business.

"Tuwafah is a profession generally passed from generation to generation. It is also seasonal work. I was leading pilgrims around the Kaaba when I was no more than 11 years old. When you have been doing a job as long as that and when you have a passion for the work, it controls your thinking and the way you plan your future work. I found I could implement certain models, discussed in lectures, into the way we operated the family Tuwafah business. As a result, we were able to increase our earnings and our annual pilgrim numbers increased from hundreds to thousands. At the time, when my father was busy in the office of King Faisal and my brother Hassan was studying medicine in Cairo, I found I could run the business very efficiently myself by employing more up-to-date methods of marketing, promotion, accounts control, and, of course, by delegating certain responsibilities to others.

"In some ways Tuwafah was the actual university from which I graduated."

Saleh Kamel was known as something of a stickler for precision in his business dealings; every "i" had to be dotted and every "t" crossed before he was satisfied. As he would insist, however: "I do not call it precision, I prefer to regard it as giving due attention to detail, giving respect and loyalty to what I do. My colleagues all know that I am basically an accountant, so they are the ones who are usually most keen to be precise.

"I developed a keen sense for this when I worked at the Ministry of Finance. As a financial representative my job was to visit various ministries and government organisations to approve or reject claims for certain items. For example, if a claim was submitted for the purchase of a new vehicle, or several new vehicles at a particular government ministry, I would be dispatched to examine the situation, to decide whether the purchase was essential and, if it was, to ensure that we were getting the best possible price.

"We were not universally popular, but in truth, financial representatives were just control tools to ensure the best possible use of funding within the limit of government budgets.

"At this time, I was also involved in a number of small enterprises of my own. I kept the printing press and my business selling student notes for a couple of years or more after graduating from university in 1963. I had also started up a restaurant and then, observing there was a real need for a women's dress shop in Riyadh, I opened one and named it Ghadeer Fashion, after my young daughter. I recruited a number of skilled tailors from Pakistan to help produce a range of designs which were sold in the shop.

"In the evening, when I came back from work at the Ministry of Finance, I would concentrate on developing opportunities at the printing house, the restaurant, and the dress shop."

Saleh Kamel was ambitious and knew from the experience of his father Abdullah, who had been a trusted employee of King Faisal for more than four decades, that public service would never grant him the rewards he was aiming for. His was not a quest merely for money for money's sake. He was genuinely anxious to see how much he could achieve in building a brand-new business empire – just how far he could push himself.

"I had already registered the Dallah Establishment as a commercial enterprise while I still worked for the government. My intention had always been to gain a secure training before launching my own company. It was just a matter of waiting until the time was right.

"The first bid I made was for the tender to circulate mail around the Kingdom. It was a service that was badly needed, even if the country was not yet aware of it. The only postal services, at the time, existed in the cities, in Riyadh, Jeddah, Makkah, and Taif, but the towns and villages in between were completely without a postal service of any kind. At that time, the company that delivered mail between the cities was the Arabian Auto Company, founded and based in Makkah.

"I thought long and hard about how I could manage to get something more efficient off the ground. Obviously, it would not be possible to establish a post office building in every village, but it occurred to me that if we established a network of drivers, they could both deliver mail and also receive it, by hand, to be delivered elsewhere.

"I put this suggestion to the Ministry of Transportation but heard nothing back from them. Some months later, and just when I had convinced myself that they were not interested in my idea, they announced a tender inviting bids for a contract very much along the lines I had suggested.

"In order to properly research the project, I travelled across the region by van. I calculated the miles covered; the timescale involved, and the costs of fuel. I travelled the miles and did all the costings myself; in that way I knew they were accurate. I was thrilled when I was told that I had won the contract."

However, the contractor who had previously delivered mail between the four main cities was extremely annoyed that the contract to serve the whole of the region had been snatched from under his nose.

"The contractor was very angry and threw a spanner in the works by complaining to King Faisal. By doing so he held the procedure up by months. He was an important man with considerable influence and at one stage it looked as though I may be on the ropes.

"In the end I resorted to a type of silent protest to bring the injustice to the attention of the King. When I was first told I had won the contract, I bought 30 Toyota SUVs, painted them with the new Dallah logo, and had them fitted with strong mailboxes.

"I had gathered up a considerable amount of money, from the profits of the printing house, the restaurant, and the clothes shop, but the cost of each vehicle at that time was SR12,000, which meant my investment in them took just about everything I had. I had our 30 SUVs, each with a uniformed driver, line up in a row close to King Faisal's palace, so that His Majesty would pass them every day as he entered the palace and every evening as he left.

The vehicles and drivers formed an impressively long line down the approach road to the palace. It was clear that they were ready to start work. Of course, this drew the King's attention and he subsequently made some inquiries."

To Saleh Kamel's delight and with King Faisal's blessing, the new company was allowed to begin its deliveries as had been promised eight months earlier.

Saleh Kamel's old friend Siraj Ghurab takes up the tale:

"Sheikh Saleh was thorough in his research but also aware that there were going to be some matters beyond his control. He did his best to minimise these. He realised that however stringent the vetting process, there would always be some drivers who would attempt to fiddle a few extra riyals.

"He therefore looked at the fuel costs he had personally calculated to drive from point A to point B, and if, for example, it amounted to a cost of 15 riyals, he would pay the driver 20. Oil changes and maintenance work were always done by Dallah in the company workshop. The drivers knew they were getting a more than fair deal, and very few would risk pushing their luck and, perhaps, losing their job, especially given that Sheikh Saleh – in a touch of genius – agreed that every driver who kept his vehicle in tip-top condition for three years, thus minimizing maintenance costs, would be given ownership of the vehicle. This deal certainly contributed to the success of the project, since every driver felt he was essentially driving his own automobile," Siraj Ghorab recalled with a chuckle at his old friend's brilliant strategy.

Winning the postal deal was a landmark in Saleh Kamel's career. His investment in securing the contract had been massive, in that it involved pretty much every riyal he had saved from his various enterprises over the preceding years. However, he had seen an opportunity and seized it; the dye was cast.

CHAPTER THREE

THE GOLDEN YEARS

Dallah Establishment began operations from a modest office in Alwazir Street, Riyadh, in 1969. Today the group is active in 44 countries around the world and employs more than 85,000 people. The company name, Dallah, had been Saleh Kamel's grandmother's pet name for her son Abdullah, Saleh Kamel's much-loved father.

Saleh Kamel made no secret of his deep love for both his parents. He was a dutiful son who did everything in his power to make them proud and comfortable. His older children recall how the lives of all the generations were inextricably entwined.

"My father deferred to his mother and father in all things," explained his daughter Ghadeer. "He would visit their home at least once a day and when he was not in the same city, he would make a point of keeping in touch by telephone."

Saleh Kamel's years with the Ministry of Finance would stand him in good stead throughout his career and he always gave credit to the instruction he received there. To have a winning idea is one thing, but to be able to methodically cost the project from beginning to end was something that would always put Saleh Kamel and Dallah ahead of the game. In later life, as his commercial interests expanded, he would increasingly depend on the expertise of trusted colleagues and advisors but at the beginning – and for some years to follow – most, if not all, the groundwork was conducted by him.

"The turning point was when I tendered for the contract to deliver postal services between the villages. I had applied for commercial registration for the Dallah Establishment while I was still a government employee, which allowed me to 'hit the ground running' when the opportunity arose," Saleh Kamel explained. "I had done my homework, and through my position with the Ministry of Finance, received years of invaluable training."

Despite his early successes as an entrepreneur, it must have taken considerable courage for Saleh Kamel to give up the security of his Ministry of Finance position, with all its associated benefits, to go it alone.

His new family, including Mayda, young son Abdullah and baby daughter Ghadeer had been joined in their Riyadh villa by his parents, Abdullah and Fatima, who supported their efforts to combine family life with the demands of a new business enterprise.

Mayda remembers how the encouragement and aid of her husband's parents played a vital role.

"Sheikh Saleh was working hard to get his business off the ground but he loved to spend time with his children; from the beginning he adopted a 'hands-on' style of parenting," his wife recalled. "The children who came later, when Sheikh Saleh was more successful and possibly even more driven, did not see him so frequently. He was forced to be away from home a lot and, in this way, they missed out on what Abdullah and Ghadeer were able to enjoy. Sheikh Saleh was very proud that his parents were around to share the joy of bringing up our children, especially since our firstborn, Abdullah, was named after his father and, of course, for me it meant that I was never alone or lonely, despite having moved to a new city."

While this period of Saleh Kamel's life was not the most financially lucrative he would ever know, the early 1970s were, in many ways, golden years for the Kamel family, as he would later acknowledge.

With his beautiful new wife and growing family, the support of his parents and his newly established Dallah Enterprise going from strength to strength, there was much to be thankful for.

Saleh Kamel was not, friends and family insist, a political man, but politics impact us all in one way or another, however much we may attempt to steer clear of the machinations of governments, both regional and global. At the time Saleh Kamel was adjusting to his own altered domestic and commercial circumstances, Saudi Arabia was also undergoing a period of significant change. King Faisal, following differences with King Saud, ascended to power in 1964 and immediately implemented a programme of modernization and transformation. Within a few years, Faisal's economic management had reduced the national debt and set the country on a new path. Outside influences further impacted the Kingdom's fortunes when, on October 6, 1973, the Egyptian Army crossed the Suez Canal to attack Israeli military positions in Sinai, occupied since the Arab humiliation of the Six-Day War in 1967.

King Faisal had been consulted by President Anwar Sadat before the attack. Sadat was frustrated by unconditional American support for Israel and saw this as the only way to break the deadlock caused by Israeli intransigence. Faisal told Sadat that Saudi Arabia would support Egypt financially and be prepared to use oil as a weapon by restricting supplies to any country that assisted Israel. Like Sadat, Faisal had become increasingly frustrated by America's failure to address the Arab/Israel question. The King had been signalling this in private to the Americans, but in July 1973 he gave an interview to American media outlets in which he made clear that, in view of America's complete support for the Israeli position, the Arabs would find it extremely difficult to continue to meet America's oil needs.

Most American policymakers believed this was a bluff. Throughout the 1960s, oil prices had rarely reached above $2 a barrel. But on October 16, 1973, OPEC announced that the price of oil would rise from $3 to just over $5 a barrel; the increase would enable Saudi

Arabia to halve its production without any significant loss of revenue. The Kingdom subsequently cut production by 5% but stopped short of implementing an embargo. Faisal still hoped that the US would stay out of the fighting.

However, in the face of massive American support for Israel, both materially and financially, King Faisal announced, on October 20, 1973, that all oil shipments to the US would be halted immediately. Within days, every other Arab country (with the exceptions of Libya and Iraq) had joined the boycott. Although the boycott did not achieve its primary objective of deterring the US in its support of Israel, it led to a quadrupling of oil prices and an energy crisis that transformed how Saudi Arabia was viewed in the wider world.

King Faisal rose to a prominence not seen by any Arab ruler for centuries. The oil embargo was lifted in March 1974, and although it had not achieved its objectives, it did create a new dilemma for Saudi Arabia. Before the embargo Saudi Arabia had an annual income of around $9 billion. By early 1974 annual revenues were over $34 billion. Excess petrodollars led to a huge surge in development in the country with the expansion of industry, hospitals, services, and hotels. King Faisal had launched Saudi Arabia's modest first Five-Year Plan in 1970. By 1974, Saudi planners faced the prospects of a vastly expanded Second Five-Year Plan, and Saleh Kamel was well-placed to surf this economic wave.

Throughout the early part of the decade, Dallah successfully tendered for lucrative government infrastructure projects, including roads, maintenance, operations, and sewage networks. Among them, there was the exclusive contract, won by Dallah in 1974, to operate and administer driving schools in Riyadh and Jeddah – a significant event for the young company. The name Dallah rose in prominence to become a maxim in a number of important new service industries.

His work as a financial representative for the Ministry of Finance had given Saleh Kamel valuable insight into just how much money was being spent and where, as Saudi Arabia continued to develop and grow at an increasingly rapid rate, and it was a knowledge he would not squander.

"During the period I was working for the government, I witnessed the development boom taking off in Saudi Arabia. The early stages of urban renaissance and infrastructural projects were evident everywhere. The last ministry I worked with as a financial representative before taking up private work was at the Ministry of Defence and Aviation. A large part of my work there involved reviewing the large financial sums paid for maintenance and operation contracts to foreign companies.

"I was impressed not only by the huge amounts of money being paid out, but also by the way foreign companies had managed to gain a monopoly on maintenance and operation activities, generating massive incomes for themselves.

"Tenders were open to all our national Saudi companies and institutions, but they rarely expressed a desire to participate, possibly for fear they lacked the technical or human skills that would qualify them to compete.

"Consequently, there was no way for the government to sidestep the foreign monopoly and avoid the massive amounts of money those firms were able to command. The importance of maintenance in both day-to-day operations and also in prolonging the lifespan of major projects was well recognised. If local companies did not possess the expertise to carry out the work, the contracts must be given to those who did.

"The wheels of development were accelerating, and the country could not afford to waste time. Of course, at this time the problem was not limited to the Ministry of Defence and Aviation but included all the facilities and institutions of the state with varying degrees.

"I desperately hoped that one day, Saudi companies and institutions would replace foreign entities, and their gains and profits would be incorporated into our national economy, but I was also realistic. I could see that such a situation was probably years into the future.

"For the record, I should say that the Western companies were not in complete control of all the country's maintenance, industry, and construction markets. There were a few respectable Saudi companies in the field, but probably no more than four had a share of the national cake, leaving the field wide open.

"The state was pretty much forced to contract foreign firms, especially American ones, to build most of the Kingdom of Saudi Arabia's infrastructure, especially technically advanced projects such as those in civil defence and aviation. American technology was dominant globally, and US performance was widely recognised for its levels of quality and efficiency. As far as the government was concerned, there were no other global competitors who could be entrusted with these sensitive works at the time.

"It was wise, therefore, and necessary – the government reasoned – to give most maintenance and operation deals back to the original manufacturer, no matter what the cost.

"I had watched developments for some time and strongly felt that if I didn't follow through on my aspirations and at least pitch for the work, any idea or ambition of Saudi companies eventually taking over their national projects would forever remain a pipe dream.

"Maybe due to my early upbringing and environment, I had no fear or hesitation. I had been seizing opportunities from an early age, implementing my own ideas without fear of failure, relying only on Allah for guidance. When I learned of a tender coming up for the Air Defence Academy maintenance contract in Jeddah, I knew this was my opportunity and I had to grasp it.

"However, it would be untrue to claim my attempt was not fraught with anxiety and the horror of anticipated failure.

"I was meticulous in my research and costings. It was a

unique tender among all those I would later win and fulfil. The specialisation was ambiguous, the provisions were vague, and the developments and modifications during implementation were unexpected, especially within the limits of the budget. However, what scared me more than anything was that the other Saudi companies – that might usually compete for such civil tenders – appeared reluctant to do so this time. The field was monopolised by Western companies.

"Finally, after much consideration, I gathered together my courage and my national pride and submitted my final tender bid, which, I discovered, was for an amount equivalent to just 10% of the amount proposed by my closest competitor, Raytheon, from the US."

"Everyone was surprised; more than once the prospect of the government teaming up with Dallah was described as being a 'risky venture'. We were accused of not doing our sums and of not calculating the possible consequences of bidding too low but, naturally, there was also a huge amount of pride at official levels and much speculation that this could be the deal that marked the beginning of a new era of participation and success for the Saudi private sector."

The process known as 'Saudisation', which calls for replacing foreign workers with Saudi nationals, was gaining traction at the time and becoming a very popular policy. Decision-makers in Riyadh desperately wanted to see a local firm emerge that was capable of competing with, and beating, the big foreign names, but not all were convinced that the time was right for Dallah.

"His Royal Highness Prince Khalid bin Sultan bin Abdul Aziz, then Assistant Commander of Air Defence, was surprised and concerned when the contract was awarded to Dallah, fearing a failure to deliver on our part might just kill off the first Saudi experience and jeopardise the future of any others that happened to be in the pipeline," Sheikh Saleh confessed.

"In truth," he went on, "his concerns were well placed. How could there not be fears given the vast financial gap between the cost proposed by Dallah Establishment for Agencies, Contracting, Maintenance, and Operation and those submitted by its US competitor, with a long, tried and true history in the industry?

"Nevertheless, national pride won out – the Dallah bid was approved and we were officially commissioned, under contract, but Prince Sultan placed me under strict supervision, which I had not been used to before in any of my previous civil contracting undertakings.

"I will not claim the first year of Dallah's contract for the Ministry was without incident. There were a number of teething problems brought about by a lack of sufficient liquidity. It was a learning process for both parties. But over time, I managed to convince the government to give Dallah a fairer deal, with greater flexibility and an increase in the value of the contract. Nevertheless, through all the considerable number of years we held the contract, the value of the Dallah deal never reached even half the value of the amount demanded by the principal US rival in that first bid.

"In his book, Desert Warrior, His Highness, wrote about this deal, which marked the first important steps on the Kingdom's road towards technical self-sufficiency and for Dallah, with the Saudi Royal Air Defence Academy as its first client, towards becoming one of the largest contractors in the Arab world.

"The contract taught me a great deal about the business of maintenance and operations," Saleh Kamel observed. "I was keen on learning all I could about the technical side of our operation and achieved this by tirelessly frequenting our warehouses, workshops, laundries, and all the other facilities Dallah had put in place, until I was able to understand the ins and outs of all operations ... this intimate knowledge of all aspects of what we were doing helped me bid for – and frequently win – subsequent tenders put out by the Ministry. To keep up with constant change in the industry, I would make it my business to regularly travel overseas to learn about the latest techniques. When I saw a development that we lacked in a certain field, be it construction, technology, engineering, or another related operation, I would recruit the relevant experts to work with us in Saudi Arabia, to help us improve our expertise.

"The air defence deal was a good opening for us in terms of providing the liquidity that allowed us to bid for other tenders and, most importantly, it helped Dallah win the trust and confidence of officials as a national corporation with both the financial and technical capacity to compete with foreign companies at a competitive price.

"Strict standards were applied, with deductions and fines imposed immediately in the event of any shortcoming or failure on the part of the contractor. This routine of careful inspection and close supervision imposed on the contractor resulted in intense discipline to achieve the highest possible quality of performance and, consequently, in a marked lack of accidents on site. Western companies had somehow managed to convince the authorities that they and only they were able of meeting such stringent standards. Of course, as Dallah was able to prove, that idea was a complete myth.

"Our Dallah workers were and are trained to a very high standard, which is why if they leave Dallah for any reason, they are considered a valuable gain by the company they join. Clearly, we were doing something right because by early 1975, we had signed a contract to maintain and operate the Kingdom of Saudi Arabia's thirteen civil airports. With the help of Allah, our experience and good reputation, we won more and more contracts until we became responsible for the maintenance and operation of all 22 airports plus all the air bases in the Kingdom.

"This was not easily achieved because success and building trust are not matters of luck. We worked hard and earned our rewards, by developing our own techniques and systems, according to the latest international standards. We imported any technique or product that could add quality to our project, no matter how much effort or money was involved. Part of what we were doing was a keenness to participate in our country's development. We were determined to meet all our contractual obligations and then to give even more.

"Our goal was not only to satisfy the customer but to meet the expectations of everyone who might become involved – for whatever reason – in the process. We evaluated ourselves from the point of view of every person, be they a citizen, resident, or visitor to our country.

"These were exciting years for Dallah. We did not win all the tenders invited by the Ministry of Defence and Aviation – competition was open to all nationalities, and while American and other Western companies had years of experience behind them and all the trappings of success, I am happy to say that Dallah was able to make a significant name for itself and hold its own in the market."

Mahmoud Hassouba, a lifelong friend from "the alleys" of Makkah and later Vice President of Dallah for several decades, recalled how Saleh Kamel became aware of the need to enrich his expertise in the industry by establishing some sort of joint venture with a long established and more experienced operator:

"Things were going well for Dallah", Mahmoud Hassouba said. "But Sheikh Saleh was always ambitious, he liked to test himself. When he came up with a new idea, he enjoyed putting it to the test and, of course, helping it succeed. He set his sights on aviation, which, by the 1970s, was already an important global industry with the potential for immense growth."

Hassouba, who, before becoming VP of Dallah, had worked in the

Ministry of Finance and for the Kingdom of Saudi Arabia's national
carrier, Saudi Arabia Airlines, observed:

"That was where the Avco Corporation, registered in the US state
of Delaware, came in. Sheikh Saleh wanted to go big, but he
knew he needed the proficiency and capability of a well-estab-
lished foreign partner to achieve maximum potential. We knew
we had a lot to learn, so we did our research and decided that
the US aviation giant known as AVCO, which had pioneered
aviation in the US from the 1920s through several decades of
significant growth, was a perfect fit for Dallah.

"AVCO had grown from a group of small airlines delivering
mail around the US to become a multi-million-dollar conglomerate handling growing numbers of both cargo and passenger
traffic. Sheikh Saleh knew that with its wealth of experience in
the industry, AVCO could help push Dallah to another level
and he was not wrong."

In 1975, the joint venture company between Dallah and AVCO –
the Dallah AVCO Trans Arabia Company – was finally declared.
Within a short time Dallah AVCO dominated Saudi Arabia's military
and commercial aviation industry development, from construction
to cleaning and maintenance. Some years later Saleh Kamel, with
many important lessons learned, bought out his American partners
to establish 100% ownership of the company.

Mahmoud Hassouba explains the thinking was as much ideological as commercial:

"Sheikh Saleh had travelled widely, initially in his work recruiting
pilgrims but later in pursuing business opportunities. As part
of these travels, he had seen progress in action and wanted that
progress for his own country. He looked at AVCO and knew
their knowledge and expertise could make a massive contribution to achieving such progress. Sheikh Saleh had a real passion
for his homeland and wanted to see it take its place on the world
stage. He was willing to do everything he could to make that

57

happen. Of course, in doing so he became a successful and wealthy man but that was not the driving force behind Saleh Kamel, not at all."

As Saleh Kamel recalled:

"I decided the most efficient way to compete with the US companies, which at that time monopolised the aviation industry in Saudi Arabia, was to partner with one of them. I met with one of the leading lights in the US-based industry, Avco, and we agreed to form a new pan-Arab company together, Dallah Avco Trans Arabia, which would specialise in the implementation of defence and civil aviation contracts, advanced maintenance work, such as air navigation systems projects and associated high-tech support ventures. We pioneered that and even after we gradually wound up the original cleaning and maintenance contracts in the late 1980s, making way for other national companies to take up the torch, we continued to carry out advanced maintenance such as the high-tech air navigation support systems until after the year 2000.

"The period from 1974 to 1985, I personally consider to have been golden years for our maintenance and operation works. Dallah played an important role in its own right and also contributed – with other nascent national companies – to establishing professional codes of values and ethics, in addition to breaking the psychological and technical barriers that had previously prevented Saudi contractors from grasping the nettle and competing in certain fields, including air defence and civil aviation facilities."

Although Dallah was a serious force to be reckoned with in the aviation business, it was not the only area in which the company was registering enviable levels of success. Saleh Kamel had started to diversify the business almost as soon as the company name Dallah was registered. When an opportunity was identified, research would begin to explore how best to turn the opening into a financially lucrative prospect.

Spiralling oil earnings were already fuelling a surge in infrastructural development by the early 1970s. Large-scale construction and other urban development processes were well underway in the major cities of the Kingdom. The demolition of old buildings to make way for the new, improved, streamlined Saudi Arabia resulted in a problematic scattering of building debris throughout the country's towns and cities. Failure to deal with the disposal of this rubbish, which left some roads and public areas impassable, inevitably led to issues with the removal of other types of waste, and the problem soon escalated.

Saleh Kamel swiftly recognised that the municipality of Jeddah, where he had a home, suffered from a distinct lack of expertise in this area. There was little or no trained manpower in the field. Regular street cleaning methods – usually comprising a man with a broom – were out of date and completely inadequate. In addition, the overall concept of cleanliness, which should have become more keenly developed with the growth in scientific awareness, was not keeping pace.

When Jeddah Municipality announced a public tender for city cleaning, Saleh Kamel swiftly seized the opportunity. Dallah was the successful bidder out of a list of applicants that included twelve specialised American companies, one Australian firm, and three Saudi companies. Dallah became responsible for city cleaning on June 20, 1974, and the company left no stone unturned in fulfilling its brief. International specialists in public cleaning and environmental health were commissioned to conduct studies on the conditions of public cleanliness in Jeddah, and all made their various recommendations.

John Marriott, a civil engineer specialising in town planning, president of the Organisation of Environmental Health Inspectors in Britain, consultant to the World Health Organization (WHO), fellow of the Institute of Municipal Engineers, and fellow of the

Institute of Environmental Health Engineers, along with George Allen, member of the British Public Cleaning Authority and consultant for dry waste management, were recruited to lead the initial investigations. The two experts conducted a two-month field study of conditions in Jeddah and subsequently submitted a detailed report.

Their suggestions included the introduction of a waste collection and disposal scheme, a far-reaching street-cleaning programme, and the introduction of a variety of methods to optimize the fight against disease-carrying vermin, flies, and other insects. They proposed establishing a factory locally where a selection of cleaning tools could be produced, eliminating the need for expensive imports, and suggested opening a vocational training institute, where locals could learn the necessary skills to operate the plant.

The contract marked another milestone for Dallah, as Saleh Kamel noted:

"The task required military precision, involving adequate manpower, sufficient transportation, and a public information campaign covering radio, television, and newspapers."

Abandoned cars, of which there were many, were towed away and disposed of; warnings were issued to those who dumped waste on the streets; unpaved areas were paved; and damaged road surfaces were restored. All undeveloped land was required to be fenced by owners to prevent them being turned into landfill sites, and all waste was henceforth to be disposed of in accordance with World Health Organisation (WHO) procedures.

Dallah was the first Saudi corporation to venture into public maintenance, both mechanical and electrical. Its impressive results helped it secure further contracts to maintain equipment at the Jeddah Islamic Port, the General Security's International Shooting Range in Riyadh, and the Government Complex in Madinah, among many others. In the days before Dallah, this type of maintenance work had always been given to foreign companies, mainly American, with the total contracts with ministries and departments worth around SR100 million annually.

"Dallah also carried out the maintenance contracts for civil aviation facilities throughout the kingdom, which included everything – airports, corridors, buildings, microphones, aircraft panels, refrigerators, air conditioning, cleaning, cars and extinguishers. This left the government with responsibility for only the security and the customs officers at the airport.

In addition to a number of government-owned companies and institutions, Dallah also won the contracts for the cleaning of Makkah airport, which receives 120 thousand pilgrims daily from different parts of the world, during the Hajj season.

Saleh Kamel insisted all Dallah's cleaning operations should be accompanied by awareness campaigns directed towards the general public. He launched cleanliness drives to promote the city's clean image, to make people proud of what had been achieved, and issued general guidelines dissuading the public from anti-social practices, such as spitting, to help cut down disease. As he confirmed in a magazine interview:

"We distributed more than one hundred thousand pamphlets to school students, outlining general guidelines on cleanliness, and we asked the Department of Education to launch competitions to spread the word. We also lobbied local journalists to conduct campaigns in their newspapers; made tapes in 16 different languages and distributed them to all airlines flying into Makkah, to be played to pilgrims coming into Saudi Arabia during the Hajj period – about all the bad habits that must be avoided in order to keep the Kingdom clean and prevent the spread of diseases.

"We also distributed more than 50,000 plastic bags, containing enough cleaning products to last the average family a month, to local homes to get individual households started on a new regime of cleanliness. We built a factory to manufacture garbage bags and distributed these to homes for free, after arranging weekly collections, also free of charge, from homes and local markets to help keep household waste under control. In Jeddah alone, we employed a thousand cleaning personnel, along with forty street-sweeping cars, as well as dumpsters and winches. I was immensely proud to be part of the city's ongoing battle against dirt and disease, as well as the campaign to educate its citizens. Our mission was to make our country a better place to live and, with God's help, I think we were able to achieve that.

"The enviable results of the mammoth clean-up campaign in Jeddah were soon noticed by other municipalities, which then wanted Dallah onboard to mount similar campaigns across their areas of the country. We raced towards initiatives and ideas, sparing no effort … Maximizing profit was never the main goal. Our country has never failed us, and all of us are winners in it. None is a loser except those who choose to be so by refraining from work and from shouldering the duties that they can do."

Saleh Kamel went on to praise the leaders of Saudi Arabia, describing them as having established a model of wisdom and justice, providing equal opportunities to all citizens to compete in the service of their country and earn their just rewards. "Since the founding of our country, they have believed in the importance of involving the private sector in achieving development, prosperity, and economic success. They have cradled this sector with care, leniency, good guidance, and the most exquisite forms of wise management, which adequately rewards achievement and punishes misbehaviour."

Talking about Dallah's journey in the field of maintenance and operation was always a source of pleasure to Saleh Kamel, who considered the sector the gateway to his personal wealth and success. He once commented:

"Contracting and maintenance is the profession that I cherish and proudly declare belonging to. It has been the source of my well-being and the means of earning the trust and esteem of my rulers over long years. I have enjoyed this profession, befriended, and loved it."

From its modest beginnings, Dallah would expand to take on multiple projects in a wide variety of sectors over the years, and to become a regional powerhouse of innovation and proficiency. The name Dallah Albaraka has become synonymous with professionalism and integrity.

The company's portfolio is diverse, its multiple operations range from agriculture and real estate to hospitals and healthcare. However, Saleh Kamel firmly believed that it was Dallah's early success in the cleaning and maintenance operations that opened the doors to the myriad opportunities that followed.

In later life, he would observe:

"I am happy, content, convinced, and satisfied with what I have done with no regrets, but there are always projects that I consider more important, or love for personal reasons, regardless of profit and loss. Carrying them out successfully was, for me, the ultimate goal, while failing in them would have been the ultimate loss.

"Of all these, and there are many, the project closest to my heart – the jewel in the crown of our contracting and maintenance portfolio – was for me the cleaning, maintenance, and provision of water to the Two Holy Mosques, in Makkah and Madinah. It will always remain the most prominent, brightest, and most beloved project to my heart and soul, among all Dallah's other business endeavours, companies and the partnerships, I have known and participated in.

"I could not have allowed a foreign partner to share in this project. In any case, a foreign partner would not have wanted a project that would cost more than its income, but I did, at any cost. Besides, I would never have allowed anyone to say that the Kingdom of Saudi Arabia entrusted a foreign company with cleaning the Two Holy Mosques."

Dallah has always been closely aligned with domestic development in the Kingdom of Saudi Arabia. The ventures it launched in its early days were, of course, designed to be lucrative, but each of them also contributed to the expansion and development of a country that within just a few generations would become a major player on the world stage.

Dallah was a name Saudi Arabians would learn to trust. Across the board, Saleh Kamel was admired for his drive and tenacity, for what he achieved. He was not a prince or a privileged royal, rather he was one of the people, a hardworking man from the alleys of Makkah who had proved his worth and made his fortune by his own efforts – he was the proud Saudi who snatched one contract after another from the jaws of big foreign conglomerates. It is entirely fitting that both the man and the company he built became, over time, a focus of national pride.

CHAPTER FOUR

PIONEER OF THE ISLAMIC ECONOMY

Saleh Kamel is frequently referred to as a pioneer of the Islamic economy, and with good reason; his contribution to spreading the concept around the globe cannot be overestimated. By the time of his death in 2020, Standard and Poors, the international financial information company, estimated the value of Islamic banking at US$2.3 trillion – a healthy expansion for a modern business model that Saleh Kamel was fundamental in creating, repurposing a moral Islamic tradition into a functioning financial code for the modern age. Islam was Saleh Kamel's true North, the direction in which he constantly travelled, balancing religion and ethics on his journey through life, much as a mariner might monitor wind and tide to navigate his chosen course. He brought his own set of ethical religious values into play in the way that he handled banking matters, and indeed his entire business empire.

Today, still relatively speaking a modern fiscal practice, Islamic banking fascinates many. How did its modern interpretation and practice come into being? A mixture of talent, faith and upbringing, plus an unusual coincidence engineered the crucible in which the idea started to simmer in the young Saleh Kamel's mind. Brought up in a household where Islam played an important role, in a city where religion was paramount, Saleh Kamel's devotion to the faith of Islam is unsurprising. However, most who knew him well insist that, while he was devout, he was not obsessive. Ahmad Al Hamdan describes Saleh Kamel's fascination with learning and his constant bid to know more about all things. "This was also his approach to religion," Hamdan observes. "There is a code of ethics by which a true Muslim strives to live life, and Sheikh Saleh Kamel, as a true Muslim, applied his inquisitive mind to seeking the truth in faith as much as in anything else. When he was satisfied that he had established the truth, this truth for him could not be 'unlearned' and he was then bound to abide by it."

One important component in the story of Saleh Kamel's principles of Islamic banking seems to have been established by a conversation he had with his mother. This exchange would change not only his approach to Islamic finance but, in time, would have repercussions around the world. It was a dialogue Saleh Kamel would often speak about, and, as both family and friends recall, it was a story he took pleasure in relating. Some three years or so after he had resigned from his government job with the Ministry of Finance and was doing well independently with his new business, his mother asked, out of the blue: "Do you work with banks?"

"Of course!" he replied. It was an automatic response since it seemed to him both obvious and natural that he would work with many banks as his business interests around the world expanded. His early days of trading as Dallah had been successful. He took pride in letting his parents know about all the contracts for which he had secured successful bids. He was perhaps a little surprised, then, that his mother might question his need to deal with banks. She said the practice was *haram* (prohibited in Islam). He assured her that he accepted no profits as interest from the banks he dealt with. But she questioned him further. Would he need, eventually, to take loans? Since he had no control over the banks, he would be compelled to accept their terms. "Yes, I would have to," he replied. Saleh Kamel recalls that he was taken aback when, on hearing his words, his beloved mother, who was deeply religious, looked downcast. She repeated her concern, pointing out that it was "*haram* in Islamic teaching not only to charge *riba*[8] (interest), but also to pay it." His mother's words took up permanent residence in his thoughts. He repeatedly recalled the encounter and set his mind to addressing the point his mother had raised. It was clearly a huge concern to her that dealing with terms imposed by international banks might be something not permissible, according to Allah's holy law.

Looking back on that conversation, which, in his own words, was "never forgotten", Saleh Kamel recalled that he made a slight assumption at the time that his mother was being rather naïve. He did not want to upset her, and, thinking that she knew perhaps relatively little about the subject, his initial response was to say, "We shall see," comforting her and closing the conversation.

However, the matter was not closed. Saleh Kamel valued the opinions of both his parents highly, and the issue continued to bother him. Moreover, his mother brought it up again a few weeks later. She described a dream she had had, featuring her own mother. The older lady was much loved by Saleh Kamel and his siblings who had often sat together listening to her wisdom and stories. In the dream, his grandmother was sitting at the foot of a water fountain, sprinkling water – which, in Arab and Islamic culture is emblematic, frequently linked to concepts of purity and plenty – from her hands onto the floor. In the dream, the water was leaking through a hole in the bowl of the fountain. This was interpreted as being highly symbolic: the hole was seen as a reference to something haram – wasting something of value. His grandmother's instruction to her daughter was that she must "tell Saleh to seal the hole."

Saleh Kamel's mother reminded her son of her dream at every possible opportunity, impressing on him his grandmother's message. To reinforce the significance of the communication, she called upon

---

8 *Riba*: commonly translated into English as 'interest', but the Arabic word has its root 'unjust or exploitative gain', so is more akin to 'usury', a term which has become archaic in English.

a family friend, the Egyptian cleric and Islamic scholar Muhammad Metwally, (better known as Sheikh Alsharawi), to share his thoughts on the matter.

Sheikh Alsharawi, at the time, was a Muslim jurist with Umm Al-Qura University in Makkah and King Abdul Aziz University in Jeddah. He had also acted as a government minister in his native Egypt. A highly prominent Islamic evangelist in the 1970s through to the 1990s, he was widely known as one of the most popular and successful Islamic preachers at the time.

Saleh Kamel explained to the Sheikh all the realities of dealing with international commercial banks, whose rules and ways were beyond his control. Alsharawi pressed him to explain the meaning of being "compelled to accept their ways". Would resisting them lead to starvation or freezing to death, the cleric asked?

Surprised by the Islamic evangelist's simple questions, Saleh Kamel asked him for Islamic guidance in dealing with commercial banks. He later related how Sheikh Alsharawi patiently and diligently explained the concept of *mudaraba* in Islam, which is a contract whereby one party provides the capital, while the other makes the investment, with both parties agreeing beforehand how any profits should be divided between them.

Although fascinated by the idea, Saleh Kamel later admitted that, at the time, he doubted many banks, if any, would accept such an arrangement. But Alsharawi further surprised him with a simple response: "Allah will find a way for those who are mindful of Him."

The following day Saleh Kamel went to the main bank handling his affairs, Banque du Caire in Jeddah, and spoke with the manager, Bahgat Saad Khalil. He explained what Sheikh Alsharawi had told him and was relieved to find that Khalil did not lightly dismiss his concerns but instead, requested a meeting with the Sheikh to share his thoughts on the matter. Saleh Kamel duly set up a meeting between the three of them. Sheikh Alsharawi explained the concept of *mudaraba* contracts to Mr Khalil and expounded on how the risks were shared. "Khalil was interested in the concept," Saleh Kamel recalled. The bank manager wrote to his Cairo headquarters requesting clarification and guidance. Several weeks passed without the arrival of any response, but Saleh Kamel did not give up on the idea and he visited his bank repeatedly every few days. Eventually, Mr Khalil agreed to try to work with the concept of *mudaraba* without waiting for the formality of any official direction from head office. Both, Saleh Kamel and the banker were interested to see the result of the experiment but the Saleh Kamel was particularly keen to establish an arrangement that would work as he knew it would bring his mother a great deal of peace on a matter that troubled her deeply.

"It was a great success," Sheikh Saleh recalled. "From that day forward, all business dealings between Dallah and Banque du Caire were conducted using the principles of *mudaraba*."

At the end of the year, the results exceeded the expectations of both Saleh Kamel and the bank. At that time the annual interest rate the business received on savings was around 4% but by applying the ethics of *mudaraba* on all Dallah's transactions over the course of the year, the bank returned a profit of 24%.

"Meanwhile, my own returns increased tenfold," Sheikh Saleh' remembered. "Our business turnover went from three million riyals annually, to 30 million riyals and, in the following year the 30 million soared to 300 million, with Banque du Caire's profits increasing accordingly."

At that time, the Saudi government issued its payment cheques through Citibank, which later became SAMBA. Cheques made payable to Dallah for government contracts were paid to Citibank by the Ministry of Finance. On receipt of the cash into Dallah's account, funds would be immediately transferred to Banque du Caire. Saleh Kamel recalled:

"One day the manager of Citibank came to see me at my office. He wanted to know why I was angry with them, since he had noticed that I transferred all my money to Banque du Caire as soon as I received it. I explained that I wasn't angry but very much wanted to operate my business according to an Islamic system – something that his bank did not make provision for.

"He wrote down details of the service Banque du Caire were providing and sent them off immediately to Citibank headquarters in New York. Within a month they had agreed to apply the same system. We worked together from that time on, and both of us gained a healthy profit from our partnership.

"For some time, I was their most important client and when Citibank eventually became the Saudi American Bank (SAMBA), they invited me to be a partner and chairman.

"I explained I would only consider their proposal if they would agree to deal exclusively in the Islamic system of *mudaraba*. However, they felt they could not comply, therefore I was obliged to decline their offer."

Although neither one of them knew it at the time, his mother's concerns had opened up a wellspring that would engage Saleh Kamel's intellectual curiosity and imagination for the rest of his life. As a result of the deep-seated desire her son should remain true to the teachings of his religion, Saleh Kamel would become one of principle pioneers at the vanguard of introducing the Islamic banking concept – in a commercially translatable form – to the Arabian Peninsula and beyond.

It was only a matter of time before this enterprising businessman would look at his financial ledgers and decide that if he truly wanted a bank that catered for his religious commitment and precise commercial needs, as well as turning him a healthy profit, he should form his own. Through Bank Albaraka Saleh Kamel would find an instrument to help him continue with his quest to better understand the complexities of Islamic finance and to spread the word globally.

Yasser Yamani, the nephew of Saleh Kamel and son of Mohammad Abdo Yamani, as well as the CEO of the Iqraa Charitable Society, established by Saleh Kamel, noted:

"Saleh Kamel was always a practical person. He was interested in the intellectual aspects of the Islamic economy, but particularly in the way it runs parallel to our society. He spoke at many conferences and forums on this subject. He had the ability to look at any particular Islamic concept in the round – to see things from a 360-degree vantage point and then come to a decision on how the concept should best be executed. He was always happy to share his thoughts on how he had come to a particular decision, his listeners would then have to make their own decision about his interpretation. Some would agree, while others would disagree with his logic.

"The concept of the Islamic economy – as we speak about it now – was not common at the time Sheikh Saleh began his commercial operations. He was among the first people, if not the first, to encourage debate on Islamic financing theories, which are very much open to interpretation. Since then, the field has been growing and developing internationally, gaining traction in the world of high finance for more than 40 years."

Islam encourages discussion and debate on all aspects of Muslim society, encouraging the evolution and development of ideas. In this tradition, scholars are deeply revered, so in his pursuit of a broader interpretation of Islamic ethics, Saleh Kamel consulted widely, following a centuries-old religious tradition of seeking a deeper understanding of life.

There are five pillars of Islam – the foundation stones on which the religion is built. These are Shahadah, the profession of faith; Salat, or daily prayers; Zakat, which refers to the giving of alms as a percentage of what is earned; Sawm, the obligatory fasting in the holy month of Ramadan; and Hajj, the required pilgrimage to Makkah.

For centuries Islamic scholars have deliberated on all manner of issues, both simple and complex, and it was just such discussion that enthralled Saleh Kamel. He would relish coming across a conundrum related to the teachings of Islam and would enjoy exploring the subject, frequently seeking clarification from Islamic scholars, until – in his mind – there was no ambivalence. Once he had formed an opinion, according to those who knew him best, he could be quite intractable.

From the time he conferred with Sheikh Alsharawi at the behest of his mother, he was captivated by this complex but somewhat obscure and flexible blueprint for life. His particular, although not sole, interest was naturally in relation to finance and how it might be best utilized to serve God and mankind.

More broadly, Saleh Kamel shared his thoughts on the nature of Islamic economics quite widely, both in the media and through his writings. In a 2017 essay on the subject in titled My Understanding of the Concept of Capital in Islam, he laid out some very detailed thoughts on exactly how he perceived Islamic economics. He specified nine core principles, the first of which is:

"The *Istikhlaf* of man (human stewardship of the earth) and his mission to develop the earth are among the supreme purposes of his creation. The improvement of the earth is an act of worship in itself. Among the elements of *Istikhlaf* is the harnessing of heaven and the earth for man, and guaranteeing his sustenance. The wealth we have is not ours, but belongs to Allah, who granted it to us as a test. Man should use this wealth in line with the requirements of faith."[9]

Saleh Kamel firmly believed, contrary to the opinion of some economists, that the resources made available to man are unlimited. "The wisdom behind the diversity of nations is to seek 'developmental integration'," he insisted. Entrepreneurs should first set out to develop their own countries but then aim to spread the benefits of development to other lands. They must, as a duty, be at the forefront of those redressing the imbalance in the global economy and they must work towards establishing a moderate global financial system. There should be commitment to piety and morals in all fields but

9 For the full text of this essay, please see the Appendix at the end of this book.

The young Saleh Kamel.

The Saudi Arabia that Saleh Kamel was born into was a world away from for which the country it has become today. Those making the Hajj pilgrimage flowed largely through the port of Jeddah *(archive photo above)*. The city was the mainstay of the Saudi economy with large numbers of international travellers visiting to the holy sites in Makkah *(below)* and Madina. Saleh Kamel's father, Abdullah Kamel *(above right)* worked as a *mutawif*, guiding visiting pilgrims around the holy sites, a job the young Saleh Kamel also took on. It was here that he fine honed the "Makkah mentality" of hospitality and cosmopolitan trading which would stay with him for life.

A gathering of the Kamel family *(right)*, Abdullah Kamel (Saleh Kamel's father) standing on the left, carrying his daughter Mariam, with, to the right, his brothers Abdelsalam and Muhammad Saeed (holding his daughter Aisha). Saleh Kamel is seated front right next to his siblings, from left to right: Hassan, Muhammad and Laila.

Saleh Kamel was a keen member of the Scout movement, and is shown here *(below right)* in uniform, with his best friend, and later brother-in-law, Mohammed Abdo Yamani *far left)*, and the President of King Saud University, Dr. Abdul Aziz Al-Khuwaiter.

Saleh Kamel (standing to the left) with his younger siblings, from left to right: Omer, Mariam, Mohammed, and the baby Abdul Aziz who is carried by a family friend.

Saleh Kamel *(above - far left)*, aged about 20 years old in the early 1960s with his mother, aunt, sisters and younger brothers enjoying a family vacation in Lebanon. He would have been around 20 years old. With friends, wearing a cloth wraparound *futa* traditionally worn in southern Arabia *(below - second from right)*.

The young Saleh Kamel, aged 14 *(above)* with his elder brother Hassan on the left.

With his father and brothers performing Hajj *(below)* - from left to right - Abdul Aziz, Omer, Mohammed, their father Abdullah, Hassan and Saleh.

Saleh Kamel in Europe in the late 1960s *(above)* with his father and two of the children of his brother Hassan, Eyad and Ammar.

Saleh Kamel with his two sons *(above right)*, Abdullah and Mohyuldeen in the late 80s.

With HRH Prince Mohammed Al Faisal *(right)*, one of the three pioneers of Islamic Banking.

Saleh Kamel accompanied by Sheikh Muhammad Metwalli Alsha'rawi *(right)*, who was to be a defining influence on the moral underpinning of his banking empire.

At his office in Dallah Tower in Jeddah *(right)*, where he installed a whole wall of TV screens so that he could personally watch and monitor Arab Radio and Television (ART) channels from his desk.

With a charity group on a trip to Africa *(right)*.

With lifelong friends and colleagues, instrumental in the early years of Dallah who went on to accompany him through his life *(above - left to right)*: Mahmoud Hassouba, Dr. Mohammed Abdo Yamani, Saleh Kamel.

With his brothers *(right - left to right: Saleh, Omer and Hassan)*.

At the suggestion of King Fahd, Saleh Kamel entered into a partnering arrangement with Sheikh Waleed bin Ibrahim to found MBC television. The channel was officially launched in London in 1991 and the two men *(right)* worked closely together, making the station a pioneering service across the Middle East.

especially in the financial sector: "Wealth must not be merely a factor for individual advancement, but rather a lever for achieving community balance and harmony."

A concerted effort to promote a love of work should prevail across all sections of society, Saleh Kamel believed, for to work is honourable and to be able to employ others to work, to support themselves and their families, is a privilege that should not be taken lightly, he insisted.

Saleh Kamel considered the phenomenon of money remaining in the hands of the rich as something that jeopardised the general financial well-being of society, leading, eventually, to social disintegration. He was of the opinion that consumerism, extravagance, and thriftlessness must be combatted. To these ends we should start out by exhibiting positive bias towards financing the "real economy" such as the store, the farm, and the small factory, he advised.

One of his core beliefs was that the market is the beating heart of every community. Originally, a place for the exchange of "benefits" and not for the exchange of "damages", he noted that the latest "values" expounded by management experts are nothing new. On the contrary, the basis of these ethics has already been taught to us by our respective religions. Each person knows in their heart what is right and what is wrong. Our faith — whatever that faith might be — has taught us morals more real than any offered up by the so-called market experts. Businessmen, Saleh Kamel insisted – especially the young ones – must be instrumental in restoring market morals and observing them, especially with regard to dispensing Zakat charity, which was something he regarded as a miraculous "development" scheme to be upheld, encouraged, and applauded throughout society.

Following on from this core basis is his Fifth Principle, encapsulating the concept of sharing risk, and this lies at the heart of the Islamic banking model:

"Participation – the agreed sharing of loss and gain – represents the mainstay of the equilibrium of financial centres and remains the pillar of rational development for the personal, national and global economy.

"Once a bank fails to engage in such ventures, it becomes an unethical and un-Islamic bank. Consolidating the participatory financing of medium, small, and micro enterprises is one of the most important elements involved in combating this phenomenon."

Speaking at a conference of bankers in London, where he shared the platform with Britain's future King Charles, Saleh Kamel noted how he had been impressed by the content of a lecture given by the monarch, then heir-apparent, in 1997, in which he referred to Islam as "a religion of culture from which the world should be enlightened". "Islam", Saleh Kamel reminded the conference, "has created a coexistent human society cooperating with and complementing others, for the sake of prosperity and the welfare of all humanity". It was one of his dearest wishes that such enlightenment should be allowed to spread around the world without hindrance, and he saw the concept of Islamic finance as an invaluable tool in nurturing such cooperation.

The concept he so admired is based upon sharing, with the bank taking on a portion of the entrepreneur's burden by shouldering some of the risk – an expectation setting it firmly apart from the criticisms levelled at certain other international banks, frequently accused of being mere money-lenders, profiteering off the backs of their clients.

The sometimes controversial[10] Saudi cleric, Sheikh Saad Al Shethri, who served on the Council of Senior Scholars and was appointed advisor to the Court of King Salman, had many conversations with Saleh Kamel, on the subject of Zakat – Islam's call for all Muslims to contribute a percentage of their earnings to charity. Zakat has

---

10 In 2009 Saad Al Shethri sparked some media debate in connection with the then newly established King Abdullah University of Science and Technology (KAUST) when he suggested that the academic curriculum should be overseen by religious scholars, and also questioned that it was set up as a mixed-gender institution.

been a thorny issue over the years, with Islamic scholars frequently at loggerheads about how and where their charitable contributions should be paid. All are agreed that the concept is a good one in principle, but opinions vary on the best and most efficient methods of collection and disbursement, and it is here that controversy most frequently arises.

Saleh Kamel was a long-term advocate of institutionalising Zakat so that it could unleash its full potential for the benefit of Muslim communities around the world. He strongly rejected the opinions of some Sharia scholars that Zakat is merely a payment to the poor, and he continuously urged its use to fund education and training projects. In Saleh Kamel's opinion, Zakat should always be invested in projects capable of stimulating local economies in a way that would bring benefit to the whole community. In this way, the fruits of these investments would be maximised over time, providing more for the poor, than would occur simply by dispensing handouts. Saleh Kamel's thoughts on the matter were much in line with the old adage that to give a man a fish is to feed him for a day, while to teach a man to fish will help keep him fed for life.

His specific proposal was that 50% of Zakat funds should be invested in industry, agriculture, and trade, or in establishing income-generating handicraft schemes, with the other 50% of funds allocated to meeting the immediate needs of those not able to sustain a livelihood for themselves. Following this method, the poor would make a living from the wages earned for their work, while the neediest would receive financial help in meeting their needs. Part of the investment allocation, Saleh Kamel believed, should be used to establishing training institutes to teach income-generating professions, in order to enable the creation of a self-reliant working class, ultimately leading to self-sufficient communities where begging would no longer be required. To achieve this, Saleh Kamel developed an administrative organisation model, starting with small communities and targeting self-sufficiency so that the Ummah[11] might benefit from the surplus in due course. Establishing the International Zakat Organisation, he stated:

"I believe that such a contemporary application and modern organization in disbursing Zakat will reflect the concept that Zakat should not aim simply to extend ad hoc assistance to feed the hungry or provide clothes to the needy. It should aim to establish sustainable institutions that can respond more fully to the needs of the poor and those in need, enriching and transforming their lives. It should play a role in promoting Islamic dawa[12], developing facilities, encouraging rationalised spending, and establishing vocational training institutes, promoting health, religious, commercial, and other types of tourism, as defined by agreed disbursement categories. I did my best to determine the disbursement categories of the various beneficiaries. I could be right or wrong about some of them, but if the right organs and committees are established, working with their Sharia Compliance Boards, they can exercise their judgement while overseeing implementation of the project. If this economic perspective is taken on board, with the help of Allah, our conditions will change for the better. Let us keep in mind the exemplary Islamic state that existed at the time of Omar bin Abdul-Aziz (the reformist Muslim Caliph), when no one needed Zakat – not only because of the abundance of resources available at the time, but also because of the pre-emptive treatment provided by Zakat, which uprooted poverty, and in many cases, prevented it from arising in the first place."

It was an important point, and one that demanded a significant change in mindset if it was going to be put into practice successfully. In some sense this might be seen as a new "modernising" interpretation of the Prophet's message that has parallels with the increasingly

11 Wider community of Muslims.
12 Call to embrace Islam.

globally adopted ethos of Corporate Social Responsibility and the duty of corporations to shoulder the care of those around them beyond the primary goal of profitability.

Sheikh Saad discussed the matter at length with Saleh Kamel, and recalls the events that followed:

"Saleh Kamel suggested that I raise the issue of Zakat for debate by the Council of Senior Scholars. He was happy to present his own thinking to the Council, and the subject was discussed at length from a religious perspective. I always admired the way Sheikh Saleh brought a fresh approach to discussions and in doing so, made a valuable contribution to the ongoing debate. I did not always agree with him, but I always appreciated his enthusiasm and commitment."

Saleh Kamel was an early advocate of this interpretation of Zakat, an argument he won both intellectually and in practice, as can be seen in the increasingly widespread acceptance today of the ideas he proposed so many years ago. In this, as was so often the case, Saleh Kamel had the vision and the courage to tread where others from the region had shown a reluctance to go.

In 1983, he founded Albaraka International Bank Limited (AIBL), but sadly, it was a brave venture that was not to end well. After more than a decade of operations and much painful upheaval, Saleh Kamel opted to surrender his UK licence. In the end, he could not meet, in the time allocated, the demands of a restructuring proposal issued by the Bank of England, which would have seen his equity in the venture diluted to a minority stake. From strong beginnings, AIBL was eventually forced to close. The pressure it came under, and the way events played out, was the subject of much media speculation and controversy.

The story of banking regulation in this era cannot be told without reference to a landmark event: the scandal of the collapse of Bank of Credit and Commerce International (BCCI) in July 1991. The crash of BCCI was a high-profile banking failure that shocked the industry and exposed serious weakness in London's bank regulatory system. The failure was all the more alarming since warning signs of BCCI's vulnerability had existed for some years, and, indeed, as early as 1982, one internal memo described BCCI as "on its way to becoming the financial equivalent of the SS Titanic!" When the bank did finally go down, spectacularly, in 1991, leaving depositors high and dry, the Bank of England came under scrutiny and was obliged to clean up its shop, checking for any other potentially unstable banks. One area they identified as a source of concern was banks operating on Islamic banking principles – notably Al Rajhi Banking and Investment Corporation (Arabic) in Saudi Arabia, Dubai Islamic Bank, Qatar Islamic Bank and the Faisal Islamic Bank of Egypt.

In an article published in June 1993 by the London-based magazine *The Middle East*, financial analyst Mushtak Parker commented:

"Albaraka International Bank in London has fallen foul of the tighter rules imposed on international banks after the collapse of BCCI. Nobody questions Albaraka's viability. Nor is there any suspicion that it is being targeted because it is an Islamic financial institution. Nevertheless, its problems reflect the changing environment in which many Arab-owned banks overseas must learn to operate."

To quote Parker again, he noted:

"AIBL can justifiably claim to be the unwitting victim of tighter international banking regulations imposed after the Bank of Credit and Commerce International (BCCI) debacle. Albaraka International is a highly liquid bank, a fully owned subsidiary of the Jeddah based Dallah Albaraka Group, headed by Sheikh Saleh Kamel, which has worldwide assets exceeding $6bn."

One remarkable element in the story is that quite a few of AIBL's customers initially refused to accept their money back, even though the bank had been instructed to return funds to them. Some reported that as many as 43 of AIBL's major depositors confirmed that they wanted to leave their funds with the bank until a resolution of the problem had been found. Alison Dodds, Saleh Kamel's PA in London at the time, recalls:

"The morning after the news broke, we had about a hundred people descend on our London offices, Muslim account holders, wanting to see Sheikh Saleh and offering to become shareholders because they wanted to save the bank."

In all of this, the Bank of England was keen to reassure the public that its actions, and the curtailing of other Islamic banks, were not discriminatory, and it issued a statement noting:

"We have no difficulty in principle with Islamic banking, it has been possible in the UK for Islamic transactions to be conducted in conformity with UK law. Our only concern is that the conduct should conform to UK laws and the Basel Concordat."

For his part, Saleh Kamel issued a clear statement defending the strength of his bank: "Our capital-to-risk assets ratio is 50% and our capital-to-deposits ratio is 28% – well over the 8% target of the Basel Concordat."

Those closely involved remember how the Bank of England decision was devastating news to Saleh Kamel, who had devoted so much time and energy into getting his London-based Islamic bank off the ground. In the end, the Bank of England gave Saleh Kamel a time-frame in which to find other outside investors.

Although initially reluctant to follow this course, Saleh Kamel did eventually give it close consideration. In a bid to address the problem, a management committee was established with a view to overseeing how AIBL might be converted into a British public entity, with majority ownership held by British Muslims. Under this arrangement, Saleh Kamel's holding would drop to a minority stake of below 10%. An arrangement along these lines would have potentially brought the bank's management in line with the Bank of England's demands, addressing the core concern that too much control was held by a single non-resident shareholder.

Saleh Kamel was able to generate interest from the Islamic

Development Bank (IDB) based in Jeddah, which offered to play a role in AIBL, thereby addressing some of the Bank of England's concerns. Negotiations to this end were underway but sadly, the time-frame given to Saleh Kamel fell over Ramadan and Eid, a period of roughly four or five weeks where traditionally work in Saudi Arabia is scaled down dramatically to accommodate a national workforce fasting during the hours of daylight, and then the ensuing Eid holiday, which immediately follows the holy month. It is a period of public holiday much like the Christmas/New Year break in Europe or the US. Saleh Kamel's team requested an extension to the timeline but their appeal was turned down.

In a move some industry observers and commentators felt might be over-zealous, the Bank of England forced AIBL to surrender its British banking licence in April 1993 and to stop receiving customer deposits. The Bank of England was resolute that in the future no single shareholder could own a bank. Although each individual member of the Kamel family was technically categorised as a shareholder in Albaraka Bank, the fact that they were all members of a single family was not acceptable to the Bank of England.

Although they were clear that this was in no way to be taken as a criticism of Saleh Kamel, their demand had been that the AIBL should have a change in ownership. Saleh Kamel, who had invested so much in the bank, was bitterly disappointed but also personally offended by the Bank of England's refusal to extend the timeline. He was, as he said himself "very upset" with London. "As a result, we didn't see him back in here for at least a couple of years. He sent other people to manage his affairs in London, whereas previously we had seen him maybe three or four times a year," explained a former colleague.

One industry expert, active at the time but since retired, believes the matter of restructuring could have been handled better, noting: "Albaraka Bank was successful, thriving in fact, and had done nothing wrong. The Bank of England was trying to protect itself from another BCCI scandal, but the timeline it gave Albaraka was most unfortunate. However, handled more sensitively, with proper negotiation by both of the parties involved, this should not have been an insurmountable problem."

Saleh Kamel and his Albaraka Group had forged strong relations with indomitable British institutions such as Kleinwort Benson, Flemings, Midland Montagu, and Morgan Grenfell during the 1980s, at a time when Islamic banking was still a nascent industry. Today, it has been the stated policy of successive British governments to promote Islamic banking as part of its financial inclusion policy, and in the post-Brexit era to attract inward Islamic investment, trade, and financial flows. It is fair to say that Saleh Kamel made a huge contribution to the emergence of London as the capital of the Islamic finance industry in the West. It was, then, no real surprise to anyone that he should feel so bitterly let down by the turn of events.

Disenchanted with London, Saleh Kamel continued to forge alliances in other countries around the world. He had, since long before his foray into UK banking, been highly active setting up other banks across the world. He was active in – and had great regard for – Malaysia, and was full of praise for its leadership and its proactive policy, legislative, and regulatory support in promoting Islamic banking, finance, and *takaful*[13]. It was, Zeti Akhtar Aziz, former governor of Bank Negara Malaysia (the country's central bank), who appointed Saleh Kamel as a Member of the Governing Council of the blossoming new International Centre for Education in Islamic Finance (INCEIF), Global University for Islamic Finance Education. Although Albaraka never managed to get a standalone banking licence in Malaysia, it did own a 40% stake in the local RHB Islamic Bank through its local entity Dallah Albaraka Malaysia Holdings (DAMH), which had years earlier acquired a stake in Bank Utama, which subsequently took a controlling stake in the RHB

---

13 *Takaful* is a type of insurance system, devised to comply with the Sharia laws, in which money is pooled and invested.

Group. And DAMH had earlier divested its stake in the flagship Bank Islam Malaysia and in Southern Bank.

Over the years, Saleh Kamel's interest in Islamic economics and his conviction of the need for a comprehensive international system of Islamic banking remained constant. Undeterred by the many and varied challenges the pursuit of his dream entailed, he was focussed on his quest. In 1977, he was instrumental in establishing the Faisal Islamic Bank in Sudan and Egypt, spearheaded by Prince Muhammad al-Faisal. In 1979, he helped set up the Jordan Islamic Bank. The original plan had been to set up the bank as a joint venture project, with Saleh Kamel and Prince Muhammad Al-Faisal as equal partners. However, when Prince Muhammad was obliged to step away from the enterprise, Saleh Kamel took up the slack with enthusiasm, participating in the executive management of the bank, as Chairman of the Board of Directors, between 1980 until his resignation in 1995, after which time he became honorary president.

Saleh Kamel continued to pioneer exploratory visits to different parts of the world with the aim of opening further banks that would work in line with the provisions of Islamic Sharia law. One of the major difficulties he encountered was the lack of existing structures compatible with Islamic banking legislation in the places he visited. In true pioneering spirit, helping the existing financial authorities of these foreign states establish the necessary legislation to facilitate Islamic enterprise became his mission. Technical delegations from Al Baraka Investment and Development Company would be dispatched to help train the existing authorities on how to operate and govern the operation of their own Islamic banks, starting at the grassroots level. Once the laws were properly established, Saleh Kamel would proceed with incorporation through local partnerships in line with the existing financial sector rules and regulations of each country. In 1983, a series of institutions were established following this model. They included Al Baraka Islamic Investment Bank – Bahrain, Al Baraka Türk Housing Finance in Turkey, and the Saudi-Tunisian

Finance House. Al Baraka Bank Sudan, Al Baraka Bank Mauritania, and Al Baraka Bank Bangladesh were established in 1984, 1985, and 1987 respectively. Meanwhile, 1989 witnessed the inception of Al Baraka Bank South Africa and Al Baraka Bank Djibouti. A year later, in 1990, Al Tawfeeq Investment Bank was established in Pakistan followed by three further banks in 1991: Banque Al Baraka D'Algérie, Al Baraka Bank Kazakhstan, and Al Baraka Bank for Finance – India.

In 1992 Al Baraka Bank was established in Lebanon, the same year Saleh Kamel established the Egyptian Saudi Finance Bank, originally set up in 1989 under the name Al-Ahram Bank. In 2002, he established Albaraka Banking Group in Bahrain, and continued expanding across the Arab region by opening Albaraka Bank in Syria in 2009, and Albaraka Bank in Morocco in 2017.

Today Albaraka Banking Group (ABG) has more than 600 branches across three continents, and can proudly declare that it was central in introducing Islamic banking to markets as diverse as Turkey, Lebanon, South Africa, Sudan, Tunisia, Egypt, Syria, Morocco, the UK, and beyond.

However, as Saleh Kamel was always at pains to point out, as well as his successes he had also had to deal with his fair share of projects that did not succeed. As he commented himself in an essay on the Islamic economy:

"One should not be ashamed of one's failures. There is nothing wrong with failure; what is wrong is to repeat the same mistake."

The banking arm of the Saleh Kamel empire was no exception to this rule and may have been all the more vulnerable to difficulties since the various international arms of Albaraka Bank were generally not set up with the aim of making profit the priority. Saleh Kamel saw Islamic banking, and the broader stimulation of an Islamic economic system, as an ideological goal, more about spreading good practice and supporting Islamic values than the mere making of money. He was always careful not to use the label "Islamic" for personal gain – while some banks made clear how they sought to operate according to an ethical Islamic system, Saleh Kamel chose not to use the categorisation in any of his financial establishments. So, when Albaraka Bank did not manage to build sustainable operations in Djibouti, Mauritania, and Kazakhstan, it was not the lack of commercial profitability of the bank itself that disappointed Saleh Kamel, as much as the projects' failure to stimulate sound Islamic economic practices in these countries. In the case of Kazakhstan, Saleh Kamel, as one of the first Arab investors who went to knock on the doors of the newly independent Muslim republics after the dissolution of the Soviet Union, built a strong personal relationship with President Nursultan Nazarbayev. He established the first Albaraka Bank Kazakhstan in the then capital, Almaty, in 1991. However, the bank stumbled after a few years of operation and finally had to be liquidated as a result of the practices of the local partners who controlled the administration. In fact, that stumbling was a natural result of the state of the business environment at that time. As Saleh Kamel noted, the former Soviet countries lacked economic knowledge and experience in commercial and investment transactions and accounting principles, as well as in control and supervisory policies. They were just emerging from totalitarian communist rule and, with hindsight, Saleh Kamel believed the new bank had been charged with taking on too much of a challenge.

Nevertheless, he remained philosophical:

"Some may be surprised when they hear me say that I owe as much to the failures in my life as I do to the successes. The patience Allah bestowed upon me after every failure was a reason to hold fast and not collapse in the middle of the road. The lessons learned from each failure led to several successes."

At one stage, however, Saleh Kamel did become deeply disillusioned with the lack of progress in the Islamic finance sector and once famously said that if he had to start his business empire again, he would not get involved in Islamic banking, as he doubted the industry had achieved a qualitative breakthrough. Islamic finance, he explained, differs in its mechanism and more importantly in its spirit and philosophy, from conventional finance. The problem he identified was the perception that the two systems are more-or-less the same. But if he failed in changing this attitude it was certainly not for the lack of trying. However, Saleh Kamel's contribution to Islamic banking cannot be accurately measured in terms of the number of contracts signed or the amounts of cash accumulated. His real success was the progress made towards his personal goal of steering more financiers to think of the banking process as being closely tied to personal ethics. His vision enlightened the hearts and minds of a whole generation of people who had previously only considered banking in terms of profit and greed. In his countless newspaper columns and television appearances, Saleh Kamel was relentless in attempting to reinforce the message that avarice did not have to be the driving force behind achievement and, because of the sheer extent of his success and his wealth, people were more willing to listen to the message he tried to convey. Speaking about his understanding of the situation, he remarked:

> "For years, my interest in the concept of capital in Islam was in terms of thought and practice. I was keen to attend seminars and keep company with religious scholars and experts in finance and economics. I also decided to make *fiqh*[14], or jurisprudence, an integral part of my business. I was fortunate to be able to draw on an extremely rich source of information, and I made it my mission to apply what I could to banking reality.

> "The geographical diversity of my investments allowed me to identify different investment patterns, various work and behavioural patterns, as well as patterns of legislation and regulation. This led me to meet with a great many leaders of Arab, Islamic,

14 *Fiqh*: the theory or philosophy of Islamic law, based on the teachings of the Quran and the traditions of the Prophet.

and Western countries and to engage with them on a number of top financial issues.

"I strongly believe that Arab and Muslim businessmen must act as a medium for integrated development in our region at the level of both the Arab world and the Muslim community. Historically and geographically speaking, Arab countries are one nation and one people, united in their faith, customs, and even their food and drink. However, colonialism and politics have caused the fragmentation of this community. If we take the relationship between Egypt and Saudi Arabia as an example, we will find labour, fertile soil, and water in Egypt, while Saudi Arabia has natural resources and advanced industries. Therefore, to focus on developing exports between them would be in the interests of both.

"If we look at the proportionality between resources and production, we find that although the Arab world has many rivers it does not grow enough wheat or rice. How does this make sense? We have all the natural and human resources, not only to be self-sufficient but to be the world's food basket. We have fertile soil, water, labour, and the right climate. That is why I say that nothing except laziness and indolence can keep us in this state."

A close colleague noted: "Saleh Kamel did his level best to keep his principles front and centre of his burgeoning Islamic banking domain. But to say it was sometimes an uphill battle would be an understatement. He took his expertise and his new ideas to places he felt they were most keenly needed but sometimes these were the very places that resisted change the most."

One place where Saleh Kamel's philosophy of ethics in finance sowed an important seed was in Germany. In May 2017 German Chancellor Angela Merkel visited the Kingdom of Saudi Arabia with a high-ranking ministerial delegation. It was a brief visit, but she made time to go to the Jeddah Chamber of Commerce, where she met Saleh Kamel and fell into conversation. She was keen to hear his insights into the success of the Islamic banking model. While most of the world had recently been experiencing a distressing global financial meltdown, the Islamic banking world seemed to have ridden out the storm relatively well. Saleh Kamel later related the conversation:

> "I told Mrs Merkel: 'We operate and believe in the real economy, not the hypothetical economy in which the world's banks operate. It is a matter that our religion has shown us and our Prophet Muhammad, may Allah's peace and blessings be upon him and the Prophets of Allah, guided us to.' She said: 'Tell me more.' I said: 'There is the Hadith (saying) of the Prophet: Do not sell what you do not own! If only this Hadith had been followed, no bank would have gone bankrupt, no individual would be broken, nor would any nation have lost.' The Chancellor asked me to elaborate. So before she left, I sent her three pages on the subject. Two months later, Chancellor Angela Merkel telephoned me to say: 'Do not sell what you do not own' is now the law in Germany!'"

Despite his age and increasing ill-health, even after he had stepped back from Dallah Albaraka, Saleh Kamel was deeply involved in a project that involved trying to bring together Islamic Chambers of Commerce to thrash out a unified policy that would massively benefit a free exchange of trade among them.

His nephew Abdul Aziz Yamani had spoken to him about developments not long before Saleh Kamel died. As his nephew pointed out:

> "He died with his work undone but that would have been true had he lived to be a hundred years old. Even though his achievements were immense, he always had a vision to strive for. There was always at least one more thing on the horizon."

It was perhaps inevitable that Saleh Kamel's work would be left incomplete, since his goals were high, indeed perhaps unattainable. Future generations of philanthropists already have a roadmap drafted, for which he will be remembered:

"On a personal level, and as I belong to this region, I have done my best to embody this spirit of economic integration and also to promote it from an intellectual point of view. I am from a generation that entertained the hope of realising Arab integration and unity.

"However, unfortunately there has been little or no progress in that direction. Sadly, we are now experiencing Arab disunity, possibly more than at any other time. The Arab common market is an aspiration easy to achieve if we apply ourselves collectively to its success. As for Islamic countries, there is a real need to establish a common market between us too, and to bring about comprehensive economic integration in both the Arab and the Islamic regions. We must all strive to achieve this goal and do our best as investors, kings, and presidents to push towards realisation of the dream as Arab countries and an Islamic community."

Profitability was never the prime motivator in what Saleh Kamel did. With regard to the Islamic economy, like all true pioneers he led from the front, a key leader in Islamic thinking as well as an enthusiastic practitioner, his skill greatly influenced by his enthusiasm to teach the wider world about the knowledge he had accumulated and to spreading a deeper understanding of what he regarded as a remarkable economic model. As part of this plan, he did all he could to strengthen research and scholarship programmes related to Islamic economics, from developing mechanisms for ethical Islamic finance to ensuring ethical financial products were made available to the wider public. He regularly collaborated with diverse research centres to encourage the publication of information that would help spread the word. The most prominent of these was the General Council of Islamic Banks and Financial Institutions, of which he was chairman, and on whose board of directors he served up until the end of his life. He was also an enthusiastic member of the Executive Committee and on the Board of Trustees of the Accounting and Auditing Organisation for Islamic Financial Institutions.

Throughout his banking career, Saleh Kamel was a regular participant in events and conferences held by the Islamic Financial Services Board. In the last two years of his life one of the key things he worked on was an ambitious project to establish the International Sharia Classification Authority, something he was sadly unable to see through to completion. He did not believe in ratings and classifications issued by specialised international firms, and nor did he concur with their feasibility studies. To him the suggestions of such bodies differed totally from the moral vision and theory that should support a real economy, and they overlooked such elements as the sustainable development of the planet and the practical employment of its people.

This thinking can be traced back to the principles that underpinned Saleh Kamel's earliest initiatives to help spread and encourage a better understanding of how an Islamic economy should operate. As early as 1976 he established an annual donation of 20,000 Egyptian Pounds to the Faculty of Commerce at Al-Azhar University in Egypt to be awarded to the best research into Islamic commerce. Through the years, the scope of the awards he gave was expanded, and in 1982 the Supreme Council of Al-Azhar approved Saleh Kamel's offer to build a research centre, now known as the Saleh Kamel Centre for Islamic Economy.

Another important project, undertaken through Albaraka Investment's regional office in Amman, under the supervision of another prominent pioneer of Islamic banking, Dr Sami Hassan Hammoud, was the Jurisprudence Encyclopaedia Project for Financial Transactions. Also in Jordan, since 1980, Saleh Kamel had cooperated with the Royal Aal Al Bayt Institute for Islamic Thought (RABIT), providing financial support to enable a series of analytical indices linked to Islamic Economics.

Various universities have benefitted from his support in a similar way. In 1985, he established the Islamic Economics Centre at King Abdul Aziz University in Jeddah, furnished its halls, supplied its specialised books and reference resources, and continued to offer financial support to the centre until the university took over. Nor did he overlook his alma mater, King Saud University (formerly University of Riyadh), where he established the Islamic Banking Centre. In 2005, he made a donation towards the construction of the College of Business Administration building at Al-Faisal University in Riyadh. From 1982 he also donated SAR 71,000 yearly to the Faculty of Business Studies in King Saud University to be awarded to the best research in Islamic economy.

Saleh Kamel was preoccupied with the mechanisms that achieve education and enlightenment, whether through specialised educational and training centres or scientific chairs that he funded. Among one of his most important legacies is the annual Albaraka Islamic Economics Symposium, launched in Madinah on June 27, 1983, and held annually in the month of Ramadan. This forum for discussion of Sharia-compliant economic systems is an essential reference point for the development of both Islamic banking and Islamic economic ideas in general.

Aside from the various centres of learning which he supported, Saleh Kamel was also a prodigious writer, penning regular articles in the Arab media, and his countless appearances on television shows made him a household name. He was always honest, true to himself, and did not shy away from presenting confident opinions that sometimes tested the often deeply entrenched interpretations of traditional society. It is beyond question that Saleh Kamel was a leading pioneer in implementing Islamic economic systems, something that went far beyond his own companies' business goals, but formed part of an ambitious vision to reshape society to be at once more ethical and more successful. This vision operated at the macro but also the micro level, as those closest to him are happy to confirm.

Mustafa Latif Topbas, a long-time friend of Saleh Kamel, explains:
"Our fathers – Nuri Topbas and Abdullah Kamel – met as a result of the Hajj pilgrimages between 1940 and 1960, when my father travelled to Makkah. The firm friendship between them was continued by us; Sheikh Saleh was my friend and confidant for more than forty years. Sometimes a friend becomes closer than a relative, he stands by you and keeps your secrets, and this was this case with Sheikh Saleh. I was never disappointed in him, he never let me down. When he was launching Albaraka Turkish Finance House, we worked together closely and also with the late Turgut Ozal, who was then Prime Minister and later became the President of the Turkish Republic. Mr Ozal once offered to give Sheikh Saleh Turkish citizenship and a Turkish passport but Sheikh Saleh declined – he was always a proud Saudi Arabian.

"I had many conversations with Sheikh Saleh about business law, *zakat*, and his interpretation of other Islamic directives. He not only discussed Islamic teachings, he also lived by them. Kings and princes ate at his table but also drivers and other employees. His home was open to all who knocked on his door. "During the Iraqi invasion of Kuwait in 1990, the Kuwaiti dinar became worthless and banks would not accept it. To reassure Kuwaitis who were far from their homeland, Sheikh Saleh instructed Albaraka to convert 500 Kuwaiti dinars per Kuwaiti passport holder into dollars or Turkish lira for those staying in Turkey, regardless of who they were; all these transactions were backed by funds from his own personal account.

"I was also present when he intervened with the authorities on behalf of three Palestinian-Jordanians who travelled on the same aircraft as us from Morocco to Tunisia. Everyone had cleared passport control except for these three, who were being denied access to the country. Government ministries swiftly became involved when Sheikh Saleh threatened that if the

Palestinian-Jordanians were not allowed in, he would not be entering Tunisia either, not then and not ever. While the matter was addressed at the highest levels, Sheikh Saleh sat with his friends and waited. Only after the last one was safely through passport control did he leave the airport.

"He was a remarkable human being, always informed and interesting, forward thinking, open to innovation, hardworking, and he also loved to teach and learn. When he was involved in a new project, he would be thinking of the families that would benefit from it, the children who would be fed from the wages it generated. I miss him, but as we always used to say, Inshallah (God willing) we will be together again in Paradise."

CHAPTER FIVE

MEDIA: FIRST STEPS

For Saleh Kamel, media was a passion as much as an investment and, much as he might be loath to admit it, Dallah's commitment to some of his personal media dreams often pushed the company close to the financial danger zone. That said, the billionaire businessman made some groundbreaking decisions that opened up the then relatively closed Saudi society to a host of outside influences which extended far beyond his homeland.

"I have been in love with the media industry since I was a young man," Sheikh Saleh explained: "What began as a hobby as a schoolboy would follow me in various guises most of my life.

"In 1969, I founded the Arab Media Production Company (Aramid) in Riyadh to specialize in importation, marketing, and production of media. We began to import television products, including TV series, recorded concerts, films, plays, and children's shows, in addition to educational programs from Egypt, Syria, Lebanon, and Jordan. We distributed them all over the Kingdom, in other Gulf countries, and beyond.

"The company was originally established as a distributor but swiftly became involved in the production side of things. It produced its own television programs and some movies. We were considered pioneers in the Gulf region by producing the first 35mm colour television film and a host of colour TV productions. It was Aramid that provided Saudi television with what would eventually amount to thousands of different television programs over the years.

"The Media Production Company was my first practical experience in media, which developed into a whole range of a broader investments."

Egypt was a key source of material but things were not always straightforward. "I was on vacation in Cairo at a time when the relationship between the Kingdom and Egypt was tense," Saleh Kamel recalled.

At the time of this visit, relations between Saudi Arabia and Egypt were at their lowest ebb since Nasser's time. The peace agreement that Egyptian President Anwar Sadat signed with Israel in March 1979 had split the Arab world in two, leading to Egypt's expulsion from the Arab League, the withdrawal of the Saudi and other Gulf ambassadors from Cairo, and the imposition of economic sanctions. Egypt had become a pariah within the Arab world.

"During my stay in Cairo, I visited Egypt's television headquarters. My quest was to be appointed their representative in the Kingdom, a role that would allow me to market plays, serials, and some films to Saudi television, then in its early years. Our programmes in the Kingdom of Saudi Arabia were simply not comparable with Egyptian productions, which were at their zenith at that time.

"People across much of the Middle East were familiar with the Egyptian product. Most of the regional television stations were filling their hours of transmission with Egyptian media, then in black and white, but in Saudi Arabia this was not the case.

"While working as a Ministry of Finance representative on secondment to the Ministry of Information, I learned there were no Egyptian productions in our Saudi Television Library. Despite being widespread elsewhere, they simply did not exist in the Kingdom.

"I immediately realised that this could provide a unique opportunity for me to bring home something new and exciting.

"I presented the idea of acting as an agent to supply Egyptian-made programs and films to the Minister of Information, who at that time was Ibrahim Al-Anqari. He seemed to like the idea in principle but was reluctant to take an immediate decision. My proposal remained on the table for some weeks until, out of the blue, the Minister invited me to his office – towards the end of the month of Ramadan – and asked me if I could produce a number of comedy plays to be broadcast during Eid.

"I was surprised by the urgency of his request. The timeframe was tight but I accepted the challenge and managed to bring him a series called 'Ella Khamsaa', the first Egyptian television comedy to be broadcast on Saudi television.

"In the mid-1980s, in partnership with Mohamed Yassin, one of the major producers and distributors in the region, I established the Sunnyland Company, with outlets in Cyprus, Beirut, and Egypt. Sunnyland would eventually become known as the largest Arab and Western film distribution company in the Arab world, and we had many smaller agencies as well as production and distribution companies, working on maintaining its premier position.

"Even before my first foray into the world of television, I had maintained a close association with the media through my involvement with Tihama. I became one of the founding members of the Tihama Group for Media, Public Relations, and Marketing Studies in 1974, and was Chairman of the Board of Directors for several years. The company did well, accumulating a history of achievements to become one of the best-known in its field across the Arab region, competing with the largest international companies in the advertising market. I enjoyed being part of its lively, innovative operation and retained my shares in the company until 1996, when other obligations took over."

Saleh Kamel was also a founder member and majority shareholder in the Okaz Press and Publishing House and, later, in the Okaz Press and Publishing Corporation, as well as the Okaz Bookstores Company. He remained a member of the Board of Directors of Okaz Press and Publishing Corporation from 1993 to 2002. Separately, he was also involved in a group of other media-related ventures, including the Iqra Company for Printing and Paper Trading and the Iqra Company for Development, Publishing and Distribution. He contributed to the Saudi Research and Marketing Group, the International Information Company, the Asir Foundation for Press and Publishing (which publishes Al-Watan newspaper), Dar Al-Qibla Company for Islamic Culture, Tara Company for Media Production and Distribution, the Rotana Company for Video, Audio, and Advertising, and the Arab Media Foundation for Artistic Production and Distribution.

Outside the Kingdom, at one time or another, Dallah owned shares in the Arab Company for Press, Publishing, and Information in Beirut and in the Alexandria Printing and Publishing House, as well as majority shares in the Video Cassette Manufacturing Centre in Egypt and a stake in the United Journalists Company, which published *Al-Alam Al-Youm* (The World Today) newspaper and *Kol Al-Nas* (Everyone) magazine.

In 2012 Saleh Kamel became Chairman of Makkah newspaper – previously known as Al-Nadwa – a small publication but one which, he confessed, gave him as much pleasure as any of his mega-media projects. "This small acquisition has had a big impact on me," he explained, "because it is so closely associated with Makkah Al-Mukarramah [the official name of Makkah], the place to which the hearts of Muslims everywhere yearn and the city in which I spent my childhood years."

The newspaper was concerned primarily with news and society related to Makkah but, despite the best efforts of its publishers, was foundering. Drawing on his considerable experience, as Chairman of a very willing new Board of Directors, Saleh Kamel was, within a short time, able to transform the publication's fortunes.

Saleh Kamel was never far away from a media-related scheme.

"Media has long been a long-term love and my passion for it remained undiminished. Following developments in the industry, I could see a growing global interest in developing the more visual aspects of the industry, where words and pictures were beamed directly into peoples' homes.

"Around 1985 I decided to stake my claim. My ambition was to own a private television station and although I knew the decision might be fraught with risks and possibly even dangers, I was compelled to go forward.

"At the time, most television channels in the region were government-owned and their content closely monitored. Some of the programmes lacked – shall we say – inspiration?

"Because of my business interests, I was constantly travelling and therefore familiar with what was on offer in the rest of the world. I knew I could make a huge difference even if, in the process, I risked stirring up a hornet's nest."

It was to be a contentious step, shaking some entrenched thinking and causing a ripple.

"When it was first confirmed I would launch a private TV channel, a famous Arab newspaper mocked me in an article, implying the move was an extravagant ruse to show off. The article was part of a wider propaganda campaign by some journalists who had their own particular axe to grind. They later realised their mistake and retracted their opinions or, as one commentator put it, "were forced to eat their words'. Such attacks did not wound me, I knew that my aims were true and had the potential to bring many benefits to my homeland and, perhaps, eventually the wider region."

From the outset, Saleh Kamel was clear that the idea of launching a private television channel was first and foremost a way of achieving a serious financial return. Because of his frequent visits to the West, especially Britain and other parts of Europe, he was aware of the large numbers of expatriate Arabs living and working in those countries. He wanted to provide a means of linking these communities, many of whom were living in a cultural and social void, away from their language, religion, and origins. He was clear that there was a need for a media vehicle that could absorb and highlight their skills and achievements, as well as capitalize on their energies.

"People in our region, as in much of the rest of the world, needed a variety of channels with different types of content. Channels that were more impressive, attractive, and interactive with contemporary issues. Perhaps, I reasoned, such exposure could help free them from the hegemony of the linear government media they had become bored of, especially as the upcoming new technologies were increasingly slipping through the censorship net, further alienating them from the lack-lustre state-owned channels."

At the time, broadcasting systems such as satellites, uplinks and downlinks, as well as receivers, dishes, and connectors, were scarce and subject to strict regulations, including a law deeming their possession, without a license, a criminal act.

"The new thinking to open up communication channels was not universally popular. We faced a considerable amount of opposition. Certain groups regarded the presence of a satellite dish almost as a symbol of corruption by foreign non-believers. Despite the potential problems and the antipathy from certain quarters, however, I was entirely confident the sort of channel I proposed would be a force for good.

"Anyone who knows me will confirm that I love a challenge and have a strong urge to press forward towards achievement, rather than fall back into defeat, but honestly, I think establishing a state might have been easier than establishing a television station back then!"

Saleh Kamel spent much of 1987 talking to Western communications

experts in the United States and Europe, exploring the more technical elements of the industry and their transferability to Saudi Arabia,
where the backup network was woefully lacking.

"I was also interested in exploring the possibilities of cutting
costs, supported by the Dallah Telecommunications Company,
which I had set up specifically with the television project in
mind. I was also in regular contact with the offices and lawyers
of Dallah Albaraka in London, who had been instructed to keep
their finger on the pulse of industry advances."

It is hard to underestimate how contentious these media steps were at
the time. Saudi Arabia was evolving fast, but there were elements of
the establishment, reflecting broader opinion, who felt the changes
were too rapid and threatened the balanced traditional values of
society. For Saleh Kamel to succeed, he would need endorsement
from the very top. He reports his encounter with the king:

"Around 1985 I was granted an audience with His Majesty King
Fahd to discuss my idea to establish a private television channel.
Although he didn't say it explicitly, I felt the King rather pitied
me for what he saw as my somewhat 'woolly' notion, but at the
same time, he did not want to discourage me from the project.
His Majesty strongly advised me to partner with Sheikh Walid bin
Ibrahim – the owner of ARA International Company for Media
Production and Advertising – who, King Fahd informed me, was
also dedicated to the development of television in local markets
and had expressed an interest in launching a similar venture to
the one I suggested. It was clear the King hoped we would pool
our experiences and resources to unite as Saudi entrepreneurs."

Sheikh Walid Ibrahim describes how they came together:

"King Fahd suggested we consider working together, which made
sense as we had similar goals but different skill-sets. It's true
that Sheikh Saleh had a talent for 'thinking outside the box'
much more than me. So, although it had not been our original
intention, we joined forces and divided the roles. I focused on

99

the creative – programming and the like – while Sheikh Saleh concentrated on the structure of the new venture, specifically the financial and legal aspects."

It was a key point in Saleh Kamel's business life, and he recalled the details clearly:

"Following negotiations with Sheikh Walid bin Ibrahim, we signed a joint agreement on January 11, 1988 to establish a television broadcasting company based in Europe. The station (which would become MBC – the Middle East Broadcasting Centre) had not been named at this point, nor had we decided in which European city it would be based. However, we agreed Sheikh Walid would be the Chairman and I would be his deputy in this groundbreaking new venture.

"The first meeting of the Board, chaired by my dearest friend, brother-in-law, and former Minister of Information, Dr Mohammad Abdo Yamani, was held in Cairo on Thursday April 14, 1988, to discuss the establishment of an Arab satellite channel in Europe.

"Several decisions were taken, the most important of which was to immediately establish an office for the station in Cairo under the management of Ms Hemmat Mustafa."

Ms Mustafa was described by Saleh Kamel as "a great woman with a demonstrated experience in media and administrative fields", who was President of Egyptian Television for a period of time. She was the first director of the Middle East Broadcasting Company, working between Cairo and London – where a second office was swiftly established – until 1991. Later, Saleh Kamel would enlist her help in the management of the Arab Radio and Television broadcasting centre in Italy.

The decision to operate from Cairo was a strategic one. The Egyptian capital was, and still is, the main hub of regional TV programming material of all kinds. The Egyptian influence in the industry during the 1980s cannot be over-stated. The amount of media experience there exceeded that of all the other countries of the region put together. Beirut was also an enthusiastic player in the entertainment industry, but nothing like on the scale of Cairo.

The new MBC Egyptian-based satellite network was the pioneering channel that would institute the breakthrough of reaching an Arab audience in Europe, through agreements with satellite service providers in numerous European capitals.

Saleh Kamel noted:

"We had a programming schedule featuring documentaries, entertainment and news, although our news was always bought in from elsewhere in order to minimise any accusation of political bias, which would have been strictly against our code of conduct.

"We were very aware of our position as the world's first Arab private channel and the expectations we would be required to meet. There had to be a good and varied library of programmes set up and ready for when the completion of establishing the technical infrastructure was in place. This would enable the channel to launch with a bang.

"Arab films were at the forefront of our programme stock. They had a universal appeal to our prospective audience and their length covered a conveniently large portion of broadcasting time. Thankfully, our Arab audience was hungry for such entertainment, especially at that time when, other than in the cinemas, there were few alternatives available.

"State-run television channels had failed miserably in meeting the needs of the public. There were, of course, videocassette tapes to supplement the meagre official offerings, but these were also strictly regulated by governments.

"There was no competition over acquisitions in those days."

Not much later, purchase and monopoly agreements would begin to emerge everywhere. But the market in the mid-1980s was limited to government channels – with restricted resources – and just a few private entrepreneurs with progressive business ideas, active mainly between Cairo and Beirut.

Although the people at MBC were thrilled with their achievements, the move was not popular with everyone and would bring some sharp criticism down on the heads of both Saleh Kamel and Sheikh Walid Ibrahim, as well as their associates.

Saleh Kamel was sanguine on the opposition the new venture inevitably faced. He had always been aware that he would be ruffling feathers, and was ready to deal with what would follow:

"When you embark on working in the media industry, you must expect a lot of criticism and attacks from within the existing industry.

"These arise out of professional insecurities, fears, or simply particular individual whims; it is important to try and understand that the motives are usually not personal. One cannot afford to get bogged down in questioning the intentions of others. It is preferable to remain open, flexible, and patient if you want to succeed in accomplishing your mission and achieving your goals.

"We tried always to stay true to our strategic media plan for the station, adhering to guidelines for material that reinforced the importance of upholding human values and Islamic ethics. "We pulled out all the stops to research satellite companies – although they were few and far between in those days – in order to obtain optimum services at the best prices and conditions. I do not exaggerate when I say that during that period, I personally read more papers, documents, and reports than I had throughout my entire university education."

The hard work paid off, and by the end of 1989, the company was able to conclude an agreement involving the Eutelsat 2 satellite broadband with the British Telecom Authority, enabling the station to cover six European capitals, namely Amsterdam, Bonn, Brussels, Geneva, Paris, and, of course, London, where the station – duly registered as the Middle East Broadcasting Company – had its headquarters.

Now, it was possible for individual subscribers to receive the channel's signal directly, via satellite dishes and, in Europe, via cable networks. At the same time, the engineering department was researching how to efficiently spread coverage across the Arab region. Eventually a deal was signed with Arabsat and a station in Italy began receiving and re-transmitting the signal from London directly to Arabsat, which covered the region from Morocco to Iran in one direction and into the south part of Russia, in the other.

Not wanting to rely entirely on Egyptian ingenuity, MBC began to take in productions from various other Arab countries in its programming schedule. The channel hosted a rich variety of Arab productions, and an essential part of the thinking was that it should represent all Arabs and not limit the target market to just one country.

It was a bold venture but was frugally run and budgets were not lavish. In the early days, it was not clear what level of revenue the corporation could expect to dependably generate. Saleh Kamel recalls:

> "We were looking forward to having advertising income as a major contributor towards covering our costs. From the outset, we were working with a limited budget that, we agreed, should never exceed what the parties contributed to the capital, without bank loans or support from any third party. That said, on one or two occasions we were forced to resort to paying from our own pocket to meet urgent operating expenses.
>
> "We entrusted our advertising to the Tihama Advertising, Public Relations, and Marketing Company, of which I was Chairman back then. The company, by that time, was in control of the advertising market in the Kingdom of Saudi Arabia and had international offices, proprietary media outlets, shareholders, and brokers in most Arab and Western countries."

MBC's agreement with Tihama was celebrated with a party in London in November 1991. The event was chiefly a vehicle to allow

MBC to promote itself as a new media outlet to prospective advertisers. The industry was more restrained in those days when it came to
spending on companies promoting their goods. The prevailing idea,
especially with big companies, was that their products were already
well known to consumers, so the advertising was not an easy sell:

> "Most companies felt that spending additional money on adver-
> tising to promote their products and services was an unnecessary
> extravagance, or even a complete waste of money. I confess I was
> one of them; I do not recall dedicating a large amount of money
> to promotional advertising for a single one of my companies or
> products."

Despite the prevailing opinion on advertising spending, in December
1991, MBC would install – at considerable expense– no fewer than
60 free dishes at strategic sites, including influential media outlets,
advertising and political locations. These allowed decision-makers
and other people of consequence to monitor the output of the new
channel and, hopefully, encourage them to take out advertising.

The MBC test broadcast began on September 18, 1991 and initially
ran for six hours a day. Its General Manager, Tariq Ahmed Riri,
headed up a team of about two hundred Arab and Western employees as well as news correspondents and broadcasters. Riri's brief was
to target the five million Arabs living in Europe and a potential
audience in excess of one hundred million in the Arab world and
bring a healthy majority on board.

MBC's official launch was celebrated at Claridge's Hotel in central
London on October 24, 1991, in the presence of a distinguished
gathering of influential Arab and Western leaders from the worlds of
media, politics, and finance, as well as a bevy of Western journalists
and media people, including publishers, broadcasters, and heads of
television channels. Saleh Kamel describes the event:

> "The Chairman of the Board of Directors, Sheikh Walid bin
> Ibrahim, delivered an excellent speech in which he stressed that
> the goal of the channel was to link Arabs residing in Europe to their

culture and their homelands. I was alongside him, welcoming the attendees and looking forward to a long and prosperous association." Unfortunately, despite the mutual respect between the two entrepreneurial Saudi businessmen, cracks soon began to appear in the partnership, although, as Sheikh Walid noted, the two had started out 'on the same wavelength'. He describes how they worked together:

"Sheikh Saleh had produced television dramas for government-funded television and already had contacts in the business that we could – and did - use. He was familiar with demand and really appreciated the idea of delivering quality work, as did I.

"We had what I would consider a father and son relationship. I learned a lot from Saleh Kamel and I respected him. He would sometimes refer to me as being his 'son'. But, as we all know, even in the closest of families, things do not always work out as planned. The roadmap for MBC was designed by us both ... we had a vision and wanted it to grow. But sadly, something went wrong along the way."

Saleh Kamel noted that the first signs of disagreement occurred within a few months, around the beginning of 1992. He was clear on where the fundamental disagreement lay. With swiftly increasing operating costs. a deficit had begun to appear and the partners disagreed on how to finance the shortfall. The view of the Chairman, Sheikh Walid, was that they should draw partners into the venture. Saleh Kamel felt there might be a better way. He explained:

"Among my proposals to overcome the liquidity problem was to jointly establish a company under the name the International Satellite Services Company (Fadaa), that would distribute an encrypted MBC transmission signal, providing services to other TV stations, together with leases for satellite broadband, broadcast channels that suited the needs of the Kingdom of Saudi Arabia, and other ideas for services capable of generating large profits.

"We discussed the matter at length but sadly, could not reach agreement. The liquidity issue continued to deteriorate and I felt action had to be taken. I was totally honest with my partner; a radical solution had to be found if we were to keep the company running and avoid collapse."

In January 1994 Saleh Kamel suggested three or four scenarios, including his own exit from the company and an offer to sell to Sheikh Walid his shares. However, the partners could not find a way to make this work. By the end of the same year, Saleh Kamel had received an offer to sell his shares at three times their nominal value. It was an attractive offer and he agreed to it immediately. By 1994, Saleh Kamel's association with MBC was at an end. It must have been a source of considerable sadness, having put so much into the venture, but Saleh Kamel did not harbour ill-will, and set his sights on moving on:

"I continue to have great affection for the channel, I still follow its progress avidly, and I have immense respect for Walid Ibrahim. I am proud to have been part of the venture with him.

"Of course, it is always disappointing when a venture fails to meet one's expectations but I was not downcast … I had gained useful experience with MBC and, armed with that, I felt the time was right for me to go it alone. I decided I would follow my heart and attempt to set up a specialised pay-to-view channel, implementing some of the ideas I had wanted to see in operation at MBC. I would launch a completely new channel where I could focus on bringing my own ideas to fruition and call it the Arab Radio and Television Network – ART."

For his part, Walid Ibrahim later acknowledged that Saleh Kamel had been keen to introduce the idea of an encrypted pay-to-view channel at MBC but noted he had disagreed, being of the view that the Arab world – with its free state-controlled television networks – was not ready for such a thing.

Paying tribute to the bravery of his former partner, Ibrahim noted:

"Sheikh Saleh was always a risk-taker and he certainly took a risk with ART. Looking back, I wish I had been bolder in our partnership. He had much wider vision than me at that time.

Eventually, some years down the line, around 2002/2003, we broke even at MBC and the station did begin to make money. Ultimately, Sheikh Saleh and I had the same idea, it just took me longer to get there."

The establishment of MBC was an important milestone in the regional media industry and one that gathered together, for the first time, a unique band of talent and unequivocal expertise and experience. King Fahd, in inviting Saleh Kamel and Walid Ibrahim to combine their knowledge and expertise to launch a new channel, had made them what some might describe as "an offer they could not refuse". It is, after all, unusual to turn down the request of a King. However, going forward, Saleh Kamel channelled his media aspirations through ART, where any decisions on the channel's future would be made by him, and him alone. He was back in the driver's seat which, according to those who knew him best, was the only position he truly enjoyed.

Through all of this, Saleh Kamel maintained a strong filial bond with his father, Sheikh Abdullah, who had his own office on the top floor of Dallah Albaraka Tower, the company's Jeddah headquarters. Mohammad Moussa, who served loyally as trusted Jeddah office manager for more than 30 years, remembers warmly how Sheikh Abdullah would leave his desk in the late afternoon and go outside to feed the pigeons that clustered on the spacious private balcony outside his office. Saleh Kamel would often join him there, and the two men would sit talking and laughing together, perhaps comparing a particularly hungry pigeon to a local politician, or a nervous bird with a fretful business contact of their acquaintance.

Saleh Kamel would consult his father on all manner of things and greatly valued his opinion. We can now never know if the complex business of establishing a media empire were among the topics discussed up there among the pigeons, but certainly many hours were spent out on the large balcony at the time Saleh Kamel had important industry issues on his mind. Sheikh Abdullah's words were weighed carefully by his son as they fed the pigeons together, but ultimately, as all were well aware, it was Saleh Kamel who made the final call.

"I saw a similar thing with his sons, who followed him into the business," Mohammad Moussa recalled. "Sheikh Saleh was proud of their business acumen and would sit with them debating developments or potential problems but, at the end of the day, it was the path of Saleh Kamel we would usually follow." The Arab Radio and Television Network (ART), being the first Pay-TV television in the region and an exciting, groundbreaking experience in its own right, was the cause of much general family debate and more than a few dilemmas. As Saleh Kamel would later admit:

"ART– the narrative of its details, the explanation of its parts, the diving into its philosophy, the purpose of its creation, the obstacles encountered, the difficulties endured, and the conflicts fought at both official and popular levels – almost derailed the process on several occasions. But with patience, perseverance, education, enlightenment, and above all faith in what I was doing and confidence in its ultimate success, the channel eventually came into being.

"I did not plan to leave my investment in television and media behind when I left MBC. The idea of developing specialised channels was particularly attractive to me. It was a new and different concept for our region. I also saw it as being very much in line with the strategic investment objectives of Dallah Albaraka, where the creation of job opportunities has always been high on our list of priorities. And since the smallest media achievement requires the input and involvement of many people, administrative, creative, technical etc., I felt it was a perfect fit for us."

A running theme through Saleh Kamel's projects was that moderate Islamic values and social traditions must be respected at all times. As a business, the fundamental goal of achieving profit was an important, and indeed was essential in order to expand and develop as a company, but the financial goal had to dovetail with other objectives. Alongside maintaining Islamic values, there was also the goal of maintaining a leadership. Innovation was key to this, and Dallah Albaraka sought to lead the field rather than imitate and compete with others. As competitors inevitably came close to catching up, Dallah would move on to something else in the quest to continue making an impact. On the ethical side, Saleh Kamel was also keen to steer clear of activities – such as speculation - that he felt could add no genuine value to any projects or to the national economy. Today corporate social responsibility is a cornerstone of all major international corporations, upheld as part of the commitment to shareholders. Saleh Kamel considered this to be part of his personal responsibility as a business leader, and he was acutely aware that a media network – with all the massive influence it could bring to a developing and potentially vulnerable social system – had to be careful to balance commercial considerations with an assessment of what was morally right. This came sharply into focus when it came to the programming decisions of the network:

"When I was partner at MBC, I was intrigued by the idea of launching specialised Arabic channels that would meet the needs of the whole family. I had seen this model in operation in various parts of the world. In America, for example, there are networks with more than 200 channels, with each channel dedicated to a specific topic, thus meeting the requirements of viewers of all ages and inclinations.

"By 1993 it was already clear there was media content that would be wholly incompatible with our society, being beamed into the Arab region - programmes totally discordant with our Islamic religion and the traditions and the customs of the Muslim and Arab family, our social and educational values.

"We could not blame their mainly western producers. They made programmes for their own consumption, according to their own customs, traditions, and preferences. But I strongly believed that these productions brought no value whatever to our Arab society.

"The solution to confronting this tide clearly did not lie in strict methods of authoritarian prevention, which had proved to be a total failure. However, it was equally obvious that geographical separations and the barriers between countries were blurring, in light of satellite convergence and, as far as we were concerned, not in a positive way.

"It became clear that to compete effectively in what had become a small global village we must create a product no less attractive or impressive than that of our foreign counterparts. There was certainly no such possibility available through government channels, and the frantic demand to buy satellite dishes – despite the ban in many areas – was an indication of the public's desire to break away from the official option."

The Arab public had a thirst to experience the new era of information and visual entertainment. Banning access to these contemporary channels was almost impossible. The markets were awash with skilled professionals illegally deciphering and decoding encrypted channels that were totally incompatible with the values of Saudi Arabia's conservative societies. It was clear that an avalanche of material, entirely devoid of all respect for our religious and social traditions, was fast approaching. And to stand in its way was to take on a potentially controversial role as gatekeeper to the future of society's values.

Whenever a solution to block this illegal trade was discovered, the 'pirates' would find a way to undo it. The ART network had much bitter experience of this, to the extent that encryption codes had to be changed almost daily during major sporting events:

"I learned, pretty quickly, to deal with the furious verbal attacks against me, which didn't bother me too much because I knew my intentions in building the station were entirely honourable.

"My goal was to engineer reform by putting into practice insights and experiences I had accumulated over years in the media industry, with the aim of launching a television channel whose content would promote Islamic and family values.

"Of course, I took a risk but there can be no reward without doing so. The whole essence of Islamic economics is based on a spirit of adventure. If you want to profit, you must also be prepared to take the risk of suffering a loss. I have always accepted the label of being a risk-taker but I have never regarded myself as a gambler – more of an adventurer.

"I decided that I would take a risk on ART and, if I discovered I had erred in my judgment, I would have the courage to withdraw and accept the result of my miscalculation."

As with any new venture, ART experienced its ups and downs. Things did not always go well, and whenever the network was going through challenging times, rivals were not slow to try and seize the opportunity and jump in. At times, rivals came to the conclusion that ART was financially bankrupt and on the verge of closing, but when things looked uncertain, Saleh Kamel would always inject more money into its veins and the channel would come back stronger and more challenging than before. Eventually, as time went on and the situation stabilized, ART was absorbed into the industry and became unshakeable. It was a process that took a long time, but gradually the encryption of TV channels became a reality accepted by both the people and their governments. Saleh Kamel benefitted from being the market leader in this, but leading the charge naturally also takes its toll. In his own words:

"I believe I paid the dowry and the tax for leading the concept of the Pay-TV industry in the Middle East region, often at the expense of my time and my health."

With ART, leading the way eventually paid off. But it was not always so. Saleh Kamel's forays into the media sector in the former Soviet Union did not work out at all well. By early 1992, shortly after the dissolution of the union, he was forced to withdraw. He recounts the tale:

"I was too hasty. I invested before the essential laws and legislation to established new business structures were in place and before communities there were familiar with the nature of private business. Clear partnership guidelines had not been established and areas of responsibilities were not defined.

"When I saw, with the system weighted against me, I could not succeed, I had the courage to withdraw; I shut down my operation and left the country. I bear no grudge against the people I tried to do business with in the ex-Soviet Islamic republics, they had been languishing in complete isolation under totalitarian socialist regimes and were not ready to embrace the changes I wanted to institute."

In September 1998, Saleh Kamel had launched the satellite channel "Iqraa" on Arabsat. It was the first Islamic satellite channel, an achievement of which he was immensely proud. The channel ran programmes variously aimed at adults, young people, and children, covering a wide range of topics, which it examined from an Islamic perspective. The aim at Iqraa was to provide a 'safe haven' for family viewing – a way of showing the true face of Islam to Muslims and non-Muslims alike. Iqraa's international programming was aimed at educating Muslims living in the West on proper Islamic practices. The network covered five continents and broadcast in several languages, including Arabic.

"Of all my media investments over the years this was a real stand out moment ... For me, establishing the Iqraa channel gave me the same sense of achievement as winning the contract for cleaning and providing water to the Two Holy Mosques of Makkah and Madinah years before. It was a way of paying something back, an attempt to partially fulfil my Islamic duty.

"The day the cleaning and maintenance contract in Makkah and Madinah was announced, I received phone calls and messages from all corners of the globe. Those who knew me well knew just how much being given the responsibility meant to me, and after establishing the Iqraa channel I experienced the same sort of thing.

"I have never let the destiny of Iqraa be decided by the income of sponsorship or advertising and I have made sure its aims of promoting moderate Islamic tolerance in matters of faith, Sharia and human interaction, will live on after me by providing for its continuance in my will," Saleh Kamel said.

Programme selection, across all channels, was ever a sensitive matter, and certainly not as straightforward as might be assumed. Saleh Kamel's range of activities was far removed from the news field – a particularly controversial subject for broadcasting, and endlessly prone to the fickle winds of political change – and entertainment also had its own sensitivities. Members of the audience would take issue with content, or with the programme's creator, or even broadcaster. The channel frequently faced the challenge of having to deal with complaints – some during late-night transmissions – demanding that it cease broadcasting a 'live' programme, for a supposed breach of guidelines, or simply because a poem, a verse, a poet, or even a particular presenter caused someone, somewhere, offence. On many occasions, controllers would receive late-night calls demanding that this or that programme be censored, or demanding the immediate end of a live transmission, or officials from this or that country would be enraged at some sensitivity breached and would force through protests at the highest levels to reject the broadcast of a poem or verse on political grounds, or to silence a poet, or even the person presenting.

ART never officially announced that it would not tackle political content but it was careful to say that it would not present news coverage. When it hosted political figures, conversation obviously covered diplomatic or constitutional matters, but they were always careful to steer clear of issues known to cause conflict among Arabs.

Such material was left to the news channels, of which there were many. That said, a clear and consistent stance was taken on certain key matters such as, for example, Palestine and the plight of its people. This was a particular issue which received attention, and indeed ART saw part of its role as connecting Palestinians at home and elsewhere in the world with their homeland.

The policy of broadcasting programmes that would support social cohesion and unity was deliberately maintained. Saleh Kamel's networks were, for example, the first TV station in history to broadcast *taraweeh*[15] prayers live from Jerusalem, and they also aired Friday prayers every week from the Al-Aqsa Mosque in Jerusalem. This was seen as important in keeping Islamic heritage at the centre of what their viewers received.

In 2001, Saleh Kamel launched a study into establishing an Arab-Islamic news agency under the name of the Fair Vision Network, an integrated channel seeking to introduce events from the Islamic region to the world with a neutral, logical vision that reflected the positive aspects of the Arab and Islamic nations in a variety of languages. He was clear on the thinking behind this:

"All too frequently I have seen our news become dominated and distorted by those actively working against the interests of Arabs and Muslims. I had hoped it might be possible to take more responsibility for our own news, to spread information on the successes and activities of the Muslim world in a positive way, to help redress the imbalance. However, the initial indicators of participation and contribution by Arab and Islamic governments were not encouraging.

Rather than seeing paid TV as a force for good, many were inclined to see it simply as a money-making exercise with Saleh Kamel raking in vast amounts of profit by charging for a service which had, hitherto, been free.

---

15 *Taraweeh*, also known as Ramadan nightly prayers, are long prayers with readings of the Quran.

"Naturally I wanted the television station to be profitable and to make money but I also felt a strong moral obligation towards our subscribers. At the beginning, providing the region with a new and fascinating entertainment channel and making a profit from it was not an easy task. I had many, many sleepless nights and, during the hours I was awake, my life seemed to be dominated by watching, monitoring, and policing the programmes we broadcast.

"It would, of course, have been easier if the work had all been directed to a single country, in which case just one set of established traditions and prohibitions could have been adhered to. But we were covering several countries, with different norms applying in each. What one nation sees as completely acceptable can be interpreted by another as hostile; it often felt as if we were navigating a minefield!

"To produce work satisfactory to all Arabs requires craftsmanship and considerable knowledge of the various cultures and history. Pursuing these different and diverse aims took time and effort. We established production centres in several Arab countries which, naturally, increased our costs.

"I don't believe I shall ever forget that period of time when dozens of bags of all shapes, sizes and materials, accompanied me wherever I went – on my plane, to my office, in meeting rooms and even in my bedroom, each was packed with broadcasting schedules, budgets for approval, papers, contracts, and scripts to read and endorse or reject.

"In my office I have a bank of small screens with a large one in the middle; each screen showed what was being broadcast by a particular ART channel. I monitored them constantly. If I noticed a deviation or violation on one of the small screens, I switched to the larger screen and immediately made contact with the responsible employee to correct the situation. To say that for those years I lived and breathed ART would not be an exaggeration. It was never-ending."

Signal piracy and the sporting events – particularly football, with league broadcasting rights, World Cup events, exclusive rights, and geographical distribution – occupied a great deal of the network's administrative time. The fiercest wars were over sport. Legislation concerning intellectual and programming property rights in the region was weak at that time, causing a continuous headache for the channel as it exerted every effort to stabilize and protect the legal rights it had invested in. Massive profits were lost to piracy, and this would frequently prevent ART from achieving the target subscriptions for certain events.

Whenever ART aired the World Cup games, or any major competition, it faced mass outrage from members of the public who had elected to stay with state television channels and consequently, could not now access the top games. Saleh Kamel describes how some of the key rival channels could easily have made a deal with him, or with the owner of the rights, to broadcast and provide coverage to their viewers, but they chose not to compete in an open market. Their tactic, instead, was to try and shift the blame to ART, depicting it as being too controlling. These rival channels would attempt to bamboozle their audiences, using false arguments as a smokescreen against the reality, which was that they had simply not managed to organise anything for major events. ART became the focus of a concerted campaign to undermine it – live events and prime-time programmes attacking ART were aired on rival channels and there was a push to mobilise some sort of boycott of ART. The network was never given an opportunity to defend itself or reply to any of their charges. However, Saleh Kamel fought back with energy:

"I personally responded by holding press conferences and by publishing articles in newspapers, even though the headlines were frequently misleading and further aggregated the situation. They simply could not forgive us. Monopolising sports events was considered a breach of patriotism, and encrypting the signal to allow only subscribers to view was regarded as a heinous crime and an infringement of the rights of the masses.

"While I was being described as the demon of the piece – single-handedly responsible for the loss of free-to-view sports from television screens around the region, the truth was that an explicit policy had been imposed by the International Federation of Football Associations (FIFA), who could see the raft of opportunities generated for the improvement of the game, by attaining another lucrative revenue source. ART and other encrypted or free, private, or state-owned channels all around the world did not have the power to change or violate this situation.

"Sport had become a lucrative industry, a commercial commodity which involved companies, investments, rules, and regulations, as well as profit and loss calculations. There was no going back. Free streaming no longer exists as a right for the citizens of any country; the laws and traditions of the international sports associations have changed, and the old days have gone for good. These changes were already in train elsewhere in the world when ART started to adopt its pay-to-view policy. Government officials propagated misinformation to the public that TV encryption in the region was a punishing innovation invented by Saleh Kamel, and that he was the one who had deprived the masses of their right to watch sports events for free. It was a ploy to let the governments off the hook."

It was an arduous and exhausting battle. The critics who refused to see the writing on the wall opened the door to insults and abuse, especially from the younger generation. Saleh Kamel argued that governments of the region should have directed efforts towards educating and enlightening people about the international change in the concept of watching sport events; he believed they should have played a role in making clear that the era of free sports was gone forever. It was far easier, however, to attempt to blame Saleh Kamel. There was a feeling held even at government levels that resistance would decrease the numbers of subscriptions and that the networks would then have to give up and withdraw from the region, resulting in a return to national sporting events being broadcast for free – something that would, in turn, have increased their popularity with the voters.

They were, of course, disappointed, and their wishes did not come true. As season followed season, the international and continental associations for sports, along with their affiliated companies, intermediaries, and brokers, raised the prices until they reached amounts that exceeded even the capability of individual investors like ART. No matter how ART struggled to decrease its subscription fees, many people still could not afford them. The income generated from advertisers in the region was not high enough to bridge the gap.

Consequently, in 2009 Saleh Kamel took the difficult decision to sell all the sports channels with their programme contents, periodicals, World Cup and other championships to the Qatari channel, Al-Jazeera, which had emerged as a powerful new force in the world of media and, with its state-backed support, was probably the only player in the game able to offer what the network was worth. The outcome was not something anyone would have foreseen, but it rounded off Saleh Kamel's involvement neatly. As he reported himself:

"The successful conclusion of the deal was a surprise even to some of my closest relatives, who had taken pity on me and thought that ART and those encrypted channels would devour everything I had built. Ultimately, the experience proved the opposite.

"There was much speculation at the time, but I am happy to confirm that the revenue generated from the sale of ART sports channels covered my entire invested capital and all my media expenses from 1993 until 2009," he said. "I would say the deal achieved a good return on investment."

It was, in some ways, the end of an era. But Saleh Kamel had reached a point where he no longer wanted to be constantly preoccupied with the media and its wars. Investing in the sector had deprived him of the time to explore and enjoy so many of his other interests. He had taken on the role of president of the Islamic Chamber of Commerce, Industry, and Agriculture in 2005 and the Chamber of Commerce and Industry in Jeddah in 2009. It was time to explore these new directions.

CHAPTER SIX: MEDIA:

BUILDING AND DIVESTING AN EMPIRE

Most of the people around the Chairman were delighted to see the removal of the ART channel from the Dallah Albaraka portfolio. ART had been an ambition and a passion, although one that involved constant struggle for Saleh Kamel. It was clear to those around him that ownership of ART had taken its toll, both physically and emotionally. With its sale to Al Jazeera there was a happy ending for Dallah and for ART – at least in the eyes of the accountants – but for Saleh Kamel letting the channel go was tinged with sadness. He had witnessed in the US and Europe how pay-to-view TV could bring a new and exciting experience to viewers and had been passionate about bringing it to Arabia. In retrospect, it is probably fair to say that the region was not yet ready for the upheaval that it entailed – everyone wanted the benefits without the price tag. Saleh Kamel had thrown himself body and soul into making ART a success. While he always maintained he did not care about the criticism which the idea brought down on his head, there can be no doubt that, at least at some level, he was disappointed that the dream had not fulfilled his expectations.

Saleh Kamel was an extremely popular figure in the Arab world, a self-made man who proved success was attainable even for those not born with a silver spoon in their mouth. People loved the idea of the boy from the alleys of Makkah flying around the world in his own private jet, raising the profile of Saudi Arabia and the Arab world in general with his business and banking ventures. But suddenly he was asking them personally for their money and, critically, money to watch their beloved football. It was more than many could endure.

The press encouraged the belief that their all-time hero, Saleh Kamel, had turned on them. The newspapers demanded to know how the successful billionaire businessman could ask clerks, van drivers, and small shopkeepers for money in order to enjoy one of the few pleasures they had always experienced for free.

Similar outrage was voiced in the press a few years later when, in an attempt to curb the outrageous traffic violations taking place on the highways of Saudi Arabia, traffic-calming measures were introduced. Along with other independent contractors, Dallah Albaraka was involved in the operation of speed cameras, which were installed on the streets of Saudi Arabia as part of a wider traffic-control project. An automated traffic management system covering major cities in Saudi Arabia was gradually introduced, using a network of digital cameras connected to the National Information Centre (NIC). When the press got wind of the fact Dallah was involved in what was, for them, essentially a light engineering project, they printed stories that made it appear Saleh Kamel himself was taking every riyal earned by the fines imposed on those traffic violators caught on camera. Saleh Kamel appeared to shrug off the criticism, but he once mentioned to a friend that while his name was always included in any story criticising the new regulations, he was never mentioned in the articles reporting the substantial reduction in road accident rates and deaths recorded, after the cameras were installed.

Saleh Kamel observed shortly after the sale of ART:

"I console myself that virtually all the criticism and conflict that resulted from our ART channel was a direct result of sports, and football in particular, with just a small percentage arising from problems with music.

"But, of course, it is sport that generates the real income. People

121

will pay to watch a sufficiently high-profile football match in a way they would never pay to watch a particular geographical, wildlife, or movie event.

"The fact I was the person who instituted pay-to-view TV in our region enraged many people who genuinely believed free view was their right. My involvement caused extreme agitation, to the point of some media outlets even calling into question my patriotism.

"I regret any embarrassment my actions might have caused officials in state-owned television channels but I believed then, as now, that a government should have far more important issues to concern itself with than squabbling over the screening of a football match.

"Looking back, there were so many ups and downs, mayhem became almost commonplace; anyone who believes owning a television channel is just a matter of accumulating vast revenues could not be further from the truth."

One of the most stressful events ART faced was the Asian championship in Lebanon, in October 2000. ART had bought the exclusive rights to all matches from an affiliate company of the Asian Football Confederation. However, the company proved to be weak and inefficient. It did not respect its contract or comply with its obligations.

Saleh Kamel noted:

"Under the terms of the exclusive deal we signed, whoever wanted to broadcast the matches played in Lebanon had to purchase the rights from ART. So I was very surprised, two days before the first match, to see advertisements on some Arab television channels publicising the fact that they would be broadcasting the entire event.

"I swiftly discovered a conspiracy had been launched by several Arab channels working together to exploit the weakness of the Asian affiliate company, the very same channels that had so bitterly objected to our monopoly.

"I immediately obtained a court order against the offending Arab channels, empowering me to stop them from broadcasting, but for two reasons I did not pursue this end. Firstly, because I did not want to snatch the opportunity of watching the live games from an enthusiastic audience; in which case I would have been punishing ordinary people for an illegal act they had taken no part in. The other reason was that the games were being played in Lebanon, a country that I genuinely love.

"Although the Lebanese Courts upheld my right to interrupt the broadcasts, I made the decision to sacrifice my own interests instead of depriving the Lebanese people of watching a greatly anticipated sporting event.

"Eventually, the Asian company was forced to return all the money we had paid, plus our litigation expenses, but we had learned a hard lesson. Sadly it was only one of a series of 'dirty tricks', from a variety of sources, that would afflict us over the years.

"Popular hacking was another problem that plagued us. This practice, which came in myriad forms, frequently including illegal broadcasting by commercial establishments such as hotels and apartment blocks, that would share the value of a single subscription between several dozen screens. This piracy cost us dearly.

"There were also many illegal wired and wireless networks in operation that delivered our signal to a single dwelling, from which the hackers would run an illegal network, sometimes covering an entire neighbourhood.

"Another type of hacking involved the activation of devices that decipher Pay-TV channels. This method put us in an ongoing race with hackers. In order to block their access to our channels we were obliged to constantly change our encoding and encryption techniques.

"These factors and others had a significant impact on reducing the company's projected revenues and decreasing our chances of returning a profit."

In an attempt to overcome the problem, ART recruited specialist detection teams who scanned entire cities, from shops, to office buildings and apartment blocks, and subsequently prepared lists of violations and duplicitous subscriptions. But the reality was that their hands were tied. All they could do was deliver lists of offenders to the authorities and wait for them to take the necessary steps to bring the hackers to justice. No legal action could be taken unless first sanctioned by a committee comprising representatives of several establishments, including the security services and municipal authorities.

Over time, the Middle East region would become secondary to ART in terms of subscriber revenue. The number of subscribers in the United States alone was equivalent to the total number of subscribers in the Middle East and North Africa. As for the advertising industry in the region, from ART's point of view it was fraught with troubles, often involving transactions that paid little heed to professional ethics, frequently feeling closer to the practices of the Sicilian mafia, in a way that totally contradicted the ethos of the Dallah Albaraka Group.

The company tried, as much as possible, to be self-sufficient in advertising by establishing a company for that purpose. In this way it was able to manage the advertising rights of its network more efficiently.

The total issued capital invested over the years in the Arab Media Company (AMC) – the holding company set up to structure ART – was about $1 billion. It was an astonishing increase from the $200 million starting pot. His Royal Highness Prince Alwaleed bin Talal, a partner and friend of Saleh Kamel, was also a shareholder.

In the early 1990s, Saleh Kamel and Prince Alwaleed had worked out a financial arrangement for the latter to buy into AMC. The network, by this time, owned close to half of the Lebanese Broadcasting Corporation's satellite channel, LBC-Sat. For an investment of $240 million, Prince Alwaleed took a 30% share and became active in overseeing some operations, particularly those related to the music industry.

Alwaleed, who had also owned some 24%, increasing to 48%, of shares in the Rotana Audiovisual Company, the largest recording label in Saudi Arabia, with most of the Arab world's top recording artists on its books, eventually took over full ownership of the firm. By 2003, as his commitment to Rotana increased, Alwaleed agreed an arrangement with Dallah Albaraka whereby he would reduce his ART shareholding to just 5%, while increasing his stake in LBC-Sat to 49%. Under the terms of the deal, the billionaire Prince would convert ART Music into a completely new Arabic language and entertainment channel, which he would operate and control. For Saleh Kamel, this divestment of the music industry share came as something of a relief, as he relates:

> "My desire to give up shares in the music sector increased as I saw deviation creeping into the product we were marketing and this disturbed me. I had already noticed signs, especially in the video clips made to accompany the broadcast of songs, that did not concur with the Dallah Albaraka ideology. I was against some of the scenes featured in the videos. The producers insisted they were merely 'creative'. I did not agree.
>
> "I consulted with my partner, Prince Alwaleed, who immediately grasped the situation and understood my dilemma. My practical partnership with him ended amicably, even harmoniously, with an arrangement that suited both of us in May 2003."

In "Alwaleed: Businessman, Billionaire, Prince", the biography of the Prince written by journalist Riz Khan, Prince Alwaleed refers to the deal as being an important milestone in his personal media journey. The Prince seemed to sense that this deal with Saleh Kamel, his first serious foray into the media, was an opening to something much bigger down the line which, of course, it would eventually prove to be.

As a direct result of the hard-won confidence ART had finally earned from most Arab countries, they were able to sign contracts to become the promoter and developer of media structures in those countries, through which they would provide media services both for internal and external use. These included Media City, Jordan, established in 2001, which Saleh Kamel saw as an unprecedented model of development and cooperation for a tax-free media zone operating between Asia and Europe. The city very soon had the capability to operate more than 60 channels and provide uplink services to a range of satellites (including Hot Bird, Arabsat, and Nilesat) for more than 120 channels, in addition to production services, all incorporating the latest international technologies.

As a close, Cairo-based colleague commented: "Sheikh Saleh had every right to be proud of his achievement with ART. He turned his dream into a reality."

Saleh Kamel's nephew, Abdul Aziz Mohammad Abdo Yamani, the son of his sister Mariam and his dearest friend Mohammad Abdo Yamani, who worked closely with Saleh Kamel from an early age observed:

"To rise in Dallah, it was essential to start at the bottom. Family members and non-family members were treated in exactly the same way, each had to prove their worth and earn a place in the company.

"Sheikh Saleh was like a second father to me. Our houses were together in the same compound and, as children, we went freely between them almost as soon as we could walk. Even our holiday homes in the South of France were right next door to each other. At home we were all equal, there were no barriers, no protocols, we ate together, we shared everything, but in the office, it was all about the business.

"My uncle prepared us all to take responsibility from an early age. He was keen on honesty and discipline but at the same time he encouraged us to believe in ourselves and the power of a united family. His ethical values and his love of family were very strong."

Abdul Aziz Yamani, who would rise through the ranks to hold a number of important offices at Dallah Albaraka, including that of

CEO and the chairmanship of several of the company's subsidi-aries in the Kingdom of Saudi Arabia and across the Middle East, described how his Uncle Saleh recruited the young members of the family, as teenagers, into the family business in Makkah. He valued the continued role in the tradition of guiding pilgrims:

"We worked looking after the pilgrims. We would guide them, clean for them, look after them, and 'serve' them. As mutawifs, we enjoyed the honour and responsibility we had been given by our elders.

"I see now it was the family's way of helping to ground us. My father and my uncle were both proud to have worked as *mutawifs* and, by getting us involved, they were encouraging us to connect with our roots.

"Even as a young boy I loved to travel with my Uncle Saleh. Even on holiday, he never stopped working. There were always people and lots of activity around him as he worked on several projects at the same time, maybe two real estate schemes and one in the media sector.

"Before MBC, Sheikh Saleh was already producing movies which, of course, was always interesting to us as young people. With my cousins, we watched his progress in the sector with fascination. At the time satellite distribution was practically non-existent for anyone outside government – various countries used it to communicate with each other, but that was about it. To relay his programmes he had to launch transponders from ArabSat – launched by the Arab League – and NileSat, launched by the Egyptian government.

"He could feel there was something new in the air and got into a new investment called 'FLAG' involving a fibre-optic cable from Japan, through Asia and Africa and across the Atlantic to the United States. The project was very important to the industry, but as an investment it was a disaster. I believe Sheikh Saleh lost a considerable amount on it at the time. But since he was always working towards enlightening people – especially in terms of information and knowledge of Islamic values - while at the same time providing entertainment, it was always going to be a delicate balance.

Abdul Aziz Yamani still feels the Middle East region owes a debt of gratitude to Saleh Kamel for his services to popular media:

"After MBC came ART, which had more than 30 channels even before the sports channels were introduced. In terms of the wider media, the Middle East region owes him a considerable debt. He not only introduced colour television programmes to the area, more than half a century ago, but he also expanded the range of content available and he made sure the region was abreast of all the new incoming technologies. His money followed his imagination, rather the other way around, and today, thanks to his ingenuity and tenacity, Dallah holds the largest library of Arab films and productions anywhere in the world and remains a leading light in the regional media industry."

Saleh Kamel's son, Mohyuldeen, known to all as Mohi, admits that during the first ten years of his life his father, then at the peak of his business career, was frequently not around.

"My father travelled a lot of the time and, although we always had a good relationship, we became much closer when I started to go to work with him. It was his idea to take me into the office when I was around 12 or 13 years old. I remember in the early years seeing my friends playing together as we would be driving off to work and wishing I could stay with them, but then Dallah became involved with the sports media and, since I was very much into sports, I was happy to be involved. My father had a knack for identifying our strengths and weaknesses, as all his children would agree. He would have been very happy if we had all followed him into Dallah, but he was also content to let us follow our own path if that was what we wanted to do.

"I didn't persuade my father to get involved in sports; that was entirely his own idea, but when he did decide that developing sporting content was the way to go to increase subscriptions, I hope I was able to steer him in the right direction. He was the one to identify the potential in football, even though he wasn't actually a fan of the game, or of any kind of sport – not at all.

"I recall when I was around 13 or 14, accompanying him to a meeting in Zurich, where we were hoping to secure the rights for the FIFA championships. We were in a room full of sporting greats, even the Brazilian footballer Pele was there. Of course, I was thrilled, but my father had absolutely no idea who anybody was.

"I think I must have been quite annoying as a child as I was extremely curious about many things and asked a lot of questions, but my father always took the time to answer me if he could. He was a prolific reader and had an incredible breadth of knowledge, so he would often be able to help with the answer to some of even my most obscure questions.

"When we would buy the rights to the World Cup, the African Cup or the Asian Cup we would always see a rise in subscription numbers. I suggested we should launch an Arab Champions League Cup and offer big rewards in order to attract teams from all over the Arab world.

"My father listened to me outline my idea and asked if I could prepare a business plan, which over the next few days, I duly did. I know now that my plan wasn't very polished but he found it interesting enough to call in a couple of experts for their opinion. Between them they decided my plan was worth a trial.

"We worked hard and he supported me all the way. For a few years it was a success and helped boost the number of our subscribers, which in turn helped us buy the rights to local league games. It changed a lot within the company.

"My father's life was work. He believed in the creation of jobs, boosting the economy and helping humankind. I think the reason he would have enjoyed all of us all working at Dallah is because it would have been a way of getting closer to us. I always wanted to impress my father. It was not about making money. He had very high standards, so to gain his respect was a great thing."

When the time to make a choice about the future of ART came, it was Mohi who urged Saleh Kamel to sell the sports channel.

"It was a good business decision, but we both found it difficult emotionally to say goodbye to the sports channel we had invested so much of ourselves in, but eventually, logic won over emotion. My father's ideas were good, but when the governments of wealthy oil-producing nations start participating in the same sector, no private company can hope to compete.

"Without Sheikh Saleh's involvement and ART, I don't believe European football would have been as popular in the Middle East as it is today. My father's efforts helped the game become much more of a money-making industry in the region than it had ever been before, bringing greater prosperity to the clubs, the teams and the players.

"In addition to football, he also introduced Formula One racing into the region, creating a huge wave of popularity. We operated very successfully in the Kingdom of Saudi Arabia for 10 years, before the government of Bahrain got onboard and bought the television rights. Now there are four or five major races annually in the Gulf region, sponsored by various governments.

"Even though he didn't like sport and organized the things he did for business reasons, his intentions were always honourable. His media ventures brought employment, prosperity, and a wealth of expertise to the region. I firmly believe that overall, his impact was enormous."

CHAPTER SEVEN

EGYPT AND BEYOND

Although Dallah Albaraka's business interests had already started to creep impressively around the globe by the 1980s, it was Saleh Kamel's media investments, and the importance of the Egyptian film industry to Jeddah-based Dallah Albaraka, that necessitated more office space in the Egyptian capital.

Operations in Egypt began in 1975. The company swiftly developed a portfolio there involving banking, business, real estate, food production and manufacture, and agricultural and various other enterprises, but inevitably it was Saleh Kamel's media adventures that attracted the most attention. Many diverse investments preceded and would follow but for years, it was ART, in which Saleh Kamel had invested so much money and credibility, that dominated the headlines.

Egypt, the hub of the Arab entertainment industry, was frequently referred to as the Hollywood of the MENA (Middle East and North Africa) region, and Saleh Kamel well understood that Cairo was the city where he must keep his finger on the pulse of those developments. By now, he was spending half his time in the Egyptian capital.

Much has been written about the days when the popularity of cinema was at its zenith in Egypt, when, it was claimed, each of the country's major towns and cities boasted a cinema on every street corner, and the export revenues earned from movies produced there were topped only by its sales of cotton. Whole books have been dedicated to the subject, and Saleh Kamel's inspirational work features prominently in many of them.

The entertainment industry in the Middle East, which first got off the ground in the late 19th century, was dominated by Egyptian producers, directors, and actors for many decades. From the 1930s, through the golden years of the 40s and 50s, the country continued to hold possession of the industry, for which there was an insatiable regional appetite, in the palm of its metaphorical hand.

Yet, even in this Cairo-dominated clique, Saleh Kamel was able to prove himself a force to be reckoned with and, except for a jealous few to whom he would always be "the Saudi", the Egyptians appeared to love him.

In addition to his business interests, Saleh Kamel had a more personal reason for his increasingly frequent stays in Cairo. In his usual style of wanting to know exactly how every process and mechanism he was funding worked, he spent a lot of time with his producers and directors on set. It was during this time he met and fell in love with the popular and beautiful Egyptian actress Safaa Abo El Saoud.

Already a darling of Egyptian cinema, Safaa was, at first, largely unimpressed by the tall Saudi who turned up to watch her work:

"I had seen him on set, he was polite, friendly, and it was clear the producer of the film we were working on – who was a well-known name in the industry – had a lot of time for him, but I had no idea he was the person funding the entire process.

"If we were on a shoot and Kamel appeared on set, everyone gathered around and started making a fuss about him. I remember hearing he was from Jeddah, but I didn't take much notice of what was going on with the crew. Much later he called me on the phone and explained that he was the guy from Saudi Arabia. He asked me how I was. I answered honestly that I had a bit of a fever that day and was feeling under the weather. He immediately suggested he call his good friend the producer and tell him to give me a few days off from the shoot.

"I was horrified and said no, no, no, going on to explain that I did not want the producer to know I was feeling ill. I feared if he did, he might replace me with another actress. My new friend Saleh Kamel said he would ensure this would not happen but, after some persuasion, he agreed he wouldn't say anything to the producer."

"In time, the relationship developed to a point where Sheikh Saleh felt he needed to discuss his interest with Safaa's father. After fielding several calls from Saleh Kamel, Safaa's father took her to one side and questioned her about the nature of her relationship with the insistent Saudi. She recalls:

"I explained to my father that there was a possibility of me working on a television series with Saleh Kamel. Of course, by this time, my father had enjoyed several conversations with him and suspected there might be more to our relationship than I was saying.

"Sheikh Saleh turned up unannounced at my home one afternoon and spent around an hour speaking with my father. Papa told me they discussed all kinds of things and he felt Sheikh Saleh was knowledgeable and cultured, not at all what my father had been expecting from a married Saudi Arabian businessman.

"When I was growing up my father had always impressed upon me that there were three types of men I should not consider as potential husband material. Firstly, a man who already had a wife, secondly, a non-Egyptian, and thirdly, a businessman, who – my father reckoned – might be too preoccupied with work to devote sufficient quality time to his family. These were men I should avoid at all costs, according to my Papa.

"Yet, when Saleh Kamel asked him for my hand in marriage, he raised not a single objection!"

Saleh Kamel and Safaa were married in March 1977. Safaa continued to work in the film industry, but increasingly her time was spent on specifically ART-related projects both on- and off-screen, and she was duly appointed head of the Movie Channel. Saleh Kamel had gained not only a wife but also a gifted associate, and together they would contribute much to his media empire.

Over the ensuing years, Saleh Kamel would nurture his families in Jeddah and in Cairo. It is to the eternal credit of the two exceptional women he married that all his children enjoy close and loving relationships with their siblings and half-siblings. The children travelled together and frequently spent holidays together at their homes in Jeddah, Cairo, and other Kamel residences around the world.

His daughter Haneen comments on how it worked: "We are very lucky; we were introduced to our siblings at an early age; we grew up together; we share very close relationships; we always have."

His sons Abdullah and Mohi play a vital role on the Board of Dallah in Jeddah, while his eldest daughter with Safaa, Hadeel, is overall Managing Director at Dallah Albaraka in Egypt, with responsibility for the company's many business and media outlets there.

Today, Dallah's Egyptian enterprises continue to form a major part of the company's portfolio outside the Kingdom of Saudi Arabia. Albaraka Bank is one of the largest banks in Egypt, where it has had a presence for more than 30 years. Lamia Al Hafnawy, who worked in the Cairo office with Saleh Kamel for 25 years, points out:

> "There are a multitude of businesses run directly from the Cairo office, with their CEOs reporting to Sheikh Saleh's sons Abdullah and Mohi, his daughter Hadeel, and a number of other close members of the family, including beloved nephews."

In his office, with his large, leather armchair positioned to enjoy an unobstructed view of the Nile, she recounted, with tears in her eyes, how "it felt as if we had lost a father when he died."

Although Saleh Kamel's earliest projects in Egypt were mostly agriculture- and food-related, over time they spread to encompass dozens of diverse ventures. Lemia notes: "He loved Egypt. He spent about half his time in the country and had several homes here. He did a lot of good for the country and its people over the years."

In a country where the problems of unemployment are ongoing, Saleh Kamel's approach was certainly a welcome one. Nor was he deterred by the slump in tourism that followed 9/11; he felt that it was important to maintain his investment and commitment to Egypt through troubled times. As he told conferences of international investors on more than one occasion:

"Every business owner should be aware that giving employment to people is the reason Allah bestowed wealth on them. If we remembered this and acted upon it, there would be no unemployment in our societies. When looking at new business opportunities, we should always include the number of new jobs the project will create in our calculations. How many families will benefit from the scheme? This must always be a major part of any feasibility study."

Saleh Kamel's son Mohi confirms that this was always the case in any project his father was involved in.

"Not all my father's projects were lucrative. But financial feasibility was never his main focus. He was a businessman, so obviously he was looking to make a profit, but there were other criteria he took into consideration. For example, if there were two projects under discussion where A would earn 10 per cent profit and B would earn 7 per cent, but provide more job opportunities, my father would always choose B, with the added job prospects, over A with greater profit margins."

Mohi went on to explain how his father would never consider laying people off in a crisis: "This is a lesson we learned from him and abide by, even when the going gets tough."

Mohi noted that during the Covid pandemic, when movement was restricted and so much production brought to a standstill, Saleh Kamel issued the instruction: "Do not lay people off. If we have to decrease salaries, then we will do that instead. Everybody will get less but everybody will get something".

Mohi went on to explain how his father used to relate a story, passed on to him by his own father, Abdullah, of events that took place when Saudi Arabia was still very new.

"Apparently there were financial problems in the Kingdom, and a couple of high-ranking officials went to King Abdul Aziz [the founder of the Kingdom] and told him that, because of a shortage of money, they were going to have to lay off half the staff. The King responded after a few moments, saying: 'Then you two should be laid off first.'

"Of course, the officials were shocked and disagreed with his thinking but, under pressure from the King, they came up with an alternative solution that all salaries should be cut by half – in that way everybody lost something, but nobody lost everything.

"In difficult times, it was a policy my father would always advocate – decreasing salaries instead of laying off employees. And, because he insisted it should be done in a proportional way – those earning the highest salaries, lost the most in terms of cash."

Saleh Kamel, who, it should be remembered, had grown up in a household where a regular income was not always assured, understood people's natural fear of not having work.

"Unemployment is one of the major reasons of decline of the individual and the community, the cause of so many misfortunes", he told a gathering of Jeddah businessmen.

"The hoarding of wealth is a sin against God. The primary duty of businessmen is to employ people, according to the teachings of Islam, first with yourself, then with your dependants, your closest next of kin, your other relatives, and then your neighbour. Government money and the money of private businessmen is estimated at trillions of riyals, so why have we not used this money to create jobs for our children? The real success of every businessman is surely his ability to 'create' projects that will

Saleh Kamel with the Saudi monarch King Salman bin Abdul Aziz *(above)*.
Saleh Kamel had the honour of welcoming King Salman of Saudi Arabia (then Crown
Prince) to his home *(below)*. Seen here is King Salman *(centre)*, Saleh Kamel *(centre right)*,
Saleh Kamel's sons, Mohyuldeen *(far left)* and Abdullah *(centre left)*, and Abdullah's son
(Saleh Kamel's grandson), Saleh Kamel junior *(far right)*.

Explaining to King Fahd a project of Jeddah Tourism City in the late 80s, with Prince
(now King) Salman standing to the right.
Saleh Kamel as he receives the King Abdul Aziz Decoration, First Order, for distinguished
businessmen, from the hands of (then Crown Prince) King Abdullah Bin Abdul Aziz in
2001.

With HRH Crown Prince Sultan Bin Abdul Aziz demonstrating the Durrat Alarous project located on the coast north of Jeddah.

Saleh Kamel forged a close bond with many royal leaders. Here he is seen with Prince Charles, now King Charles III, of Great Britain *(below)*, during a conference on Islamic finance services and global supervision – London 2004.

Saleh Kamel's discussions with German Chancellor Angela Merkel were to have a lasting impact on German banking procedures. She is seen here *(above)* during her 2010 visit to Saudi Arabia.

Saleh Kamel dealt personally with many heads of state; shown here, he is with Turkish President Recep Tayyip Erdoğan *(below left)* and with the late Prime Minister of Lebanon, Rafic Hariri *(below right)*.

Saleh Kamel meets three prominent Arab monarchs: King Mohammed VI of Morocco *(right)*; King Abdullah II of Jordan during the inauguration of Jordan Media City in 2001 *(below right)*; and Sultan Qaboos of Oman *(bottom right)*.

With Malaysian Prime Minister Dr Mahathir Mohamad *(above)* during his visit to Saleh Kamel in his home in Durrat Alarous in Jeddah in 2022.
With Egyptian President Hosni Mubarak *(below left)*, and with Syrian President Bashar Al Assad *(below right)*.

With President Bourguiba of
Tunisia and his brother Abdulaziz
Kamel, reviewing the Tunis
Lake project *(right)* and with
Bourguiba's successor, President
Zine El Abidine Ben Ali *(below
right)*.

and with President Silvio
Berlusconi of Italy *(right: centre of
image, with HRH Prince Waleed
bin Talal on the right and Saleh
Kamel on the let)*, where ART
studios were located.

With former US President Bill Clinton *(above)* during his 2002 visit to Saudi Arabia to attend the Jeddah Economic Forum.
Presenting a memorial gift to President Jaafar Nimeiry of Sudan on the occasion of the inauguratiion of Albaraka Bank Sudan, 1984 *(below left)* and with President Muhammad Zia-ul-Haq of Pakistan *(below right)*.

move the largest number of people out of unemployment." Such sentiments were keenly felt by Saleh Kamel, and part of the strong code of ethics by which he tried to live his life and run his business interests. Part of his grand scheme was also to provide communities with systems and structures that would help meet their needs.

In reference to Dallah programs, he had this to say:

"The extraordinary breadth of our activities reflects the needs and interests of the diverse communities we serve. In the business sector, we provide quality goods and services and encourage a high level of international trade. In the finance sector, we strengthen the economy, while providing a solid foundation for future activities. And in the media sector, we deliver innovative content which raises awareness of important issues affecting our everyday lives.

"Through all of our activities, we aim to significantly enhance the quality of life of all people in the countries in which we operate. To this end, we are involved in a variety of programmes in education, technology deployment and application, self-sufficiency in producing food, jobs and skills training, and the careful stewardship of natural resources."

Lemia Al Hafnawy commented:

"One of his biggest concerns when he launched a project was how many people would gain employment from it. Saleh Kamel truly believed that with wealth came a big responsibility to make sure others also benefitted. However, I never knew him to throw money away; all spending had to be justified. He would ask the price of everything. He loved a particular brand of lactose-free cheese we get here in Egypt – although for medical reasons, he was not supposed to eat too much of it. If I saw it in the shop, I would occasionally buy it for him, as a special treat, but even though he loved it, he would always complain about the price, even as he was tucking in!"

Despite his wealth and privilege, Saleh Kamel was always apprecia-
tive of the small gestures made by those around him, something his
staff frequently commented on. Abed Elbasset, his personal assistant
in Egypt for more than 20 years, recalled how, when he learned of a
trip Saleh Kamel was making to Aswan, he secretly arranged for his
large, leather office chair to be shipped from Cairo to the Cataract
Hotel, where he was staying:

"We knew he would be having some long meetings during his
stay in Aswan and we wanted him to be as comfortable as possible, but we also knew he would never authorise the expense of
transporting his favourite chair over that distance.

"He was flying to Aswan from Jeddah, so while he was away from
the Cairo office, we packed up the chair and arranged for it to be
transported – at very reasonable cost – down to Aswan by road.

"When he arrived at the hotel and saw it there waiting for him,
he was over the moon. He was able to use it for all his meetings
and be completely comfortable and at ease.

"It all backfired a little however, when we arranged for someone
to collect the chair and return it to Cairo. During his stay,
Sheikh Saleh had met an elderly English lady who loved Aswan
and had made the Cataract Hotel her home. The two struck up a
firm friendship during his stay, and before leaving for Jeddah, he
insisted she should have his chair as a parting gift. Fortunately,
we were able to buy another and have it delivered to the Cairo
office before he returned," Abed Elbasset confirmed with a
chuckle.

The fact that Saleh Kamel did not allow his wealth to distance
him from the general population was something that was helpful
in the implementation of his business ideas, to which he brought
fresh thinking inspired by everyday life. As Dr Sami Abdul Aziz,
a professor in Media Studies, his trusted friend, and a marketing
media consultant at ART for many years, noted:

"I have never known anyone with the vision Sheikh Saleh

possessed. In terms of imagination, the sky was the limit; he often conceived and presented topics that were way beyond the comprehension of most people."

As long ago as 1977, Saleh Kamel had commissioned a team of experts to study a proposal to establish a giant theme park, following a Disneyland-style example, featuring activities, rides, restaurants, hotels, and completely self-contained infrastructure, outside Cairo. But instead of featuring Mickey Mouse and Donald Duck, Saleh Kamel's vision was to make the ancient pharaohs of Egypt the heroes of his new venture. Walt Disney's California theme park, established in Anaheim, California, in the mid-1950s, had proved itself an ongoing commercial success, attracting tourists from all over the world, so much so that a second, similar venture, Disneyworld, was established by the company in Orlando, Florida, in the early 1970s.

In Egypt, Saleh Kamel's team of researchers had identified a suitable site, drawn up plans, and evaluated the projected returns. Several million dollars had already been invested in putting together a master plan before Saleh Kamel took the idea to the Egyptian leader at the time, President Anwar Sadat.

The President could see the massive potential the scheme offered. The theme park, which was proposed for an undeveloped area of desert, would essentially become a small- to medium-sized town, offering close to a million jobs in various sectors, including hospitality, maintenance, transport, security and others. However, 1977 was a difficult time in Egypt. Nine out of ten Egyptians lived in poverty and half the male population was unemployed. When President Sadat cut public subsidies for flour, cooking oil, and other staples, people took to the streets in two days of violent protest, which became known as the 'bread riots'. When the army stepped in to quell the rioters, 80 people were killed, 800 were injured, and more than 1,000 were imprisoned.

President Sadat and his wife Jehan believed that under the prevailing circumstances, the timing was inappropriate to launch what they deemed an 'entertainment' project. But Dr Sami noted:

"Sheikh Saleh went all out to persuade them the project was first and foremost an industry that would provide jobs, security, and a massive boost to tourist revenues, but the Sadats refused to change their minds.

"Sheikh Saleh was a man of great ideas. Big, big ideas that were beyond the imagination of many people. But he never claimed to have the know-how to carry them off himself; rather, he would employ the best consultants money could buy to implement that side of things. From his early training with the Ministry of Finance and from harsh experience in some of his early maintenance ventures, he knew that getting the finance right could make or break a project, no matter how brilliant the concept might be.

"Before Hong Kong was returned to China in 1994, he began studying how a change in government in the former British territory might open up opportunities in the Middle East region.

"The result was his plan to establish a Suez Canal free trade zone. Sheikh Saleh reckoned the canal was in a unique geographical location, one that would be ideal for the creation of a hub for transportation, storage, and a huge duty-free trade zone, not to mention the enormous employment opportunities it would generate in the area.

"As always, his proposal was well researched and presented. It identified the opportunities this project would create for the Egyptian economy. He presented the idea to our President, who at the time was Hosni Mubarak. Sadly, the government was unable to grasp the magnitude of the proposed scheme and the financial rewards it could have generated. They felt it might, in some way, undermine the country's authority over Suez and they turned the project down flat.

"Fully twenty years later, in 2014, President Sisi returned to the idea and the result was what we now know as the Suez Canal

Economic Zone (SCZone)."

Following the go-ahead by the Egyptian government and expansion of the canal in 2015, the area adjacent to the strategic waterway was declared a 'special economic zone'. The Organisation for Economic Cooperation and Development (OECD) agreed to support the Egyptian authorities in harnessing the potential of the 8% of global trade flowing through the canal for job creation and economic growth, bringing a range of tangible benefits to the Egyptian population. In 2020, some 18,829 ships with a total net tonnage of 1.17 billion were registered by the SCZone, amounting to daily revenues averaging $15 million.

Not all Saleh Kamel's proposed enterprises in Egypt were quite so imaginative, but all were conceived and designed to add value to the lives of all those they touched. A key factor in Dallah's international success has been its ability to pinpoint the specific needs of customers in different regions, and to develop custom-made solutions to meet them. This simple concept has helped form a loyal customer base for the company.

According to Dr Sami Abul Aziz, people often commented on Saleh Kamel's pride in being a Saudi, but it did not overshadow his enthusiasm for other countries. He particularly loved Egypt and delighted in bringing together projects that married Saudi finance with Egyptian manpower.

"In reality his vision was pan-Arab. He was 100% behind free trade and he believed implicitly in the Arab Nation. He was not at all political – to him politics was the relationship between the government and the public. He was a modest man and always totally inclusive. If, for example, he had something to eat at the office, he would always share the food with his staff. They would sit down and eat the same thing and they would eat together".

Dr Sami had deep admiration for his colleague and friend of many decades. He recalls:

"Sheikh Saleh had a real interest in developing 'human-based'

141

projects. He did a lot of charitable work in Egypt and established the Egyptian Organization for Zakat, which helps charitable donations get to where they are most needed."

Dr Sami relates how Saleh Kamel, on realising that Egypt needed more hospitals and healthcare workers, embarked upon a project to deliver just that. The building and equipping of hospitals was no problem, as Dallah had vast experience in the healthcare sector and was more than equal to the task of providing more in Egypt, but it soon became clear that there was also a dearth of healthcare professionals in the country.

Saleh Kamel set up a team to evaluate the country's needs and how they might best be met. He decided, after extensive research, that to provide the best possible training, he would partner with a large German company. The training would focus on trainees from various Arab countries – which it was felt would make staff-patient communication easier.

Training would be in a wide range of disciplines. Dr Sami confirmed:

"Those who could afford to were asked to pay their own fees against the promise of a job. However, most potential candidates were sponsored by Sheikh Saleh, with training costs to be paid back when they took up work as a trainee. Many thousands of Egypt's currently practicing healthcare workers benefitted from this scheme."

Egyptians are generally a proud people, conscious of their heritage and their place in history and world civilisation. Although far from being insular, for the most part, by choice, they like to eat Egyptian food, watch Egyptian films, and hang out with Egyptian friends. They dabble in, but are in no way overawed by, the latest trends out of London, Paris, or New York. Most of his former colleagues agree that Saleh Kamel was somehow able to transcend Egypt's traditional preference for all things Egyptian. One of his Cairo office colleagues explained:

"Saleh Kamel was loved in Egypt. Being a Saudi Arabian could have been a drawback in the realm of popular culture but, from the evidence of my own eyes, it never was. He was unique. I'm not saying he was perfect; he could get annoyed and sometimes have temper tantrums when things went wrong, but he always deeply regretted giving way to any sort of outburst. He was kind and generous and despite his great wealth, he was a very modest man."

Saleh Kamel's personal assistant in Dallah's London office, Alison Dodds, recalled a meeting at a restaurant in Cannes in the South of France, where six or seven high-flying businessmen were gathered together to discuss an important venture. Alison, a fluent French speaker, sat next to her boss to ensure she could advise him should any language difficulties arise. The meeting had already begun when a man selling red roses approached the table and tried to engage one of the men in buying a bloom.

"I immediately called the flower seller over to me and asked him not to trouble anyone at the table. I explained they were involved in an important meeting and should be left alone," she recalled. "Sheikh Saleh stopped me in mid-flow and very quietly whispered: 'Don't tell him off, Alison, everybody has to make a living.'"

It seems such behaviour was typical of the billionaire entrepreneur who travelled the world in his private jet but never forgot the smell of Taif roses or the dusty alleys of his Makkan childhood. Mohammad Moussa, Saleh Kamel's assistant for many years, recalls an incident when they stopped in Nairobi, Kenya, to refuel on a journey from Cairo to Johannesburg:

"Sheikh Saleh left us for a couple of minutes and went off on his own into the duty-free area. We checked everywhere in the airport and could not locate him, but shortly he emerged smiling in full, colourful African dress, holding aloft a sack in which he had the more conservative clothes in which he had left Cairo that morning."

His wife Safaa recounts another experience, in Marrakesh, when Saleh Kamel revealed himself as very much a man of the people.

> "We had decided to go to a well-known restaurant in Jamaa El Fna Square. The girls, who were probably young teenagers at the time, decided they would not eat a full meal but planned to join us for an ice cream later. They were much more interested in exploring the exciting square they had heard so much about than hanging around with their parents."

Djeema El Fna Square has been a centre of frenetic activity in Marrakesh since the 11th century. It boasts a host of restaurants, food stalls, and shops, as well as dozens of street entertainers, including musicians, acrobats, and even snake charmers. It is frequented by local Moroccans and tourists alike from morning until night.

As Safaa and Saleh Kamel made their way through the square, stopping occasionally to watch some of the street performers and generally take in the sights, they were approached by a number of people selling things – fruit, sweetmeats and hand-carved wooden toys – but they didn't buy anything.

> "Sheikh Saleh turned them down," Safaa recalled, "but he was always polite and respectful and sometimes this could be misunderstood."

The Kamel's clothes were obviously of good quality and as they made their way across the square, they were repeatedly approached by people asking for money. Again, Saleh Kamel refused, but always politely. Safaa recounts:

> "On reaching the restaurant, we realised that we were now being pursued by quite a few people. The restaurant owners came out and started ushering them away, flapping their hands and speaking quite rudely. Sheikh Saleh was appalled at their behaviour. He asked them to stop and demanded to know 'What are you doing? These people are my guests.'
>
> "I said nothing but made my way quietly into the rather expensive restaurant, followed by Sheikh Saleh and his 'guests.'"

144

His daughter Nadeer takes up the story:

"When we had explored the square and arrived at the restaurant, as arranged, to have dessert, I saw my parents sitting at a crowded table. My mother was silent but smiling. We all looked through the window but simply could not figure out what was going on. We went inside and it became clear my father was talking and laughing with a group of seven or eight beggars he had invited to join them for dinner because the restaurant staff had treated them so rudely!

"Some might call such actions 'behaving like being a man of the people'. I'm not sure my mother would have agreed, but she knew, as we all did, that life with my father was never dull or predictable. He was always able to surprise us, and he frequently did."

CHAPTER EIGHT

KEEPING THE FAITH

Saleh Kamel did not talk about the extent of his charity work, nor did he allow those who worked with him to speak about it. Several people admitted to knowing a little of what went on, but nobody appears to have known the full scope of his commitment. Yet, after his death, the number of charity-related files, correspondence, and payment orders discovered in his offices, dating back as far as 1969, were no less than the amount of all the files related to his businesses and investments portfolio put together. There is a hadith (one of the verified sayings of the Prophet Muhammad) that refers to the great reward that awaits he or she who donates voluntary, but discretely, to charity – so discretely that the left hand does not know what the right hand donates. Doubtless this emphasis on the importance of modest discretion must have underpinned some of Saleh Kamel's thinking on the topic.

One astute associate commented that it was as if surreptitiously, he was preparing his path to the Hereafter, alongside his day-to-day work schedule. As is well recorded, Saleh Kamel did not run his businesses in isolation from Islamic teachings. The ethics behind this were built on logic and reason, and became part of the behavioural style of all his organisations.

He was conscientious in abiding by the rules regarding the management of wealth, precisely as instructed by Islam. However, he frequently found an excuse to help things along with generous contributions which went above and beyond those stipulated by Islamic teachings, believing that ultimately, all wealth belongs to Allah. Zakat was paid in accordance with the relevant rules and through the recognised channels, but his personal generosity far outstripped the demands of Zakat. And, according to Islamic teaching, it is the voluntary charity that guarantees the greatest returns, doubling the rewards from Allah.

Those who worked with Saleh Kamel say their instructions were to put the humanitarian aid file at the top of all the files presented daily for his attention. While he studied the charity file, he did not allow his office staff to interrupt him. He would remain silent and focused, almost as if praying, one of them observed.

He was not swayed by big names or personalities, but rather studied each case on the basis of whose need was greatest, and he made notes constantly on the help he was willing to provide, moving his lips gently but constantly while doing so, as if in conversation with some unseen accomplice.

When someone asked him about the mechanism he used to decide on the exact amount of help he was prepared to give, Saleh Kamel responded by saying that when he made that decision, his pen was guided by Allah. When someone was found to be well off and undeserving of aid – as sometimes happened – Saleh Kamel did not refuse help because he believed that "no one would humiliate himself to ask for help unless they were needy."

"Besides," he insisted, "we can never know the exact circumstances of any individual and should not be deceived by appearances."

However, billionaire or not, he refused to help those he believed were in need because of reckless behaviour or law breaking. He would not, for example, give financial aid to pay a large backlog of traffic fines. Saleh Kamel saw such help as undermining to the rule of law, and believed his assistance might only encourage further wrongdoing and perhaps, ultimately, cause harm to others. That said, he delighted in helping pay off the money owed by prison inmates. He would regularly make an additional payment on the night of the Eid al-Fitr feast, which follows the holy month of Ramadan, to release a group of prisoners incarcerated for debt, to allow them "to celebrate the feast with their children."

Saleh Kamel rejoiced in helping others even if, as sometimes happened, they had previously done him or one of his companies wrong. He would still treat them kindly, help them if possible, and pray for them.

He made a big effort to establish a personal connection with all his colleagues and their relatives. It was important to him that he should be there to share their happy moments and to console them during their sad times. He would frequently support them in periods of need, even before they asked for help. He frequently paid yearly or monthly allowances to a large number of his past and present employees without ever discussing the arrangement with anyone, thereby avoiding any risk of embarrassment to the individuals concerned.

These things were a part of Saleh Kamel's personal code. He not only believed in the teachings of Islam and gloried in being a Muslim, but also totally absorbed Islam into his existence, both the personal and the professional side of his day-to-day life.

"I realised that as long as I was in commerce, my steps had to be weighed against the rules of Sharia. As I did not receive a formal Islamic jurisprudence (*fiqh* - the observance of rituals, morals, and social legislation in Islam) education, I decided to be a permanent part-time student. Thus, I became a seeker of Sharia-related knowledge.

"From day one, my biggest concern was to explore the spirit, the higher purposes and ends of the provisions of *fiqh*. as well as to capture them literally. I kept company with religious scholars and experts in finance and economics and decided I wanted to make *fiqh* an integral part of my business."

Saleh Kamel was always keen on maintaining and nurturing his relationships, be they with former classmates, work colleagues, or friends. In later life, he instigated the formation of a group called 'The Seat', where friends, colleagues, and loved ones gathered at his home, initially once a week, to talk, laugh, and maintain their connections with each other. Before the Covid pandemic, he had turned these meetings into fixed, open, gatherings, held twice a week on Sundays and Wednesdays from afternoon prayer to sunset prayer. As one regular visitor said:

"He was a man who loved company and conversation. He had a unique way of making every person feel as if he was the most important to him of all those present. That continued until the implications of the global pandemic cut him off from this twice-weekly pleasure."

As the pandemic intensified and the weeks dragged into months, his only alternative was to make telephone calls with extended family and old and new friends and acquaintances across the world. During the last month of his life, in addition to the usual number of telephone calls, the number of messages and communications he exchanged exceeded three thousand, his office confirmed. His signature greeting was always the same: "Peace, mercy, blessings and well-being from Allah be with you!"

His heart was heavy – during the pandemic and until his death – when he was greatly preoccupied with the situation of the many workers whose sources of income had been disrupted or removed entirely. He made numerous calls to officials of various associations, charities, hospitals, and individual neighbourhood groups, to ask about how people were managing. Such calls would invariably result in Saleh Kamel dispatching generous aid packages to those in need.

He gave aid generously and without expectation of any return, but he was also often approached directly for loans. If approved, these were always given interest-free, in keeping with Islamic teachings. He was lenient regarding security and collateral for such loans, and, most of the time, the repayment date was not set or recorded apart from: "when the condition of the borrower allows".

Many dozens and possibly hundreds benefitted from these interest-free loans. Most repaid the amount in full. For different reasons, a small percentage did not, but it was not Saleh Kamel's policy to litigate. He would let it go as if it were an agreed charitable donation. He might ask an employee to send a kindly worded letter to the borrower asking them to repay the amount owed, in order to let others benefit from the same interest-free privilege, but there would be no angry words and no threats.

That is not to say that Saleh Kamel was flawless; he could shout and rage with the best of them under certain circumstances, but, by all accounts, he abhorred losing control in this way and, for the most part, maintained calmness in his life wherever he could.

Alison Dodds, his PA in Dallah's London office for many years, noted how, despite his great wealth and power, he was a "quiet and unassuming" man.

"He was very intelligent, very perceptive, an innovator and a trailblazer, yet he never displayed any airs or graces. Nobody would ever have guessed he was such a wealthy and powerful person. I found him always to be fair, treating everybody with the same respect, the humble and the great.

"Over all the years we worked together I did, on occasion, hear him raise his voice and speak quite loudly, but this never happened with me. He had a real presence, when he walked into a room, everybody would notice him. He also had a wonderful sense of humour and we would always enjoy a laugh together whenever we met."

Mohammad Moussa, Saleh Kamel's longstanding personal assistant in Jeddah, recalls:

"One of Sheikh Saleh's young nephews complained that when he came to visit his uncle, I was disrespectful because I didn't stand up. Sheikh Saleh simply laughed and said: 'My son, you have to know something – he does not stand up for me either, but for all that I know he loves and respects me. If he stood for everybody entering his office, he would have no time to do the work I need from him. Respect does not show itself in getting up and down. It shows itself in how he behaves. Has he harmed you? Have you heard anything bad he has said against you?' The boy's answers to Sheikh Saleh's questions were all 'No', and since that day we have been close friends."

His office staff in Jeddah still talk about the occasion when Saleh Kamel took the private elevator to his office on the top floor of Dallah Tower and it broke down between floors. The company Chairman simply slid to the floor, where he sat reading his mail and making notes, just as if he had been sitting at his office desk. Without causing any sort of fuss or annoyance, he waited there, working on his papers, until the engineers arrived and solved the problem. Everyone expected him to be furious at having been incarcerated in an airless, confined space for so long. They feared he would blame the gross inefficiencies of the office maintenance team for the breakdown, but the opposite was true. He thanked those who finally released him for giving him some time – without interruption or phone calls – which, he said, had helped him finish his work. This was just one of thousands of situations that displayed his patient good nature. He was never cruel or severe; and his unwavering fairness, even under duress, earned him people's respect, love, and loyalty, making them strive even harder to do well at their work.

Unpleasant events never seemed to frighten him or weaken his belief, maybe because his faith in fate and destiny was overwhelming. Whenever he was presented with an ordeal or a crisis, he did not panic or react angrily. He tried to accept fate gracefully, and considered any ordeal that challenged him an opportunity to reassess, learn and, hopefully, improve. He often claimed he considered problems a chance to examine his mistakes and an opportunity to correct his course.

Saleh Kamel was tolerant and gentle with everyone except himself, noted a colleague in Cairo. "He was considerate of others but too frequently hard on himself. When he was advised to take rest – as he grew older and it was difficult to maintain his activity levels due to the disparity between his strong mind and his waning body – he would get angry with himself and say to people who urged him to relax: "My rest will be in my grave. My pleasure here and now is in my work."

Some attributed his benevolent attitude to his upbringing in Makkan society, where local people generally stay close, as part of one large, cohesive family.

Above all, there was the spiritual atmosphere of the holy city, that nourished the soul, elevating feelings of virtue and humanity, as well as the understanding and application of faith.

Saleh Kamel's early career as a pilgrim guide, which taught him dedication and the meaning of brotherhood, opened his mind and expanded his understanding of people's needs. As recounted earlier, he was also a keen leader in the Boy Scout movement, which encourages friendship and social cohesion, as a boy and later at university. These factors and others probably helped form Saleh Kamel's character and nurtured his love for doing good where he could.

As with most entrepreneurs, he may have suffered liquidity problems on occasion, as happens in businesses from time to time. Yet, he never abandoned his commitment to making payments of financial aid. This obligation came before all others, those who worked with him confirm. No charity cheque was ever returned unpaid. If necessary, he would take cash from his own personal funds.

Only five hours before he died, Saleh Kamel had a meeting with the top management of his Jeddah office to discuss administrative restructuring, a necessary evil, he was informed, proposed by the executive management of the company.

By this time, he was less hands-on at Dallah, having passed the running of the company and the making of high-level decisions to his sons, Abdullah and Mohi, his daughter Hadeel, and his nephews, the Yamani brothers, who also play an important role in the Dallah Albaraka hierarchy.

At the meeting Saleh Kamel was mightily unhappy to hear there would have to be lay-offs. Advanced technology had simply rendered certain positions in the company obsolete, which could not be ignored. But when the name of one employee was read out to him, he became extremely upset. "Is there no compassion in your hearts?" he demanded of those at the table with him. "How can you terminate the services of a man knowing he has seven children and a wife with cancer? How will he feed his children and provide the cost of medication for his wife?"

He looked around at the familiar faces with real anger in his eyes before instructing: "If termination is legally and absolutely necessary, then do it but you will continue to pay this man's salary every month from the charity money and increase it by 500 riyals!"

Only five hours after giving this order, Saleh Kamel went to meet his maker.

He did not like any fuss or publicity about his charitable contributions. He would frequently say: "Oh Allah, make me better than what they believe of me and forgive me for what they do not know". Throughout his life, he never gave a statement or even a hint as to the extent of his humanitarian work or details of a charitable project he might have been involved with. Many people, companies, and institutions boast about their charitable gifts to society. Saleh Kamel saw his contributions as a duty and would have considered publicizing any such activities as being boastful.

There were those who argued that Dallah should have made a big noise about its extensive and deeply rooted involvement in charity work. The group never used its good deeds to polish its name and brand, or to achieve media exposure, as so many other companies are inclined to do. Those critics even advised that Dallah's perceived aversion to publicity regarding its charity activities was causing the company damage. Such claims never fazed Saleh Kamel. He would smile knowingly and respond eloquently in his Makkan[16] dialect: "Allah knows who brought the seeds." This phrase was taken from a Makkan proverb that tells of a child who snatched a sack of seeds bought by a visiting pilgrim to the holy city, to feed the pigeons at the Sacred Mosque. Even though the child snatched the bag and spread the seeds to feed the birds and enjoy watching them eat, the pilgrim was not fazed for, after all, Allah – who sees everything – knew well who brought the seeds in the first place.

Saleh Kamel often used this proverb when he wanted to illustrate how to those who know the truth of a situation, falsehoods are a less than fleeting distraction and of no consequence whatever.

Following an extensive study of business practices at Dallah's offices in 1986, an expert in human resources delivered his findings. His report made a number of suggestions to close certain departments and terminate the service of numerous employees. He also added some comments of his own. In an act of near-provocation, the expert wrote starkly in his recommendations: "With respect, Dallah has become more like a giant charity than a company."

The Sheikh's response was instant and equally uncomplicated. "Thank Allah for that. This is the essence of Dallah and this is its blessing."

He had expected the expert to come up with creative, outside-the-box recommendations to accommodate the employees threatened with unemployment, rather than stating the obvious.

"Sheikh Saleh's methods may have been unorthodox, but his workers loved him", noted his long-time friend and colleague Mahmoud Hassouba, who held several leading positions in Dallah in the 1980s through to his retirement in 2008. "As far as he was concerned, they were all in it together and he made this clear." This

---

16 As noted earlier, the official Saudi spelling of the holy city of Makkah is used throughout this book, in lieu of the spelling 'Mecca' widely adopted internationally. 'Makkan' is the adjective accordingly, rather then 'Meccan'.

point was perfectly illustrated by a well-documented meeting in Egypt when Saleh Kamel was touring one of his own dairy projects.

Hadeel recounts how a young worker, who was not known to Saleh Kamel, approached him as he was touring the new factory and said: "Thank you Sir, we pray for you because you provide for our households." Saleh Kamel grasped the worker by the hand and replied, "No, my son. It is the opposite. Your hard work provides for my household. I thank you."

Saleh Kamel was constantly looking for ways to improve the efficacy of charitable funds disbursed. The benefits of charity are rarely quantifiable. Who can tell, for example, how many lives will be improved by setting up a school in a rural village? Will it benefit only the 20 children attending class, or will they pass their knowledge on to parents and siblings? If one of them becomes a doctor and saves 100 lives, how many does it now benefit? And if another becomes a politician and prevents a war, how many people benefit then?

But although Saleh Kamel knew any charity would always have many imponderables, he had a real yen for seeing what a well-organised charitable foundation might achieve if it is imaginatively structured and efficiently operated.

Towards the end of the 1970s Saleh Kamel and the man he frequently referred to as "my dearest friend", his brother-in-law Dr Mohammad Yamani, a well-respected and accomplished scholar and the author of over 300 books, hit upon the idea of launching their own charity. Yassir Yamani recalls:

"Our families were always very close. My father and Sheikh Saleh were classmates in Makkah and my father married Saleh's sister. Because they all came from Makkah, they thought and acted in much the same sort of way. I know a lot of people think the so-called 'Makkah mentality' is a myth, but our family lived that culture, it does exist. Going to the mosque is not good enough, you have to live by Islamic principles.

"My father and Sheikh Saleh shared the same charitable values. Both of them were proud Saudi Arabians but they had also travelled extensively and absorbed – or rejected – the new ideas they had seen.

"They both had similar humanitarian ideals, based roughly along the lines of 'you share my country, you may not share my faith, but together we can succeed.'"

As well as growing up together, they were at University in Riyadh, where they shared a villa with some other friends. The ties that bound them as young men never loosened.

Yassir Yamani points out that both his father, who was Saudi Arabia's Minister of Information between 1975 and 1982 and also worked at Dallah, and Saleh Kamel were men of culture and conscience who wanted to see their beloved homeland move forward in global society.

"They both felt driven to do something and believed they could start by solving some of the problems in their own community, the Muslim community. Sheikh Saleh's father, my grandfather, Abdullah, had been forced to leave higher education because his family could not afford for him to remain at school. Both my father and my uncle were passionate about making sure the potential of young scholars should, if possible, never be lost for lack of funding.

"Uncle Saleh had the resources and, after he retired from government, my father had the time to devote to the project."

As Dallah's business around the world grew, despite Saleh Kamel's strong convictions, not all company business could be conducted through Islamic-compliant banks. For example, certain deals conducted with governments or companies overseas had to be paid through central clearing banks in London, New York, Paris, or Geneva. There was nothing he could do to prevent the interest accumulating and, because of the huge amounts involved, it accrued at a pretty rapid rate.

These payments, he calculated, were amounting to in excess of a billion riyals a year. He therefore decided that all interest payments made to Dallah should henceforth be channelled through the new charitable foundation, known as Iqraa, and in that way used to provide support to disadvantaged communities.

It is common knowledge that Saleh Kamel authorised a billion riyals to get the ball rolling on the Iqraa Charitable Society project. The interest from his overseas deals kept turnover high, although as Yassir Yamani observed:

"Sheikh Saleh was not interested in discussing the money side of Iqraa, so I am not prepared to discuss it in detail either. However, it is well known he left one third of his personal fortune to the Foundation, so clearly, we are speaking about an operation worth billions, rather than millions, of riyals.

"Sheikh Saleh put my father in charge of Iqraa right at the beginning and he worked with the Foundation until he died, following a stroke, in November 2010. Of course, losing him was a devastating blow for all of us but I had helped out at the Foundation for six or seven years before he died and, when the time came, I was proud and privileged to follow in his footsteps as head of the Foundation.

"Saleh Kamel's main concern was always that Iqraa money be used wisely to benefit those in need. We have partnerships in Africa, India, across Asia and Europe. We are very particular about who we partner with. We seek local entities that share our ethics and our goals for mankind. We deal only with people who are totally law-abiding and have 'clean' books that have been professionally audited.

"Mostly we create and manage programmes that fall into one of three categories – those who need help immediately, those who can be helped over several months, and those who can be helped over years.

"We are an Islamic Foundation and we believe, first and foremost, in developing communities. So if, for example, we build a school in West Africa, we do not say the children who attend must be Muslims. We are open to every child in the community, regardless of his or her religion. We want everyone to move forward together – this is the real Islam."

The late 1970s were fraught with radical activity in the Middle East region. In Iran, directly across the waters of the Arabian Gulf from Saudi Arabia, the Shah was ousted and the Ayatollahs came to power. Afghanistan, once the British Empire's bulwark against the Russians in what became known as 'The Great Game', was now invaded by Soviet Russia. Closer to home, the Holy Mosque in Makkah was seized and held through November and December of 1979 by a group of Islamist insurgents – something that sent shockwaves through the Kingdom and beyond – all the more so since Saudi Arabia's leader is traditionally given the title 'Guardian of the Two Holy Places'. Saleh Kamel was greatly concerned with what he saw going on around him and believed it entirely contrary to the teachings of the Islam he knew and loved.

Yassir Yamani explains the approach Saleh Kamel had throughout these troubled times:

"Sheikh Saleh hated anything to do with radical Islam and believed it was something unnatural and in complete contradiction to genuine Islamic principles. He was of the opinion that the only way to fight its spread was with development. Force imposed by governments, the police, and the courts had all proved to be ineffective. It was clear that poor people, living on the breadline with little or no hope of any change in their circumstances, were the easiest to radicalise.

"Sheikh Saleh wanted to use Iqraa to fight this situation by improving the conditions of those in need. Saleh Kamel and my father spent hours speaking together of how this might best be achieved. If people have work and a regular income, if they can feed their children and build a comfortable home, they feel more secure, in which case they are not such easy targets. Radicals

158

play on deprivation to stir up discontent."

He went on to describe Iqraa's approach:

"Iqraa aims to give help where it is most needed. If we learn about a natural disaster, for example, a landslide or an earthquake in a poor area – in the Arab world, Africa, Asia, or wherever – we will send in our medical teams. We go to poor communities to see what they need. We don't start planning to build a hospital eighteen months down the line; we look at how we can help now, how we can help by feeding the hungry, ensuring a potable water supply; bringing doctors and vaccines; taking care of pregnant women. Only then would we look at the best area to establish a medical centre or hospital but always involving the local community.

"After they see what we do, how we try to give practical help in the first early days, we then try to recruit their help in establishing longer-term solutions and, ultimately, something permanent. We want people to be invested in their own communities and in helping to build their own facilities, rather than waiting for handouts. After we put a programme on track, we hope to be able to leave it to the community to run. That is what we regard as true success.

"Of course, we are all aware that not all so-called charitable organisations have the same good intentions as Iqraa. But Sheikh Saleh always believed if you have noble intentions, you can and will win through. Take time, make people aware you are serious and want good things for them without any ulterior motive.

"There have been very strong objections to our presence in certain countries – particularly in southern Europe – from those who think our charity is a ruse to convert people to Islam. Let me stress there is not now, nor has there ever been, any such intention. Saleh Kamel did not believe he had a mission to convert people, his mission was to make life better for those he could help. He genuinely respected the good in all religions.

'Human beings are the same all over the world,' he would say, 'whatever religion they are. In order to be more united, we must seek to identify our similarities rather than our differences. We are all part of the human family.'"

"In England 20 years ago, for example, we launched a programme aimed at preventing Muslims in prison from being tempted towards terrorism. We learned British prisons were a hotbed for recruiting ordinary Muslims and radicalising them. We hoped – through our programme – to tell the truth about Islam and what it expects of its followers and, in this way, to help ensure Muslim prisoners stay on the right path. The British government watched developments with interest for more than 13 years and were pleased with what they saw. They partnered with us for several years after that and then took the project over completely. For us, that was a real win, the Iqraa ethos had succeeded. We had identified a need, launched a programme to fulfil that need, and left the project in the capable hands of its own community.

"Sheikh Saleh always wanted to be hands-on with Iqraa, he loved seeing positive results, although he accepted not every story could have a happy ending. One of his great strengths was his persistence. It was also a trait he admired in others. He always seemed to enjoy his work with the Foundation, as did my father, he thought it was his greatest achievement and among his most important contributions to society, after his children.

"The Iqraa Charitable Society remains concerned with development, primarily in education, aid, and healthcare, although we do assess projects in other areas on their merits. Sheikh Saleh was involved with developments on a daily basis. I think there was an element of him seeing his work with the charity as payback for his success and the blessings God had given him.

"Helping people was always a priority for him. As I explained, he liked to see details of what we had been doing on a daily basis.

If I did not send him details of our ongoing progress first thing in the morning for some reason, he would be on the phone at an early hour asking for them. It might be a morning where he had a meeting with the Prime Minister scheduled but still it was his charity activities that came first. The people who work for Iqraa always got a boost from this. They knew they were sharing his goals.

"Sheikh Saleh was always coming up with ideas about what we should try to organise – sometimes several a day. If I went to his office to give him a report, telling him we have done this, or we have done that, he would sometimes look at me and said 'Yes, my son, but this is in the past. Don't tell me where you have been; tell me where you are going next'. It made me realise I should never try to show off to my Uncle Saleh. He would always be several steps ahead.

"He might call me and tell me what he had heard on the morning news and suggest ways in which Iqraa could offer help. Then he would call me back an hour later demanding: 'Where are you with what we discussed earlier? Who have you spoken to? What did they say?'

"But the truth is that we were all happy to do what he asked, not least because we only had one job, while we knew he was doing about 15 jobs at the same time. But he always made Iqraa a priority and right to the end of his life, he retained a dynamic and lively mind.

"Despite the fact that he was a billionaire, he really didn't care about money. Of course, he enjoyed it when a project was a success, but he didn't measure his accomplishments in money. People were far more important to him.

"He was very intuitive. He could read a situation very quickly and he saw no reason to prevaricate. If he liked you, he liked you. Of course, he did not always get it right – he sometimes made mistakes about people, which could made him very unhappy

– but generally he got it right. However, he always owned his mistakes and they didn't seem to deter him. 'If you make five attempts and you fail, don't give up, get it right the sixth time,' he would advise. He once told journalists coming to interview him at the office that he wanted to talk about his failures, not his success. If you fail, he insisted, you must learn from your mistakes. You have to persist until you achieve your goal. He liked to reassure people that not everybody can get it right first time.

"Life will present you with challenges, competition and new, frequently confusing elements. The secret is to be able to adapt. Neither Sheikh Saleh nor my father was driven by any thought of money but they were convinced that good thoughts could result in high achievement in terms of good deeds. My Uncle Saleh used to tell us, as children, 'if you are serious and make good decisions, money will always come your way.'"

They were visionary men. They saw that huge changes were afoot as far back as the 1970s and early 1980s, when the oil wealth started to come through and things in Saudi Arabia began to change quite drastically. The region was clearly about to undergo profound shifts and they were concerned that the Islamic world was not ready for such upheaval. They could see that people would need to be trained to do many of the jobs that would be required as the development process expanded. Accordingly, they recruited manpower from countries including Bangladesh, Sri Lanka, and India to train people for the future. Saleh Kamel always maintained that if you set a good example, you opened the road for everybody to replicate the idea, and progress could move forward.

Today Iqraa supports a wide range of individuals in education and training programmes. These projects are 'means tested' – tailored to what can be afforded by the individual. Students and trainees pay what they can afford – sometimes nothing – at the outset and the rest is paid off when they begin to earn a salary. The idea is to be flexible and assess every situation fairly and on its merits.

Yassir Yamani concluded by saying that the whole process is not something that can be rushed:

"In charitable work, you have to be patient to see the returns; anything from three to four years, maybe even ten to see real change. Our strategy is also to involve local people in a partnership in their community and their country. Choosing a partner in another country brings its own challenges. They have to be 'serious' and successful.

"Iqraa's biggest area of operation currently is India. We operate a large medical programme there dedicated to kidney disease; it started as a research centre, then became a clinic, and is now one of the biggest hospitals in southern India. As was our intention from the outset, its experts have trained others to become experts and consequently, the knowledge and expertise increases. Some fifteen years or so after the original success with the renal facility in India, it was successfully implemented in African countries, including the Gambia, Kenya, Niger, Nigeria, and South Africa."

Saleh Kamel was keen to perpetuate the same message of cooperation and inclusivity developed by the Iqraa Charitable Society on his television channel of the same name, Iqraa TV. He made clear from the outset that the channel should always attempt to nurture feelings of belonging to the unified cultural identity of the Arab nation; to highlight the importance of Arab-Islamic civilization and the important contributions Arabs and Muslims have made to the world throughout history. Saleh Kamel wanted Iqraa TV to present the true image of Islam, the religion he knew and loved, and to refute – with evidence – any suspicions or accusations raised against it.

Iqraa TV broadcasts sought to affirm the important role played by women in building a holistic society, while also highlighting issues of education and the importance of dedicating time to ensure a proper upbringing for upcoming generations. The channel made it its mission to address the problems and issues faced by Arabs and Muslims in our global society and, wherever possible, to offer solutions.

In the years since its inception in 2009, Iqraa TV has gone on to become one of the world's most popular Muslim channels. With its unique blend of programming, including religious and educational content, it has proved itself an important and cohesive medium, providing solace and support to Muslims from around the world.

CHAPTER NINE

THE VISION

The ambition, initiative and energy were all plain to see in the young Saleh Kamel as he was growing up in Makkah. His childhood ventures of selling *baleela* and leaded sheep bones for games of *kaboosh* were early evidence of a nascent entrepreneurial spirit.

His flair for commerce was already clear when he petitioned local businessmen to support his school plays and in the way he turned his Scouting activities into a method of generating a small income for himself as well as fulfilling a need for his friends. To be real Boy Scouts, they needed the correct uniform and, with effort and imagination, Saleh Kamel was able to make that happen, right down to the special Boy Scout whistle. Over time, right through to his university years, Saleh Kamel would continue to expand this particular business, frequently making trips abroad to secure new suppliers and, on his return, selling his newly acquired wares to a growing number of ever-eager customers out of the back of his car.

Saleh Kamel describes his years at Riyadh University as a real turning point in his life.

"The university was a hub for the Riyadh community, so I came to know many government officials, which opened doors for me in later life. I made it my business to become well known in the community. During the time I was a student, at preparatory, secondary, and university levels, I built strong friendships with all my professors, some of whom would go on to become high-ranking officials in various government ministries. It was a good start, not only for my studies at the time, but also in paving the way for business in the years to come.

"The printing press I established at university had enormous financial significance in my life. My workload increased dramatically when I started printing lecture notes, not only for my own group but for most of the other groups and years as well. In order to keep up, I was forced to rent a small shop and I began to work there in addition to attending lectures and keeping up with Scouting business and my studies.

"Although my clothing was stained with black ink every day, I had never been happier, I was selling publications to students, and making real money. In operating the printing press, with the help of friends, I succeeded in creating my first real capital. I felt I was on my way to my first million.

"Out of the profits of the printing business, I bought my first car. When we took over the Tawaf Post Project (a pioneering courier service for the transmission and distribution of domestic mail between villages and remote areas), I became well-acquainted with the geography of the Kingdom because I personally went to all the places that the mail deliveries reached. I measured the distances, the gasoline consumption, and the number of driving hours, in order to have first-hand knowledge of exactly what the drivers might encounter. Travelling through areas of the country that were completely new to me also opened my eyes to possible new opportunities outside the city.

"I was later awarded the tender for a street-cleaning project in Jeddah, becoming the first private contractor to become involved in such work, which had previously always been in the hands of the government. We worked in the sector for several years. I particularly remember that on evenings during Eid, when people traditionally go to visit relatives and friends, I would stand on the street with my brothers Hassan and Omar, who helped me out at busy times, seeing the debris, accumulated during the nightly celebrations build up in the streets. In Jeddah alone, they reached several tons every night. We then had to coordinate together in organising the massive clean-up and transportation of rubbish from the city centre, so that when people came out the next day, they would find the streets clean."

We see how Saleh Kamel's various enterprises continued to develop and flourish. With his printing and publishing ventures, the postal service, and cleaning and maintenance projects – all now running alongside his full-time position in accountancy at the Ministry of Finance – he decided he was ready to go it alone with an umbrella organisation. The decision heralded the launch of Dallah and the rest, as they say, is history.

While this could have been the story of the rise of just another billionaire, that was far from the reality of Saleh Kamel.

There is no doubt that as long ago as the 1960s, he was on a trajectory to success. Married to the beautiful Mayda and with two young children and his beloved parents living in Riyadh with them, he was able to give all his attention to building up a successful business, as Dallah went from strength to strength, picking up contracts across the Kingdom of Saudi Arabia and beyond.

Into the equation, came the revered Islamic scholar Sheikh Mohammad Alsharawi who, at the request of Saleh Kamel's mother, Fatima, would educate him on the finer points of Islamic law in relation to business practises and thereby start him on a lifelong journey.

Saleh Kamel frequently made a point of telling how the words of Sheikh Alsharawi made him reflect on ways he might continue to develop his global business interests, while at the same time complying with his religious obligations.

The conversations with his new mentor had concentrated on how not to become embroiled in the usury (interest) system, either by paying or receiving such payments. As illustrated earlier, by relentless petitioning of his bankers, Saleh Kamel was eventually able to switch his company's financial system to become totally compliant with Islamic teachings. However, it was not enough to become compliant. A spark had been ignited, and his desire from that point on was to be able to explore how to meet the requirements of his faith, not just adequately but exceptionally, and to help others do likewise.

His old friend Mahmoud Hassouba explained it this way:

"Sheikh Saleh never looked on religious compliance as a hardship, indeed it was the opposite case. He studied diligently to understand how he could ever more assiduously follow Islamic teachings. However, Islam, like all religions, is open to interpretation, which is why he enjoyed speaking to scholars about disciplines and concepts. It was never his intention to improve his knowledge to avoid his religious responsibilities, his aim was to deepen and broaden his understanding and thereby improve his observance. It wasn't a chore for him; on the contrary, it was a lifelong passion."

By the nature of his business, Saleh Kamel was well placed to fulfil many of the ambitious life goals he had set for himself, both in business and in spiritual attainment. He claimed a great interest but no unique wisdom of Islam in the way business is conducted. Extrapolating from his experiences in relation to domestic workers in his homeland, be they Muslim, Christian, Buddhist, or non-religious, he commented that "there is no nationality and no religion that provides for competence."

Saleh Kamel had a deeply ingrained work ethic and was keen to nurture the same in others. He would often refer to the Islamic story about a poor man coming to seek help and assistance from the Prophet Muhammad. The Prophet told him to go home and return with something he would be able to sell. The man returned with a small trinket that he managed to sell for two dirhams. The

Prophet told him first to buy food for a meal for his family and use the remainder to buy an axe. The Prophet then spent time with the man, teaching him how to cut wood and sell it in the market, which he was then able to do to keep his family fed and sheltered. In one short story, the Prophet gave lessons in financing, education, training, and other related subjects, such as – by first feeding his family – social responsibility.

Saleh Kamel liked to use the story as an example of how proper training should always fall within the scope of the duty of care of companies and individual businessmen. He believed that with training and a love of work, almost everything was within one's grasp. It was a personal sadness to him to observe what he saw as a decline in the work ethic, so dear to his own heart.

"I believe contentment and ambition are like the two wings indispensable for a bird to fly, Sheikh Saleh noted. Although they seem to contradict each other, the opposite is true, both are necessary to keep the bird aloft."

"Contentment is satisfaction. It represents a psychological state that leads gradually to reassurance. To be satisfied with my situation does not mean that I should not seek to improve it. This is what ambition is about! The wise Muslim moves forward with his ambition on his right and satisfaction on his left, in parallel but separate lines. He continues to exert efforts and persists in his endeavours.

"I aspired from an early age to be a merchant and a businessman. I was brought up in a family that could not even be described as a middle-income and was closer to poverty than to riches. However, thanks to Allah and to my parents, contentment prevailed in our house. At the same time, satisfaction did not prevent us from dreaming of improving the reality in which we grew up. Whining and grumbling represent a lack of acceptance of the will of Allah. They do not befit a Muslim and lead only to a life marred by constant anxiety, envy, and greed that sicken the heart," Saleh Kamel once said. He firmly believed that some businessmen, by their neglect of civil and religious duty, shared the responsibility for the decline in the work ethic and the spread of unemployment. He remarked: "Unfortunately, some businessmen do not give priority to our citizens and do not seem to realize that their main duty is to employ people. Islam has set priorities in this regard, beginning with yourself, your dependents, your closest relatives, then your neighbour." He also felt that certain banks, including Islamic banks, could have served the people better:

"Instead of investing the huge liquidity available to them in labour-intensive projects, or even in projects with medium employment rates, most banks resort to trading in goods, simply buying and selling, just to achieve profits to increase their equity. The outcomes of such investment solutions, in my opinion, are not in line with the purposes of Sharia, even if they are permissible. My experience in the world of banking has allowed me to see banking practices that do not bring real developmental returns, for example those such as trading in international goods, which adds no real value to our economy other than in profits for the seller."

To illustrate his point further, Saleh Kamel asked a group of Islamic bankers who were investing $300 billion in Western copper markets.

"What did the people at home reap from that? Consider the number of workers for whom you could open up jobs if this amount were invested in labour-intensive projects or even projects with medium employment rates at home. I also hope you can imagine the number of individuals for whom you can create 'independent job opportunities' on the sidelines of these projects – transportation services, food services, industrial products, etc. I recommend you also think about the numbers of the dependents – families and relatives – who will be supported by those who employed. After estimating these numbers, please also guess the number of individuals that these workers will assist in establishing new businesses; figure out the size and value of the innovations that some of these workers would come up with in their work in factories and laboratories. Can you now perceive the volume of development being missed for failing to invest in a way that would raise employment rates? Can you imagine the number of lost opportunities? After estimating this loss, please consider the number of crimes some of these individuals might have committed had they remained in the quagmire of unemployment and idleness. Can you now see the magnitude of the socioeconomic impact of this investment option?

"For these reasons, I firmly believe that some investment options, even if not prohibited, produce many indirect damages. Although some of those options do meet Sharia requirements, such as trading in copper, their outcome is not acceptable to the ethos of Sharia."

Saleh Kamel was also a staunch defender of the concept that all work is honourable. He deplored the idea that manual work is in some way less worthy than occupations in which those involved did not get their hands dirty.

"There is nothing wrong with any honest profession. Most of Allah's Prophets had professions. Among them were the carpenter, the blacksmith, and the tailor, and our own Prophet Muhammad was a shepherd and a trader. So why do we look down on these honest jobs? This misguided cultural norm puts pressure on our youth. It did not exist in our generation. If a young, conscientious Saudi plumber, earning an annual income of 30,000 riyals, and a feckless university graduate with a 3,000-riyal annual salary, both proposed to my daughter, I would automatically advise her to take the hardworking plumber. A decent, hardworking, educated plumber with ambition is probably a better bet than a university graduate who is educated but cannot secure a decent wage even with all the academic knowledge he has acquired."

During his long career Saleh Kamel made no secret of the fact that as a proud Saudi Arabian himself, he would always prioritise Saudi employees on domestic projects over expatriate labour. He did not reject employing foreigners, and he appreciated that sometimes they were the best people for the job, but when he did, he would usually insist that part of the contract with them would involve training up Saudi labour in order that one day, a Saudi national could step into their shoes, lending weight to Saudi national expertise and the local economy – money earned in Saudi, money spent in Saudi.

"I remember from my early childhood through to my adolescence that most of the people we dealt with in our daily lives, from various professions and fields, were all Saudis. The butcher was a Saudi, as was the baker, the carpenter, and the barber, the sheep shearer, and shoemaker, all were our countrymen. None were ashamed of their profession; on the contrary, they were proud to teach their children to follow in their footsteps, so that they too would always be assured of a living. Today, this is no longer the case. Young people have abandoned the skills and craftsmanship of their forefathers, allowing expatriate workers to multiply, while our own affluent sons turn up their noses at good, honest work."

The spread of unemployment among Saudi nationals was a direct result of wishy-washy planning policies and the way these policies were implemented, according to the gifted entrepreneur. A case in point, he insisted was the way in which the Saudisation policy – aimed at getting Saudi nationals into work – was implemented.

"I do not find fault with Saudisation per se, but rather the way we handle it. It was treated emotionally. There was not sufficient preparation for young people to take interest in all honest work. There are many professions Saudis simply refuse to practice, primarily involving manual labour. We must prepare our society culturally and psychologically for the Saudi youth to accept such professions, to take pride in providing for their society and not to despise those who are able to do so.

"How can we Saudise our workforce if culturally we look down on essential jobs? If your car breaks down on a desert highway, you pray the next car along will be driven by a mechanic, not a heart surgeon. All occupations are honourable and all are vital to our society. We need to acknowledge this and reintroduce the importance of skills as well as professions into our society and our culture."

Saleh Kamel made huge financial investments into vocational education projects, both in the Kingdom of Saudi Arabia and beyond. Special training institutes were set up to ensure that those who failed to get good high school scores did not fall by the wayside.

He was an outspoken critic of the way such schemes were handled by the state. "We should be celebrating the skills of all those who contribute to our society but these days – because of the negativity that surrounds certain jobs – some refuse to work as a mechanic in a car workshop for 4,000 riyals, choosing instead to work in an office for 1,000 riyals. Billions of riyals of government money have been spent on the vocational education system, but the end result has been a fiasco. Unfortunately, education in our Saudi society has become a matter of social status. This shallow attitude is detrimental to us all. Sadly, we have become a society that values the certificate more than its holder."

In the Kingdom of Saudi Arabia, Egypt, and beyond, Dallah established factories and workshops, giving employment to many thousands of people and helping to put food on their tables. Dallah's activities took in a range of industries, including iron and steel production for use in the construction sector; a large-scale cattle production operation, including breeding, milking and the production of dairy produce, including milk, cheese and other related foodstuffs; a massive milk and fruit juice production and packaging factory; a textile recycling and manufacturing unit; several large-scale poultry-related ventures, including breeding, slaughterhouses, and freezing factories capable of handling up to 3,000 birds an hour; and a wide range of other diverse endeavours, ranging from biscuit production to high-end chocolate manufacture and even a textile and ready-made garment company (Al-Thobe Al-Saudi) established in 1979 in Makkah.

According to those who knew him well over many decades, Saleh Kamel always had an interest in what we now refer to universally as 'real estate'. His long-time friend and brother-in-law Naji Nazer recalls:

"I'm not sure we were even aware of the term back then, but I remember Saleh telling me that he had bought this or that plot of land, in Jeddah or Riyadh, not in a boastful way but just as a matter of fact. It began when he was quite a young man and his purchases were extremely modest compared to what was to follow.

"He might be walking or driving along a street and see that there was a small parcel of undeveloped land with a 'For Sale' board hammered into the ground. If he could see potential in the location, he would put in an offer and usually end up buying it. Land was relatively cheap in those days and he had a few of these plots here and there".

Speaking on his television programme, Al Souq (The Market), Saleh Kamel advised: "Real estate is a safe asset that preserves its value. In fact, land is a value-preserving asset and, in my opinion, a safer option than buying shares in a company. Investing in real estate, to build new houses and rent them to others, is a productive economic activity and will be divinely rewarded.

"I would more readily advocate investment in real estate than shares, especially if the goal is to construct new housing stock to sell or to rent. However, this should always be proportionate to the demand in the market.

"When the real estate market flourishes, this has the additional benefit of creating multiple job opportunities. Industries such as cement and steel, to supply the construction market, flourish. This type of building activity also gives a boost to men in building-related trades – carpenters, plumbers, electricians, blacksmiths, and the like. All these vital industries feed off the construction market and provide thousands of job opportunities."

When asked about the risks of losing money in a real estate crisis such as the one that hit the United States in 2008, Saleh Kamel responded: "I think a real estate crisis, like the one that happened in America, is unlikely to take place in any Arab country.

"That crisis was not caused by any shortage of real estate in America. It was caused by selling bonds that were collateralised by mortgages; these bonds were resold many times, which had the effect of them becoming aggressively overvalued. In most of the Arab countries I have visited, such activities are not present.

"However, there are some Arab states that may witness a decrease in the demand on real estate, as the result of a depression in the global economy. For instance, some Arab states have constructed many tall buildings in their towns and cities, that far exceed the needs of their citizens, and could supply a population ten times larger than they possess. Should there be a global recession, God forbid, the real estate market of these countries will likely be affected because of the decrease in demand for renting or purchasing.

"Real estate is generally a good area of investment, provided the appropriate regulations are strictly applied. In this case, property would almost always be a safe and profitable investment. An Arabic proverb reminds us: 'Land can fall ill, but it will never die.' I believe this proverb to be correct."

As the years went by, Dallah would become a major player in the real estate industry, in a variety of ways. A flagship achievement for the company was the establishment of the Prince Fawaz residential complex in Jeddah, the largest housing project ever executed in the

Middle East by a private sector company at that time.

Dallah's first major real estate endeavour in the early 1980s was the establishment of the Prince Fawaz District in Jeddah. Although the project entailed significant risks for an emergent real estate company, the construction of the 900-villa residential neighbourhood was widely heralded as a success. By introducing cutting-edge precast construction techniques to the Middle East region through the establishment of a dedicated factory, Dallah was able to contain costs, allowing the local middle class to purchase most of the properties. Forty years later, the development still looks as good as new – testament to the quality of the planning and workmanship – and has turned this community into a thriving major urban development hub that has shifted Jeddah's growth south.

Saleh Kamel believed a safe living environment should be considered an essential for all people, although he was aware that far too many millions across the globe did not enjoy the privilege. He observed:

> "Low-income citizens should be provided with the appropriate means to enable them to own the home in which they live. We should stop building excessively luxurious homes because most people cannot afford them. We need to pay more attention to the needs of low-income people. Good living conditions, like a job with a decent wage, give people self-worth.

Dallah won the approval of numerous decision-makers in its efforts to help meet regional housing needs. Mega-projects, like the one undertaken in Prince Fawaz District, were key in providing the homes desperately required to address the city's escalating housing problems.

The project created a residential suburb with integrated services and facilities, which supported the housing needs across all of Jeddah's social classes – part of the municipality's aim to make Jeddah a model city, meeting the needs of citizens and visitors alike.

Dallah Albaraka would contribute to many more such projects over the years, not only as the main contractor but frequently as technical support in a variety of specialist areas in which they were able to offer their expertise.

It was the company's extensive skill set that would put Dallah Albaraka into the history books for its invaluable achievement in solving a problem no other international company had been able to overcome.

In addition to the important projects at home, there were a number of standout schemes that would become known internationally. One of the jewels in the crown of Dallah's international achievements is the Tunis Lake project. The successful undertaking was not only a feather in Dallah Albaraka's cap, but also an important personal achievement for Saleh Kamel because it complied absolutely with his firm commitment to *Istikhlaf*, or stewardship of the earth.

Mahmoud Hassouba, the first Vice President of Dallah Albaraka, who worked closely with Saleh Kamel for almost 30 years, was also a friend and confidant. He points out that as Saleh Kamel's business enterprises went global, he developed many important relationships with leaders of governments and business institutions around the world. One of these was with the late president of Tunisia, Habib Bourguiba.

Bourguiba was a Tunisian lawyer, nationalist, and statesman who became prime minister in 1956 and was therefore well placed to become the first president of the newly liberated Tunisia when it gained independence from France a year later in 1957, a position he would retain for some 30 years. Like Saleh Kamel, Bourguiba had come from a modest background and worked hard to achieve his goals. He was born in 1903, so there was an age difference of almost 40 years between the two men, but those close to the President said he had an enormous respect for the Saudi entrepreneur, who was in his thirties when they first met.

Back in the golden years of the late 1970s, Bourguiba and Saleh Kamel made a formidable pair as their foresight and enthusiasm saw several important projects take shape. Not least of these was the Tunis Lake project.

Mahmoud Hassouba takes up the story:

"We had been visiting Tunis on banking business and were enjoying an informal dinner with President Bourguiba and his wife at their home – just the four of us. Sheikh Saleh and President Bourguiba were friends who genuinely enjoyed spending time together. Conversation was informal and had covered several topics when the subject of the sadly neglected Tunis Lakes came up and the recent failure by contractors to make any impact on clearing and re-energising the area."

There were two bodies of water, the North Lake and the South Lake, separated by a seven-mile-long navigation channel connecting the Mediterranean ports of Tunis and Goulette. At the North Lake, to the east of the capital, rainwater and wastewater, including effluent from several industrial areas, had accumulated over the years. The result was that the sediment at the bottom of the lake was severely contaminated by heavy metal residue, including iron, zinc, chrome, and copper, resulting in high levels of pollution, foul smells, and a complete inability to maintain marine life.

Historically, the lakes had been a single body of water covering around 37 square kilometres and Tunis's natural harbour. It was the Romans who first built a dam across its relatively shallow waters and, years later, the occupying French forces constructed a 10- kilometre-long canal between the North and South lakes.

Mahmoud Hassouba continued, laughing at the memory:

"I could see Sheikh Saleh was fascinated. There was nothing that spurred his imagination more than coming across a problem most people had written off as insoluble. I also knew it was a project that honoured Istikhlaf, man's stewardship of the planet, and I was aware this would be an additional attraction. Even so, I remember still how my heart sank as I heard Sheikh Saleh say to Bourguiba: 'We will take a look at it if you like'.

"I had heard about complications with the Tunis Lake on many occasions and knew of various projects launched to solve the problems – and there had been a considerable number – which had drawn a blank. I tried to nudge Sheikh Saleh with my foot beneath the table – a gesture to persuade him to hold off on making any commitment – but the dining table was too big, I could not reach him and before I knew it, the words were out of his mouth: 'I think we might be able to come up with something to solve your problem.'

"By the time we left the presidential palace that evening, it had been agreed Dallah would look into conducting a feasibility study with the objective of taking on the problem project. Saleh was full of excitement; President Bourguiba, inspired by Sheikh Saleh, was similarly optimistic. It seemed that I was the only one with any misgivings!"

Predictably, the Tunis Lake regeneration scheme and the inevitable problems it encountered attracted attention from around the world. Albaraka's objectives were to remove the polluted sediment from the floor of the lake, which was effectively poisoning all chances for sustainable plant or marine life. Once this was achieved, a system would be put in place that would see the lake flushed by sea water, based on tidal flows and, gradually, there would be a land reclamation project instituted around the shores of the lake, which would act as the cornerstone of an ambitious scheme for total regeneration of the area.

It was not plain sailing; work took several years to complete but eventually, Dallah Albaraka pulled it off, in partnership with the Tunisian government. Work commenced in 1984 and Dallah used a combination of swamp draining, habitat preservation, and water engineering – all using environmentally friendly materials – to rid the lake of its raw sewage pollution and develop the surrounding area into a safe, healthy community. Some years later, enthused by what had been achieved, an international consortium successfully tackled the South Lake, and today, some of the most expensive and highly prized homes, offices, and hotels of the Tunisian capital are established in the area that was once regarded as little more than a giant urban cesspit. And the profit margin for Dallah, Mahmoud Hassouba confirmed, was an enviable 22%.

The Tunisian publishing magnate, Afif Ben Yedder, recalled how, before Saleh Kamel took on the project, the area was so disgusting that nobody could or would ever have considered living there: "All the detritus of the city of Tunis seemed to find its way into the lakes, the area was an ugly, foul-smelling disaster, but thanks to Saleh Kamel's vision and expertise, it was transformed and work to continue what he started continues today in a range of beautification schemes surrounding some of the most sought-after property in Tunis."

This flourishing suburban metropolis hosts world-class hotels, offices, embassies, consulates, as well as commercial and residential complexes. Immersed in greenery, the area occupies almost one third of the capital's surface and has effectively become its beating heart.

In line with his commitment to communities, was Saleh Kamel's commitment to provide real estate instruments at affordable prices. Owning a small sea-view plot or beachfront house, whether for accommodation or investment, was a dream inaccessible to most Saudi Arabians, due to the scarcity of small plots as well as the lack of infrastructure in distant areas. Saleh Kamel – who strongly believed in the physical and spiritual benefits of spending time by the sea – had the idea to develop an area some 65 kilometres north of Jeddah and turn it into an enclave of properties with all the required infrastructure, services, and entertainment facilities to be a self-sufficient community. It was likely he had seen such enterprises take shape abroad and believed his homeland could benefit from something similar. In order not to limit the seafront properties to the privileged few, Dallah managed to stretch the seafront area from 4 kilometres to a 34-kilometre finger-shaped coastline. All development and reclamation work was carried out with great care given to the protection and conservation of the marine ecosystem. Hundreds of villas were built, all with good access to the beach – some, obviously, closer than others – and tailored for diverse budgets.

Durrat Alarous, as the project was named, became a hub for a new and innovative lifestyle with affordable prices. At the heart of Durrat Alarous, Dallah invested in recreational and hospitality premises, including a marina, a separate hotel resort, and other beach-related outlets. Residents and visitors today continue to enjoy a large menu of marine activities that range from fishing and jet-skiing to surfing and scuba diving, all within a gated community that was first of its kind within the Kingdom of Saudi Arabia.

The infrastructure of Durrat Alarous was highly developed, with all services available, including its own power station, water desalination plant, sewage options, telecommunication networks, satellite television, and 24-hour sea- and land-based security services. On completion of the first phase of development in the 1990s, Saleh Kamel decided he loved the concept so much that one of the largest, most luxurious villas on the compound, on the very edge of the Red Sea, was set aside for the Kamel family, who enjoyed some wonderful holidays together within their many-roomed Thai-style, teak bungalow. Saleh Kamel entertained many important international politicians and celebrities within its walls, frequently allocating his visitors their own guest villa within his own extensive compound, with its luxurious and well-manicured gardens, overlooking the open sea.

Although Saleh Kamel prioritised projects within Saudi Arabia, in line with his desire to see his homeland develop and grow, he also had a passion for Egypt. Dallah Real Estate & Tourism Development were the main developers of the Samla & Alam El Roum project on the Mediterranean coast of Egypt, a favourite of Saleh Kamel, as his Jeddah Office Manager Mohammad Moussa recalled:

"Sheikh Saleh loved to travel to the north coast of Egypt near Alexandria. He had several homes there and would – unusually for him – visit for weeks at a time, as he craved cooler weather and loved watching the storms that are frequently experienced in the area, blowing in from the sea."

Mustafa Jumaa, Managing Director of Dallah Real Estate Egypt and a close associate of Saleh Kamel Kamel, confirmed:

"Sheikh Saleh's idea was to transform Dallah's North Coast resorts into areas that could operate throughout the year, unlike the tourism villages that operate for only three months in summer and are closed up the rest of the year. Sheikh Saleh's plan was to establish international universities, educational institutes, hospitals, and specialised medical and surgical centres on a land area of around five million square metres. The project is massive and still under construction."

Saleh Kamel owned other urban development projects in Egypt near Cairo City, where Dallah Real Estate planned and constructed the Almultaqa Alarabi Neighbourhood. This district attracted investors and global hotel operators, and now boasts the Valore Sheraton Compound, the Heliopolis Gardens, Almaza Avenue, and the Leyenda Hotel.

Saleh Kamel believed there should be more regulations in place in the construction industry and more transparency in planning intentions at the point of purchase. As he commented around the time of the property slump in 2010: "The lack of financing options has left the real estate market in a coma. The result is that land remains undeveloped for many years, even though many people in our society cannot afford to buy a house to live in.

"People hold on to their property until prices rise. Too many estate investors adopt this policy, negatively affecting young people's ability to buy a home. Leaving land undeveloped causes a lot of trouble for municipalities, it hinders city planning and wastes resources, leading to increases in the cost of facilities, including electricity, water, sewage, telephone lines, etcetera. Municipalities should set a time limit for landowners who don't build on their land and, where necessary, impose penalties."

Mortgage financing is feasible in Islam, Saleh Kamel was at pains to point out.

"Once the appropriate legal tools are established, the lease-to-own solution is a very good mechanism which protects the rights of those involved. And so is deferred ownership, in which ownership is transferred only after all the payments have been made. All these mechanisms can easily be adapted to comply with Islamic law, serving Islamic objectives. In Islam, mortgages are meant to help people buy or build a house to live in; not designed to help people buy a house as an investment to sell on to somebody else as their home at vast profit."

One of the things that marked Saleh Kamel out from the rest of the crowd was his boundless enthusiasm to discover more and better ways to deal with problems. For most of his life, he ploughed much of his energies into business and business-related projects, but in his later years, the "philosophy" of business, which had so intrigued him, began to take up more and more of his time. His colleagues at Dallah Albaraka insist Saleh Kamel did not tire of the company, or of the cut and thrust of the business world, but at a certain point it is clear that he simply found something else that offered different and more attractive challenges – a new dimension to what he had been doing throughout his life – the possibilities of which captivated him. Saleh Kamel was totally confident in the leadership of his son Abdullah and decided the time was right to hand over the reins of power at Dallah Albaraka to him, in order to allow him the freedom to pursue other interests.

As his years on earth increased, he became ever more aware of the need for sustainable development and was particularly concerned for the well-being of Saudi Arabia – the country he loved – its people and also the wider Islamic community. When he was appointed Chairman of Islamic Chamber of Commerce, Industry, and Agriculture (ICCIA), he welcomed the new challenge with enthusiasm. Shortly after, he was elected as a member of the Forum of Muslim Scholars and Thinkers, responsible for the preparation of the Exceptional Muslim Leaders Summit in Makkah (December 2005) under the umbrella of the Organisation of the Islamic

Conference (now the Organisation for Islamic Cooperation). Saleh Kamel prepared proposals for the Forum, targeting the objectives of increasing trade, investment, tourism, and labour exchange among Islamic countries. He also drew up directives on developing the education curriculum to give more attention to research and studies.

Between 2005 and 2007, Saleh Kamel worked on reviewing the economic and social challenges facing Saudi Arabia, as well the new opportunities available to the country. Building on his experience, gained over more than 40 years working in investment and business, his research benefitted from his familiarity with the laws and employment regulations of a huge swathe of Islamic countries. While acutely aware of the obstacles facing the advancement of Islamic economies, he believed fervently in the dream of establishing a common Islamic market, building a strong economic bloc that would enhance their status and capabilities. To this end, Saleh Kamel compiled a booklet containing a ten-year plan, issued in Arabic, English, and French, which he promoted by touring a great many Islamic countries, meeting with kings, presidents, and other leaders, explaining the details of his blueprint with great care.

The booklet outlined 16 achievement goals, among them the revival of moral values in commercial transactions, the need to raise awareness of the concept of Islamic economics, the importance of deepening the spirit of solidarity among Islamic nations, and the development of an Islamic common market. To the best of his considerable ability, he put in place the appropriate mechanisms to achieve it, including the establishment of the International Zakat Authority, Islamic Endowment Funds, free trade zones, the removal of customs barriers, the establishment of an international Islamic construction bank, and the freedom of movement for Muslim business owners between Islamic countries.

In 2008, Dallah Albaraka set up a centre for Islamic banking studies and research at King Saud University in Riyadh. The centre is affiliated with the Faculty of Economics and Administration but has technical, financial and administrative autonomy. It has an ongoing commitment to scientific research on Islamic banking, including its origins and aspirations – through research – to meet the growing need for financing banks commensurate with Islamic Sharia rules, while also protecting and enhancing Islamic banking ethics.

No doubt impressed by his relentless passion, the Jeddah Chamber of Commerce and Industry (JCCI) in 2009 elected Saleh Kamel Chairman. This new position kept him impressively busy – even by his own onerous standards – right up until a few months before his death. At JCCI he continued to channel energy into community reform initiatives which took the form of combatting unemployment, developing work and training programs, establishing funds to support productive families, and finding ways to stimulate the local economy.

He believed the fundamental role of a chamber of commerce should be to give priority to the support of the state's balance of payments. To this end, he set out a programme of economic and investment ideas in relation to regulations governing companies and partnerships. He laboured relentlessly to spread his message, working through the media and discussion forums, as well as speaking directly to the government to highlight areas of potential economic benefit. An example of this was seen at the 13th Jeddah Economic Forum (held in 2013), where the main topic was population and housing. He later sent a letter to King Abdullah bin Abdul Aziz, in which he summarised discussions at the forum and its recommendations. One important issue he was keen to emphasise was the problem of so called 'white lands', which he felt impacted adversely on housing in Saudi Arabia, which was in crisis at the time.

'White lands' was the term commonly used to describe large areas of land in the middle of towns and cities, acquired by businessmen and then left undeveloped, sometimes for years, until the value increased. As cities naturally expand, these open lands become an obstacle to normal urban development. Saleh Kamel demanded the imposition of substantial government fees on these areas left to lay fallow, in addition to payment of zakat, to discourage the practise which, he insisted, was blatantly opportunistic and damaging to development.

Within a few years, Saleh Kamel's recommendations were put in place, which played an important role in relieving the inner-city housing calamity.

Saleh Kamel was never afraid to go to the top when he strongly believed it was in the best interests of his countrymen. When he had the idea of establishing two charitable hospitals, one in Makkah, the other in Madinah, he approached the future king, then-Crown Prince Salman, who after careful examination of the proposal, not only embraced the idea of the scheme but saw fit to extend the scope of the original idea to include additional medical facilities.

Saleh Kamel never ran out of ideas to improve the lot of his fellow man by using business as the conduit. Yassir Yamani remembers how his Uncle Saleh had a vision for a thriving business exchange among Islamic markets in the Middle East region and elsewhere – a type of Islamic Common Market loosely based on the one operated in the countries of Europe by the European Economic Community, the precursor to today's European Union.

He also had the dream of creating an umbrella bank which would enable all Islamic countries to do business together seamlessly – a 'Bank of Banks', as he referred to it, the concept of which some have likened to an Islamic International Monetary Fund (IMF). "This was a dream my father was passionate about," his eldest son and CEO of Dallah Albaraka, Abdullah, explained. "By preventing us all from travelling, the global pandemic helped focus my father's mind on things he had been mulling over for years.

"It is true he would usually lose interest in a project when it was up and running. He would then put it into the hands of a good manager and move on to something else. But the opportunities offered by the Islamic Chamber of Commerce and Industry were exactly the sort of schemes and structures he most enjoyed, interwoven and endless."

Through his work at ICCI, Saleh Kamel was able to give time and attention to creating a living awareness of Islamic economics in contemporary society and his achievements were many and varied.

Fostering social solidarity and cooperation to help overcome poverty, improve health conditions, and raise living standards remains high on the agenda of the ICCI, as it was in the days when he was at the helm. To this end, the Chamber is working diligently on a number of programmes. One which was particularly close to Saleh Kamel's heart is designed to facilitate a procedure to allow people to purchase their own homes. ICCI is also constantly looking at new tools to facilitate the tightening up of real estate law to protect the buyer. Yassir Yamani, head of Saleh Kamel's Iqraa Charitable Society pointed out:

"Sheikh Saleh did not believe in the subjugation of human beings, especially not for profit. He strove throughout his life to establish equal opportunities for men and women across the world, be they Muslim, Christian, or any other religion. He believed the conditions of poor people and impoverished countries deserved to be improved and developed. Obviously, he made a lot of his money in Saudi Arabia, but he also invested his wealth in countries that most people didn't even want to visit, taking big risks to do so. We were active in Sudan, Mauritania, Pakistan, Yemen, poor countries, with governments at times weak and with no obvious structure for investments at the time."

Saleh Kamel was also keen to promote the protection of Arabic – the language of the Quran – in all Muslim states.

"Our ancestors spread the Arabic language, and many great books were written by non-Arabs in our Arabic language. Eminent scholars such as Imam Al Bukhari, Imam Muslim, Imam Ibn Majah, Avicenna, and Ibn Rushd, all of them non-Arabs, struggled to master our language and now, unfortunately, we see Arab Muslims speaking and texting in English with each other. If Arabs do not respect their own language, who will?" Many of Saleh Kamel's objectives – shared and encouraged by his fellow Board members – form part of the ICCI strategy for the future.

Saleh Kamel was forward-looking, but he also liked to keep in mind that the past had served Islam well. He wanted due attention to be given to inventions, inventors, and research that had gone before, believing that if Muslims did not give credence to their achievements, the rest of the world would follow suit.

Speaking to a meeting of the ICCI, Saleh Kamel noted: "Our Muslim ancestors were famous for inventing many things that benefitted the world. Today, sadly, Muslims are mere consumers of the inventions of other nations."

With the weight of the ICCI and its members behind him, Saleh Kamel was able to help go some way to redressing the balance. Saleh Kamel said in many interviews that when he retired, he would write a book about mistakes he had made and what he learned from them. "After all," he noted, "those mistakes are the secret of my success".

It is unlikely those errors will ever be catalogued now, and his many successes speak for themselves. One thing is for certain: Saleh Kamel cannot be rebuked for his lack of courage in trying to attain his goals. He had a vision – one he carried with him right to the end of his life – and Islam was central to that vision. Today, Islam is widely portrayed in the Western media as a regressive force, trying to turn back time and to enforce an unenlightened lifestyle from some distant age. This is largely an untrue and wholly unrepresentative viewpoint. There are many different interpretations of the faith, but the vast majority of Muslims do not identify with the negative versions of Islam so often presented in the West.

Saleh Kamel was very much a reformer, revering tradition while embracing necessary modification. In this sense, he was probably one of the most progressive thinkers in Saudi Arabia's modern history and, as such, played a vital role in steering the established mainstream religion into something that works well within the framework of all the new economic and social developments of the time. When, for example, hard-line religious scholars spoke out against the evils of television, he asked how an invention capable of taking the teachings of the Holy Quran into millions of Muslim homes could possibly be categorised as 'evil'. He had eloquently made his point and the hard-liners were forced into silence.

Saleh Kamel believed in following the teachings of Islam with all his heart, as he believed in the benefits a unified Islam could bring to its followers in terms of providing employment, education, and the hope of a prosperous future. As he would explain it: "One Islamic Nation, One Qibla, One heart."

CHAPTER TEN

A FAMILY MAN

To the world, Saleh Abdullah Kamel was the hugely
successful Saudi Arabian billionaire businessman with the
Midas touch. To those who knew him, he was a gifted,
intelligent, complex individual who did his best to be the man his
faith demanded. However, success and wealth were just a small
part of what made Saleh Kamel so exceptional; another facet of
his exceptional personality was his outstanding ability to bring out
the best in each of his nine children. Although his work kept him
busy a great deal of the time, all his children confirm that he was a
devoted father who unfailingly remembered exactly what was going
on in their lives – always attentive, caring, and compassionate when
it mattered. His daughter Aseel recalls how her father insisted on
accompanying her to the hospital when she was diagnosed with
Covid in the early days of the pandemic, when little was known
about the disease and restrictions were at their most strict:

"When the ambulance arrived at the house, my father was in
tears. It was only the paramedic who managed to prevent him
from getting into the ambulance with me. I was admitted to
hospital but, of course, no visitors were allowed. My dad was
beside himself. He would call me several times a day, recounting
events at home, or telling me stories to keep my spirits up. He
even gave me a telephone for our exclusive use, so that we could

be in touch at all times.

She continued:

"Years before, it was my dad who first diagnosed my diabetes. I had been sick for a while but the doctors had not been able to come up with a cause. My Dad had been watching me carefully, noting my symptoms. He spotted signs of the disease before the medics and was proven correct. Because of his vigilance, treatment was able to start immediately."

Abdullah and Ghadeer, being the first born of the Kamel children, were able to enjoy more of their father's attention in the years before his business empire truly blossomed. "I remember him reading the newspaper at home, while holding me on his knee," notes Ghadeer.

His daughter Sadeer recalls his love of books:

"My father was a great reader. He took a bag of books with him almost everywhere he went. He read all kinds of things, ranging from novels, to guide books to a factual report. It gave him a wide breadth of knowledge, with the result that when we asked him anything, he would usually be able to give us some information on the topic. It might not always be exactly the information we requested but it would be – in some way – related to the subject. It certainly made for some interesting conversations."

Saleh Kamel's reading habit stayed with him all his life and when, in later life, he had trouble reading himself, as a result of an eye problem, he employed somebody to read to him. Reading helped feed his unquenchable thirst for knowledge as well as his interest in identifying the opportunity to solve a problem.

However, Saleh Kamel's passion for reading did not always find wholehearted approval with his family. His daughters laugh as they recall the hours spent in bookshops in London with their father, when they were desperate to be out enjoying the delights of the city.

They recount how, when away from home, he remained a creature of habit, always choosing to read the same daily newspapers but in

changed locations. Ghadeer recalls how Saleh Kamel always used a
well-known Paris restaurant on the Champs Elysée as a base when
he was in the French capital:

"He was good at establishing a home away from home. When
we were in Paris, we could always find him in Fouquet's. He
loved the atmosphere there and would schedule all his business
meetings in the restaurant. In Cannes, it was the Carlton Hotel.
He would spend the afternoon and early evening hours in the
lobby there, drinking coffee with his associates, after spending
the morning with us at the beach."

Saleh Kamel was a proud Muslim, a proud Saudi, and a proud Arab,
old school in some of his thinking but also determinedly forward
looking in many areas, for example in his determination that
women have a vitally important role to play in 21st century society.
Interestingly, his daughters say that he did not attempt to interfere in
their choices of partners. "Those of us who are married were pretty
much allowed to make their own decision," explained his daughter
Hadeel, "which is unusual in our society, even today. But my father
was a romantic…"

All his family agree on this point. "He loved romantic songs and
romantic stories. If someone told him a story that touched him, he
would always remember them," his daughter Nadeer recounted fondly.

Nadeer, Aseel, and Hadeel well remember a stay in Dubai when
their father, who had arrived in the city a couple of days earlier for
business meetings, met them at the airport. Nadeer recalls:

"After we had completed our greetings, with hugs and kisses,
my father told us he had a car waiting outside. The driver was
stood to attention next to his vehicle. He greeted us warmly,
offering us 'salaams' and smiling from ear to ear, but then we
couldn't believe what we saw. The car my Dad had arranged for
us was barely roadworthy. It was clean but the lack of dust only
revealed dents and scrapes and even pieces missing around the
wheel arches. I swear it must have been the very worst car in

the whole of the United Arab Emirates, but my Dad insisted, so we piled in.

"There wasn't nearly enough room for our luggage but it was squashed in anyway, at least one of the back seats was wobbly and broken, and the air conditioning was barely functioning – it was a nightmare.

"But somehow, my father had come across the driver, I think his name was Mustapha, and listened to stories of how he had left his family in Yemen, to come to Dubai to try to make a living to lift them all out of poverty at home."

Hadeel takes up the story:

"His sad story was probably true but I knew immediately it had all the romantic components necessary to appeal to Dad – impoverished man in a foreign land, hoping to improve the fortunes of his disadvantaged family back home, with only a cheery grin and a broken-down taxi – a sure winner. It was almost a film script, right there."

While they sympathised with Mustapha's plight, the sisters would have appreciated a little more comfort for their stay in Dubai but Saleh Kamel was obdurate. Nadeer went on:

"Dad sat up in the front chatting to Mustapha as if he had known him all his life, while we were crunched up in the back steaming, and that was the case for every single day of our stay in Dubai. Every morning, smiling from ear to ear, Mustapha and his ramshackle taxi would be waiting to whisk us away. We left Dubai a couple of days before Dad, who, I think and hope, would have given Mustapha a generous tip for taking care of us so well – I just hope it was enough to buy him a decent taxi!"

One of the drivers who drove Saleh Kamel during his visits to London reports how he would sit in the back of the car with his wife and sing to her when returning home from dinner or a social event. And, by all accounts, he had an impressive baritone voice with which he conveyed his romantic message.

It is clear that there were many sides to the billionaire businessman only a few were privy to. A dutiful and loving son, he never underestimated the sacrifices his parents had made bringing him up. When they were alive, he made sure he visited them every day if he was in the same city. If not, he would telephone them from wherever he was.

After they passed, he started every day with a recording of each of them offering a prayer for his continuing good health and good fortune.

In Jeddah, Mohammad Moussa still smiles when he recalls how Saleh Kamel and his father, Sheikh Abdullah, would sit on the balcony outside the latter's office in the late afternoon sunshine, feeding the pigeons.

"They were father and son, obviously, but they were also like friends. Whatever was going on in Sheikh Saleh's business life, however busy he might have been, the time on the balcony with his father and the pigeons was precious. I would bring them tea just to hear them laughing together and enjoying each other's company. They had a marvellous relationship.

"After his mother passed away, he made sure his father wanted for nothing. If he travelled to London or Paris or Istanbul on business, he would always try to persuade him to go along on the trip. If his father agreed, Sheikh Saleh would be genuinely thrilled that he would be able to enjoy his company."

Saleh Kamel's mother, Fatima, was described by her granddaughters as a quiet but strong woman. She could not read or write but she had great presence and great wisdom. They recall her as someone who never raised her voice but, when she spoke, people listened. The sisters recount an incident they were told about when Fatima's husband, their grandfather, was working in the government offices in Riyadh. Sadeer relates:

"My father was just a boy when my father was working in Riyadh and his wife, my grandmother, was forced to remain in Jeddah, to take care of the home and the family. When my grandfather returned home, after a month or two working in Riyadh without a break, he found she had built an entire new floor to their home, with the proceeds of what she had been able to save from the money he sent home."

A family member recounts Saleh Kamel's remembrance of his family in his prayers:

"His fajr dawn prayer would include him asking for God's guidance on everyone in the family, each of whom he would name and – for each –specify an area where they may need His help. He would then pray for friends and ask for Allah to guide them in certain, detailed matters. He would even mention the citizens of particular countries in his prayers. For example, after Italy was forced into lockdown following spiralling Covid cases, I heard him offer a prayer for the country and its people during the pandemic. He was never in a hurry when speaking with God."

Saleh Kamel was a man who by his own efforts rose to a position where he regularly dined with Presidents and Kings, yet he was totally grounded and never forgot the times when he and his family did not always have enough. His time working as a mutawif had taught him a great deal, and his love for Makkah and his pride in his former hometown was immense. His nephew, Abdul Aziz Yamani, explains:

"He was proud to be from Makkah and he was proud of the role his family played for generations in taking care of the many thousands of Hajj pilgrims they sponsored over the years, from various parts of the world. He believed his time as a mutawif had always kept him grounded. It was a business and one that eventually became quite lucrative, but he also believed it was a great honour to serve these people and he insisted, when we became teenagers, that we a do likewise. We were not allowed to do it half-heartedly either. If it meant rising at 4am, we rose at 4am. We organized their transport to the holy sites and did everything we could to ensure their lives ran smoothly during their time in Makkah. We even cleaned their toilets if that was what was required."

195

Kindness is another recurring word when conversations about Saleh Kamel take place. Some are known but there must be hundreds of random acts that were never recorded. His wife, Safaa, learned of one quite by surprise when she entered a hotel dining room one evening with her husband. "The maître d' was speaking with Sheikh Saleh when a young woman in her 30s approached us, threw her arms around Sheikh Saleh and embraced him warmly," she recalls.

"I stood back in surprise. She was, I remember, tall and quite beautiful. I wondered who on earth she could be! She and my husband were totally engrossed in conversation. I looked over at the maître d', who could see my confusion. He whispered to me: 'She was a waitress here for several years but had to leave when she was diagnosed with an aggressive form of cancer around 18 months ago. Sheikh Saleh found out what had happened and asked for my help in organising to send her to the United States for treatment. He paid for everything – the trip, the treatment – and now she seems to be in remission. This is the first time they have met since she was diagnosed.' It was just one of many, many times I found Saleh out in an act of kindness and generosity. They were a regular occurrence. He didn't speak about them, he just got on with doing them."

Safaa continued:

"All people were the same to him. He was at ease with everybody. He treated all with respect, both the high and the low. We were once on our way to a celebration dinner, a special event, in Cairo. On our way there we were passing through a fairly insalubrious area in the limousine when Saleh told the driver to stop the car. He jumped out of the car and I sat in backseat and watched him approach a fairly elderly woman who was sitting on the pavement; she appeared to be eating something. I wound down the window slightly and heard him ask, to my total astonishment, if he could join her. She was happy to have company and laughed as she extended her hand to invite him to sit on the pavement with her, telling him: 'Of course, of course my dear, please join me!' just as if she was inviting him to sit at her table in the finest of French restaurants.

"They started to talk and laugh together and I saw her offer him a chunk of bread and a piece of cheese, from a small bundle she carried with her. To my astonishment – not least because we were on our way to dinner – I saw him accept and, sitting on the roadside they ate and laughed together for several minutes. He finished his bread and cheese, thanked her for her hospitality, and returned to the car. While the driver was outside repaying the old woman's generosity to his boss, Saleh told me that he had spotted her cheese and knew that he must have a piece before he could travel any further that night. He was, he said, compelled to go and sit with her and eat some cheese. What could I say? The driver returned and away we went, with the old woman waving at Saleh from the kerbside."

All his children say Saleh Kamel was not a disciplinarian but, they insist, he didn't need to be. His son Mohi explains how he managed to engender such regard for the rules in his children:

"We didn't generally misbehave because we knew how much it would have disappointed him. He had a way about him that made you feel you just wanted to make him proud and happy. He would never have punished us, or even reprimanded us for getting something wrong. On the contrary, he was always at pains to say that it is far better to make a mistake, which you will learn from, than to sit on the fence and do nothing. In terms of misbehaving, or anything like that, I just didn't want to sadden him."

Speaking in a debate on the Iqraa channel, Saleh Kamel outlined his feelings on this aspect of parenthood:

"Fathers and mothers must not be too hard on their children, otherwise, the children will not be tender or merciful to their parents in later life.

"Lead by example. Before expecting your children to be dutiful, you must first fulfil your responsibilities towards them. Be fair and tender, treat your children in a good way that will help to establish a healthy, loving relationship.

"The fact that a father is head of the household, the person who supports his family financially, does not give him the right to treat his children unfairly or cruelly. Such behaviour would be a violation of his paternal duties and all the beautiful sentiments this entails. Parenthood, if carried out properly, is a form of sacrifice but children are, above all else, a blessing from God. Parents should raise their children and educate them to the best of their ability, but they should never expect to be repaid for the privilege.

"Nor should mothers and fathers be abusive or arrogant with their children; arrogance is to be abhorred, especially when dealing with others, let alone with one's children.

"We have all heard sad stories about this kind of treatment of children. I personally know of parents who humiliate their children and behave in such an authoritarian way that the children develop weak and diffident personalities.

"Developing a child's self-esteem and encouraging respect for their elders are not mutually exclusive goals, but rather mutually reinforcing. Children should show respect for their parents, but parents should always behave in a way that earns that respect.

"As parents, we also need to be constantly aware of helping our offspring to have a sense of their own self-worth, based on the independence and individuality we nurture in them."

His daughter Haneen explained this further:

"My father was always a big part of our lives, which is a real achievement when you have nine kids. But he was close to each and every one of us and totally tuned in to our individual needs.

"We all had our own problems and issues at various times which, strangely, he would usually pick up on without any sort of conversation or preamble. Whenever we had such difficulties, whatever they were, however insignificant, Dad would always be ready to discuss them and offer advice.

"He took us all around the world at various times. All his trips were business trips of one type or another, but he would always take some of us with him wherever he went. In Saudi Arabia, it is very common for a man to have more than one wife. Sometimes you hear or read about there being difficulties but, in our family, I was never aware of any problems. All credit to my Mom and to my Step-Mom for that, they worked together to make sure all nine of us had a wonderful life. I am close to all my siblings, I love them and I know they love me, we share an incredible connection.

"My Dad was very wise in the way he treated us all the same, emotionally and financially, he split everything between us equally. He was a believer in women's equality and we never felt that he favoured our brothers."

Her sister Aseel recalled how Saleh Kamel would encourage her to attend meetings at Dallah, where she could familiarize herself with a business environment.

"Dad knew I was interested in a career in finance and he would sometimes tell me to skip school and come to the office, if he thought a particular meeting or topic of discussion would be interesting to me. He would take me into the meeting but then he might leave me in there, the only woman in a room of perhaps 30 men, to be his eyes and ears.

"To know he invested such trust in me was an empowering thing. He was always very supportive of us and I still feel his absence in my daily life, for exactly this reason. He encouraged me to gain experience by living life. As children we had always been used to travelling by limousine and private jet, but when I worked as an intern in London, he encouraged me to live a local style of life, to take taxis and even to take the Tube to increase my life experience."

Recalling her time as a student in the US, Aseel continued:

"I also studied in Boston, and when I went there, Dad gave me a monthly allowance for the first time in my life but he didn't realise that I also had a credit card he had given me years before, registered to his name. I would use his card, as well as my allowance, to buy the things I wanted. My Dad was careful with money and he soon realised the extent of my spending. So, we made a deal. I would give up the credit card and learn to live on my allowance. However, to sweeten the pill, he promised that anything I managed to save from my allowance during my time in Boston he would double on my return to Jeddah.

"Looking back now, I realise what an ingenious move it was to offer me such a wonderful incentive to learn to manage my money. I really put my mind to living within a budget and putting a little aside every month, in order that my Dad would double it.

"At the end of my time in Boston, Dad was true to his word and doubled what I had saved when I got home. After some discussion, we agreed I would invest the money on the Saudi stock market. He took the opportunity to warn me that I should never invest money if I could not afford to lose it, but in this case, he would back my decision. Unfortunately, when the stock market crashed some months later, I lost my entire investment but even that, as my Dad pointed out, was an important life lesson. Later, I learned that he had operated a similar system with all my siblings who studied abroad and, I believe, all of us managed to save something during our time away from home."

Saleh Kamel was also a great fan of hobbies and had something of a reputation within the family for attempting to whip up enthusiasm for his latest pastime. Eldest daughter Ghadeer laughed as she recalled her father's enthusiasm for a variety of hobbies over the years.

"He was extraordinarily busy but he had a very active mind and his doctor had persuaded him that he needed to take up a hobby.

He tried tennis for a while and had us all on the court playing with him when his enthusiasm was at its peak. Then there was a period where he collected antiques and then beautiful old pieces of jewellery, which he roped us into researching with him. He also loved his walking canes – he started with quite an ordinary stick but gradually they became more intricate and interesting until they became quite a fashion statement. But mostly, his hobbies were fairly short-lived. Only reading was a constant. He read in Arabic but the books themselves were frequently translations from the original, which could have been in Spanish, French, Urdu – he had a fascination for them all."

His wife, Mayda, recalls:

"Saleh always wanted everyone to enjoy the things he enjoyed. When he discovered tennis, he wanted us all to play tennis and for weeks we spent hours playing matches with him. When he discovered yoga, it was the same, he would encourage us all onto our mats, finding new ways to bend and stretch our bodies. Sometimes, it was a relief – at least to some of us – when his attentions moved on."

Some hobbies were clearly better received by the family than others, but daughter Sadeer recalls the joy the entire family found in laughing yoga, which Saleh Kamel took up originally to help his breathing and improve his lung capacity.

"None of us had heard of laughing yoga but Dad's doctor thought it might be beneficial to him so he started doing it daily. He would encourage us all to join him, which we did. It was great fun. We didn't think about the health benefits, to us it was just about raising our arms in the air, maintaining eye contact with him and laughing out loud. Once he had more than fifty family members and friends gathered together in one large room doing the same thing. At first it was entirely forced laughter, as is usual, but laughing is totally contagious and before long the whole room was rocking. The staff were looking in at our antics as they passed

201

by the window. Clearly, they thought we had all gone mad!

"My father was always fun to be around. He had a great sense of humour and people were drawn, almost magnetically, to his personality."

Although most of the Kamel children were recruited to work within the family firm for a short time – maybe just weeks or months – to give them experience, Abdullah, Mohi, and Hadeel would choose to make Dallah their career, as would some of their cousins. Mohi explains: "There were no benefits to being the boss's son. My Dad didn't believe in that sort of privilege, so everybody had to prove themselves on their own merits."

Mohi had a real passion for sport and, as we have heard, was keen to get involved in the television sports channels operated by ART.

"I was always close to my father but we became closer when we worked together. I'm sure he would have enjoyed us all working in the company. He certainly tried to encourage all of us into the business, his sons and daughters, I believe in order to become closer to us as individuals. By working alongside someone you really see their strengths and weaknesses and I think Dad enjoyed that.

"I have always enjoyed sport and I could see that the company really needed something to help raise our profile. When I proposed that we launch an Arab Championship League and presented him with a business plan, he took it to a couple of experts in the game and gave me the go ahead. For him to take a risk on my idea gave me great confidence. I worked hard for several years with his full and active support until he felt I had proved myself, at which point he handed over the entire project to me."

Mohi recalls how his father would sometimes take him to prestigious events where major international sportsmen were present. Frequently he would have to explain to his father exactly who these people were and what it was that they had achieved. But he was not at all interested in celebrity. As Mohi relates: 'He loved to engage with people who had an interesting story to tell, but the concept of celebrity went right over his head."

Abdullah, Saleh Kamel's oldest son, who took over the position of CEO of Dallah Albaraka when his father moved to work full time on Chamber of Commerce business and has, since Saleh Kamel's death, been chairman of the company, describes his father's way of handling things in the company:

"My father was not afraid to let go of control but he had to be sure that we were up to the task he was giving us. We would disagree sometimes but on principles my Father didn't compromise – ever – otherwise, he was usually happy to listen to different points of view. We travelled together and generally spent a lot of time together; I knew I had a lot to learn and that he was the best person to teach me. He never really separated family life from company business, so our discussions could go on in the office or at home. Of course, we had disagreements but after he promoted me to the position of CEO, he respected the fact that he had put me in charge and that I would want to do things my way; he took a backseat from that time."

Saleh Kamel discussed parenting in one of his many media interviews, noted:

"All parents should understand that treating their children equally is very important. It is important for us, as parents, to give our children equal financial allowances but more important to be fair in offering spiritual support and kindness.

"It is wrong that some fathers and mothers play favourites with their children, perhaps sometimes favouring one son or daughter over the other children. This is incompatible with good parenting, which demands that one must be fair with all of one's children. All should be treated on an equal footing with kindness, fairness, and justice.

"Of course, parents will give more attention to one of their children if the child is sick or in need, but these are temporary conditions in which giving more attention is justified. Otherwise, all one's children should receive the same attention and love.

"Yes, children have duties towards their parents, but parents have duties towards their children too. It is the child, not the parent, who should expect love unconditionally. We should also teach them to nurture and care for their brothers and sisters as well as for their parents."

Haneen recalled a situation which illustrates this point:

"Dad believed in equality but at the same time, we live in the Arab world and he knew that when he was no longer around, our brothers might – at some point – be required to assume responsibility for taking care of us. I can remember asking my Dad for permission to do something, or to go somewhere, in my early teens and Dad telling me to ask Abdullah if it was okay. In this way I learned to accept and appreciate Abdullah's authority as my eldest sibling and Abdullah learned to accept and appreciate what his responsibilities would be in the absence of my Dad."

Saleh Kamel was a demonstrative father and reminded his children that whenever the Prophet's daughter, Fatima, approached her father, the Prophet Muhammad would stand up and kiss her on the forehead. In a television interview, Saleh Kamel noted that the Prophet Muhammad did this in order to teach parents how to be kind and tender with our daughters.

But he stressed:

"We should also treat our sons in a similar way. If your son is returning from a trip and you have missed him, give him a warm hug on his return and let him know how much you love him. Kiss your son and let him feel your affection for him by standing up and embracing him warmly.

"This is not the same as spoiling a child. On the contrary, if your children do not enjoy your affection when young, it is unlikely they will return it to you as an adult. If your sons and daughters love you and feel affection for you, they are much less likely to disappoint you in their words or deeds."

Hadeel, who now runs Dallah Albaraka operations in Egypt, agrees:

"There was not much discipline at home and, for most of the family, none was needed. His first two children, Abdullah and Ghadeer, were probably the ones who spent most time with him in terms of actual hours but we were all close to our father in our different ways."

On this theme, Nadeer adds:

"He seemed to know all our strengths and weaknesses. He made perhaps as many as a hundred business trips in the average year, but after those, he divided his time between Saudi Arabia and Egypt. It wasn't structured, he just made sure that it worked out equally. He was always totally involved with our lives and had a close personal relationship not only with us but even with our friends; they all thought he was wonderful."

Saleh Kamel was a loving and respectful son and, in that way, he led by example. He was also a lot of fun and his children learned they might always expect the unexpected. The sisters laugh together as they recall an impromptu trip in the 1990s when Saleh Kamel hired a bus and took all the family, including an entourage of household servants, to see a Michael Jackson concert:

"We were spending several weeks in Cannes when Dad heard of a Michael Jackson concert being held in neighbouring Nice and decided to take a busload of us to the event. He knew we were all keen Michael Jackson fans and managed to pull some strings with people he knew – I think it was Michael Jackson's manager – before filling a bus with family, friends, maids, and other people who worked with us, to have fun at the concert. It was a complete surprise that turned into a truly wonderful evening and that was what life with my father was like a lot of the time."

Saleh Kamel was once questioned by an interviewer on the

difficulties of being a businessman and a father of nine. His response was enlightening:

"Parents are usually busy with their work. In fact, many men make the mistake of being too busy with work to the extent that it keeps them from fulfilling their parental duties towards both their sons and their daughters. I must include myself in this group.

"Several days may elapse without me seeing my children and at a certain age of his child's life, a father should not allow work to take him away from his children for that long. He should be spending time showering his children with kindness and affection.

"I admit I have made mistakes in this area. My first two children, Abdullah and Ghadeer, received more love and attention than the others when they were young because I was still a civil servant at that time with more free time. However, when I became a businessman, I became increasingly busy. Consequently, I was not physically able to give my younger children the same attention I had given to the older ones. This had consequences in their relationship with me and I feel sometimes that my children, Abdullah and Ghadeer, are more attached to me than my younger children. As the saying goes: 'As you sow so shall you reap'.

"I did not spend enough time with my younger children. This does not mean that they are detached from me or that there is any less love between us, I just think that my relationship with those children with whom I spent most time is perhaps stronger than the bond I share with their younger brothers and sisters.

"A few days ago, I was talking to some people who are about the same age as myself. One of them, who lives outside his homeland, complained that whenever he returns to his country, he does not see his children because they are travelling for work. I told him that is the same complaint our children used to make about us, their fathers, who years ago were always busy with their business. That's life! Work often distracts fathers from spending time with their children and they, in turn, become busy and distracted from their parents. The secret is finding a way to balance professional and family life and to find that balance before it is too late."

The love and contentment of his own family was critically important to Saleh Kamel, but he very much respected the need of his sons and daughters, his friends and colleagues to enjoy the same benefits. Mohammad Moussa, who worked closely with Saleh Kamel for around 30 years, tells a poignant story about the loss of his own teenage daughter to a sudden and fatal asthma attack, just a few years ago.

"She had the attack, it came suddenly, unexpectedly, as is so often the case, and we could not save her. Sadly, she passed away. Sheikh Saleh heard the news and that night he arrived, quite unexpectedly, at our home in Jeddah. He had met all my children at one time or another and I could see he was genuinely distressed by our tragedy. He embraced me and expressed his sadness and then he sat with me; he sat, sharing my grief, mostly in silence, for hours and hours. That is the sort of kindness I will never forget and an act typical of the man he was."

It is clear that all Saleh Kamel's children remember him with huge fondness. Interestingly, when asked if they, as the offspring of a celebrity billionaire, were indulged or spoiled, all seem a little taken aback at the idea. As Nadeer commented:

"I suppose we were, in that we were used to being driven around the town in limousines and flown around the world in a private jet, but our parents were very grounded people. They did not behave in the way we see rich people on the television behave. There were no ostentatious displays of wealth. I felt our lives were very normal until I began meeting the families of school-friends and then the penny dropped that we were indeed very fortunate. It was not the wealth but the tenderness of our parents that made us all truly lucky. We were all valued, respected, and cherished as individuals but most importantly, we were truly loved."

THE LEGEND & THE LEGACY

In the skies above the offices of Dallah Tower, in Jeddah, pigeons still congregate in the late afternoon.

Saleh Kamel and his father are no longer around to feed them, as was their custom, but loyal and trusted friend Mohammad Moussa makes certain there is always sufficient corn to ensure the birds never go hungry.

Saleh Kamel's magnificent suite of offices, on the top floor of the Dallah Tower building, where every inch of space beyond its massive, carved wooden doors is devoted to the operation of a fast moving, multi-million-dollar conglomerate, remains an oasis of calm, overseen by Mohammad Moussa.

Saleh Kamel's books, files and many dozens of awards line the surfaces of shelves and tables. On the walls are photographs of Saleh Kamel with kings and presidents, captains of industry and media celebrities from all over the world. There are also souvenirs – most of them gifts – of the many countries he visited during his illustrious career. The screens of a bank of around 20 televisions where he once watched all the programmes being broadcast by Art simultaneously, remain dark and silent. In one corner stands a cylindrical container, home to six or seven elegant, bone handled, walking sticks.

In Cairo, his leather reclining chair sits alongside the large picture window in his office overlooking the waters of the Nile, which offers panoramic views of the river and the bustling streets below.

The staff who served and loved him so well for so many years are still at their desks. Dallah Albaraka values hard work, loyalty and dedication and that is unlikely to change.

Life at Dallah, the company Saleh Kamel built from scratch, continues at a frenetic pace, as might be expected of a firm with tens of thousands of employees spread across the globe. At the helm are sons, Abdullah and Mohyuldeen, daughter Hadeel, and a group of other close family, including his nephews, the Yamani brothers, who continue to play a vital part in pushing forward with new schemes and operations intended to help Dallah stay ahead in terms of international development and growth.

In a rapidly changing world, there will inevitably be shifts in the system of checks and balances to conform with the prevailing global business climate; nothing is forever.

The life of 79-year-old Saleh Kamel came to a close on 18 May 2020, quietly, at his home in Jeddah. It was during the Islamic holy month of Ramadan, considered by Muslims to be a blessed time to leave this earthly life. He had recently prayed with members of his family before going to rest and, during that time, he peacefully passed away.

The Covid pandemic, with its attendant rules and regulations, had prevented him visiting Egypt for many months but his passing was mourned as keenly in Cairo as it was in Jeddah.

"Although he was almost 80 years old and had not been well, it was a huge surprise to learn that he had passed. We all thought of him as being a force of nature, invincible", noted a colleague and friend in Jeddah. "He was a unique character, a giant of a man. I do not expect to meet anyone like him ever again. I won't deny I shed a tear when I learned he had gone."

For those who knew and loved him, life would never be the same but, during his 79 years on earth, Saleh Kamel also changed the life of many millions of people he had never met.

As a boy from the alleys of Makkah he had proved that it was possible to rise to prominence in Saudi society without being born with a silver spoon. He was a humble man but proud to admit he had worked hard to get to where he wanted to be.

All his children agree Saleh Kamel was a wonderful father; his wives say he was a wonderful husband. His presence seemed to bring great happiness to those he loved.

Clearly, he was a proud Saudi Arabian but with a love for travel and experiencing other traditions and ethnicities. Many of the ideas he had first experienced on his travels to different cultures and continents, he brought back and successfully implemented in his homeland. He had a fascination and great respect for progress, which he turned to his advantage whenever the opportunity arose.

As a young man, one year he was forced to take on considerably more work as a mutawif when his father was obliged to stay at the court of King Faisal in Riyadh and could not work with the pilgrims, during the Hajj, as usual. The young Saleh used the opportunity to streamline the family's Tawafa operations and, as a result the number of pilgrims they were able to serve in subsequent years increased dramatically, along with the family's earnings.

Saleh Kamel's devotion to God and his religious ethics were steadfast. His conversation, orchestrated by his mother, with the Egyptian cleric Sheikh Mohammad Metwally Alsharawi, was a catalyst on his spiritual journey. He had previously been a good and pious Muslim but Sheikh Alsharawi opened up new dimensions he gloried in exploring and sparked an interest in jurisprudence, which remained with him for the rest of his life.

Islamic thinking encourages Muslims to follow the Sharia principles of social equality, fairness, justice, moderation and regard for less fortunate members of society. The Quran frequently alludes to the importance of charity, honesty and fairness in business. Saleh Kamel assiduously lived by these principles and encouraged others to do likewise by his example and his charity, Iqraa, is living testament to the massive help he brought to entire communities across the globe.

He was a great believer in the concept of hard work, for himself and for others and certainly insisted upon diligence in those around him. Although Saleh Kamel was always delighted to offer any family member a job at Dallah, they were required to start at the bottom and work their way up, according to their merits. There was no such thing as a free ride.

At the Durrat Alarous holiday resort, the former Kamel family villa on the shores of the Red Sea is now in the process of being demolished. The family no longer have the will to visit their old seaside home without Saleh Kamel's presence but outside the gates of the villa other residents continue to enjoy the relaxed atmosphere created by Saleh Kamel's vision of the perfect Red Sea holiday retreat.

The festering lake in Tunis, which he dredged so successfully for President Bourguiba, once home only to vermin and mosquitoes, is today the centrepiece of the city's most desirable residential area, thanks to his ingenuity and tenacity.

Saleh Kamel was a visionary, an innovator and an inspiration. He has left behind an empire and is certain his children will do everything within their power to maintain and expand his legacy. Dallah Albaraka and its multiple subsidiaries are active in more than 40 countries and employ tens of thousands of people worldwide.

Through Iqraa and the many training schemes Saleh Kamel established, there are many thousands of people in employment in all kinds of professions, from doctors to bakers, thanks to his vision and his largesse. Their children, as a result of the fruits of that employment, will live better lives than their forefathers might ever have dreamed for them. Their children and grandchildren will go on to prosper in a similar way until, years from now, quite possibly, the name of the man responsible for their good fortune – the home they live in, the education they receive or the food on their table, is forgotten.

But in a way that hardly matters, because as the old Makkah proverb goes: Allah knows who brought the seeds.

APPENDIX

MY UNDERSTANDING OF THE CONCEPT OF
CAPITAL IN ISLAM

In the following pages I will summarize my understanding of the "the essence" of the concept of capital in Islam. By the essence of the concept of capital in Islam, I refer to those main, supreme principles that represent the pillars of the edifice. Like anything else, the concept of capital in Islam covers many principles and countless rules. These principles could be fundamental or subsidiary. In the following pages, I will attempt to focus on what I deem fundamental principles. As is well known, Allah created things in a hierarchical order.

Before proceeding with these conclusions, I wish that the phrase "my understanding" contained in the title will always be fresh in the respected reader's mind. I thank Allah, who guided me to this approach, so I used the same phrase in the title of a booklet I issued on Zakat. This book is primarily an invitation to reflection. It is also a call to launch a dialogue among all those concerned with finance, development and economics. Perfection belongs to Allah alone, and each of us can only do the best he can.

This understanding of the essence of the concept of capital in Islam is the outcome of my experience that spans over forty years and several studies and reflections. During this period, Allah graced me by illuminating the path for me to understand certain aspects of Islam in one of the most important matters that touched people's lives, namely the financial and economic aspect.

First, this understanding of the essence of the concept of capital in Islam is the fruit of a "learning journey" in the field of finance and banking that spans over forty years in which I gained a lot "on the intellectual level". Allah blessed me with a zeal for work from an early age. I worked for about ten years in the Ministry of Finance, which I joined for learning, not for employment. At a certain moment in my life about which I will talk in detail later, I realized that as long as I was in commerce, my steps had to be weighed against the rules of Sharia. As I did not receive a formal Islamic jurisprudence (*fiqh*) education, I decided to be a permanent part-time student. Thus, I became a seeker of livelihood, or a worker, and a seeker of sharia-related knowledge, or a researcher at the same time. From day one, my biggest concern was to explore the spirit, higher purposes and ends of the provisions (of *fiqh*) and to capture them literally. Therefore, I found it necessary to keep company with religious scholars and experts in finance and economics. I also decided to make *fiqh* and scientific aspects an integral part of my business. This approach prompted the establishment of sharia bodies that featured eminent scholars and scholarly councils featuring professors and experts. For years, since my interest in the concept of capital in Islam began in terms of thought and practice, I was keen to accept most of the invitations to attend and participate in the various seminars and conferences in general, and on Islamic economics in particular. Those seminars and lectures provided me with an extremely rich source through which I received contributions from our senior scholars and sheikhs, who were experts in various branches of the economics. I have always tried to apply what I could from that knowledge to the prevailing banking reality.

Secondly, the understanding contained in this booklet represents a summary of a "business journey" in the field of banking and investment in this spacious earth created by Allah, in which I learned a lot "on a practical level". Allah has enabled and prepared me to invest in forty-two countries. Since the early 1970s, I embarked on heading to various countries to study the possibility of investing in them in light of their need for reconstruction and employment. I believe that gains are not limited to this life but go beyond that to the hereafter. This is my approach. During this journey, I founded more than 340 companies. I went through this experience with a large team whose members increased over time. I have always been keen to adopt the teamwork model, as I preferred having most of my companies run by boards of directors. These boards included people with diverse and solid experiences from different countries. The dialogues and discussions that took place during the meetings stretched for hours because I was keen to take decisions after everyone offered their contributions. The geographical diversity of my investments allowed me to identify different investment patterns, various work and behavior patterns, and diverse patterns of legislation and regulation. So, I developed a matured comparative understanding. I thank Allah for guiding me to contribute to the renaissance of these countries. This led me to meet with most of the leaders of Arab, Islamic and Western countries and to engage with them on a number of top financial issues.

Third, this understanding is the culmination of accumulated experience in civil society work, particularly in relation to the regulation of the industrial trade field and its related professions. Allah honored me with the trust of parties representing various components of the commercial and economic sectors. I was assigned the leadership of a number of civil society institutions that contributed to the development of this field and related professions, including the Jeddah Chamber of Commerce and Industry, which we are proud to be one of the first chambers of commerce to be established in the region and the world, the Islamic Chamber of Commerce, Industry and Agriculture (ICCIA) and the General Council for Islamic Banks and Financial Institutions (CIBAFI). It is acknowledged that the nature of work in commercial investment is different from that of work in civil, social and organizational fields. Even the nature of teamwork in one is different from the nature of teamwork in the other.

I should point out here that this understanding of the essence of the concept of capital in Islam is a product of successes and failures. I have encountered countless failures in my life. Some may be surprised when they hear me say that I owe the failures as much as I owe the successes The patience that Allah bestowed upon me after every failure was a reason for me to hold fast and not collapse in the middle of the road. The lessons learned from each failure led to several successes. This made me think of writing a book about failures rather than successes. Why? Because the successes are obvious, there is no need to write about them. One should not be ashamed of one's failures. There is nothing wrong with failure; what is wrong is to repeat the same mistake. This is probably what prompted me in 1996, when I received the Islamic Development Bank's award, to take the opportunity to criticize myself, although the occasion was a tribute ceremony.

In short, my understanding of the concept of capital in Islam derives from a realistic, practical experience in which the theoretical dimension interacted with the practical one. This understanding was based on the view of a trader who knew the meaning of profit and loss, and recognized what profit and loss represented to him.

Therefore, I will explain my perception of the essence of the concept of capital in light of this journey and its highlights. When discussing each of the principles that, in my view, represent the core of the concept of capital in Islam, I will refer to my personal interaction with the principle I am addressing on the intellectual and/or the level of experience. I will present my understanding within the context of my human experience.

I would also like to point out that my understanding of the concept of capital in Islam to which I devote this book represents the compendium of views that matured through the landmarks of my entire career, that is, over forty years. I have explained some of them in television interviews and programs in which I took part in a number of stations, including Iqraa and Al-Arabiya. I also clarified some others in articles and interviews published in Saudi and Arab newspapers, such as Makkah and Asharq Al-Awsat newspapers. I addressed some others in the speeches and lectures I gave at seminars, tribute ceremonies and events, such as the opening of the Participatory Exchange for Development and Employment (MASFAQ). Some of these insights are also included in brochures printed in limited editions. However, I have expressed my understanding of the concept mostly verbally. Why? Because I tend to express my views orally. The content of these statements has been compiled and edited to accommodate the written form.

The book is divided into four chapters. In the first chapter, I introduce the experience of reviving the applications of Islamic economics (the experience of Islamic banks) as it represents the context in which my understanding of the concept of capital in Islam matured.

In the second chapter, I present the principles that collectively represent the foundations of my understanding of the concept of capital in Islam. In the third chapter, I shed light on the model of the mega investment bank, and in the fourth chapter I present the model of the participatory exchange for development and operation.

* * * *

THE PRINCIPLES THAT SHAPE MY
UNDERSTANDING OF THE CONCEPT OF CAPITAL IN ISLAM

The First Principle
The *Istikhlaf* of man (human stewardship of the earth) and his commissioning to develop the earth are among the supreme purposes of his creation. The development of the earth is an act of worship in itself. Among the elements of Istikhlaf is harnessing heavens and the earth for man, and guaranteeing his sustenance. The wealth we have is not ours, but belongs to Allah, Who granted it to us to test us. Man should use this wealth in line with the requirements of faith.

The Second Principle
Contrary to what some economists claim, the resources that Allah has

made available to man are unlimited. The wisdom behind the diversity of nations' needs is to seek 'developmental integration'. Entrepreneurs must serve as a medium of development integration in addition to taking care of the development of their countries. They must be at the forefront of the initiators to redress the imbalance in the global economy and establish a moderate global financial system to rescue the world from collapsing, using its resources wisely.

The Third Principle

Commitment to piety and morals in all fields, especially the financial field, is the essence of the Final Message and all Messages. It is not just a factor for individual advancement, but rather a factor for improving resource management and achieving community balance and harmony. It is also a factor for leading nations to welfare. The decline in ethical commitment is destructive. The term "ethical banking" is the precise designation of banks that seek to abide by the spirit of faith.

The Fourth Principle

Reviving "the love of work" and "the love of employing Servants of Allah" is one of the foundations for achieving the goal of istikhlaf. Originally, job creation has priority over employment.

The first category that should be taken care of is persons with special needs, as they are the most deserving and the best performing. Societies in which the flames of love of work and employment fade suffer from "mendicancy". Subsequently, even the state itself becomes accustomed and addicted to "mendicancy". Responsibility for unemployment lies with many parties, primarily businessmen and banks.

The Fifth Principle

Participation—that is, sharing loss and gain—represents the mainstay of the equilibrium of financial centers and the pillar of rational development for the personal, national and global economy.

Once a bank fails to engage in ventures, it becomes an unethical and unIslamic bank. The phenomenon of money remaining in the hands of the rich jeopardizes the general financial situation and leads to social disintegration. Consolidating the participatory financing of medium, small and micro enterprises is one of the most important elements that contributes to combating this phenomenon.

The Sixth Principle

Although the resources that Allah has devoted to creation are sufficient, it is indispensable to establish the value of "saving" as a hedge against fluctuations. So, the "saving decision" should be linked to the "investment decision".

At the same time, it is indispensable to fight "money hoarding", whose subtle forms lie in retaining huge cash flows without investment due to the failure of banks to devise new investment solutions, which raises the unemployment rate. Likewise, although the resources that Allah has made available are sufficient, they must be utilized rationally. Consumerism, wasting money, extravagance, squandering and thriftlessness must be combatted.

The Seventh Principle
Rational development should be based on the primary markets, especially those geared towards activities with real development returns, such as infrastructure projects, with investment banks playing the role of market maker. It is not appropriate to skip from the commercial bank to the secondary market -trading in shares is not a development activity- nor is it appropriate to infer the state of the economy from the state of the stock market. Therefore, we should exhibit positive bias towards financing the "real economy" such as the factory, the store, and the farm without deceptive sales, nor the purchase of shares.

The Eighth Principle
The market is the beating heart of every community. Originally, it is a place for the exchange of "benefits" and not for the exchange of "damages". Divinely revealed religions established rational norms and morals. They fought practices that run contrary to morals which prevailed therein. The values that management experts keep telling us about have already been taught to us by our religion and the heavenly religions. Our Faith taught us morals that are even better. Businessmen, especially the youth, must restore market morals and observe them.

The Ninth Principle
Zakat is a miraculous "development" scheme. The channels (masarif) of spending Zakat should be dealt in light of contemporary understanding while giving precedence to the spirit of the text. For example, if the channel (masarif) of "enfranchising slaves" has become unavailable in most parts of the world due to the criminalization of slavery, we can still observe that "collective slavery" is widely spread, as entire communities are held in slavery. Therefore, the share of "enfranchising slaves" should be allotted to "enfranchising" such communities. The basic principle is that the state

collects Zakat and distributes it in the place where it was first collected. The Creator, Glory be to Him, has harnessed to His creatures resources that meet all their needs, contrary to claims made by modern economists that resources are limited. Allah says in Surat Fussilat

﴿قُلْ أَئِنَّكُمْ لَتَكْفُرُونَ بِالَّذِي خَلَقَ الْأَرْضَ فِي يَوْمَيْنِ وَتَجْعَلُونَ لَهُ أَنْدَادًا ذَلِكَ رَبُّ الْعَالَمِينَ (٩) وَجَعَلَ فِيهَا رَوَاسِيَ مِنْ فَوْقِهَا وَبَارَكَ فِيهَا وَقَدَّرَ فِيهَا أَقْوَاتَهَا فِي أَرْبَعَةِ أَيَّامٍ سَوَاءً لِلسَّائِلِينَ (١٠) ثُمَّ اسْتَوَى إِلَى السَّمَاءِ وَهِيَ دُخَانٌ فَقَالَ لَهَا وَلِلْأَرْضِ ائْتِيَا طَوْعًا أَوْ كَرْهًا قَالَتَا أَتَيْنَا طَائِعِينَ (١١) فَقَضَاهُنَّ سَبْعَ سَمَوَاتٍ فِي يَوْمَيْنِ وَأَوْحَى فِي كُلِّ سَمَاءٍ أَمْرَهَا وَزَيَّنَّا السَّمَاءَ الدُّنْيَا بِمَصَابِيحَ وَحِفْظًا ذَلِكَ تَقْدِيرُ الْعَزِيزِ الْعَلِيمِ﴾.

"Say: Do you verily disbelieve in Him Who created the earth in two Days? And you set up equals (in worship) with Him? That is the Lord of the 'Âlamîn (mankind, jinn and all that exists). And He placed on it [i.e., the earth] firmly set mountains over its surface, and He blessed it and determined therein its [creatures'] sustenance in four days without distinction - for [the information of] those who ask. Then He directed Himself to the heaven while it was smoke and said to it and to the earth, "Come [into being], willingly or by compulsion." They said, "We have come willingly." So He formed the heaven into seven heavens in two Days, assigning to each its mandate. And We adorned the lowest heaven with stars like lamps for beauty and for protection. That is the design of the Almighty, All-Knowing."

Allah Almighty says in Surat Hud

﴿وَمَا مِنْ دَابَّةٍ فِي الْأَرْضِ إِلَّا عَلَى اللَّهِ رِزْقُهَا وَيَعْلَمُ مُسْتَقَرَّهَا وَمُسْتَوْدَعَهَا كُلٌّ فِي كِتَابٍ مُبِينٍ﴾..

"There is no moving creature on earth whose provision is not guaranteed by Allah. And He knows where it lives and where it is laid to rest. All is written in a perfect Record".

This means that when Allah created the heavens and the earth, He predestined the resources that suffice the needs of all creation, including human beings, despite their large number, in addition to harnessing what is in the heavens and the earth for man. It also signifies that Allah created and subjugated to man all that is on the earth, and that Allah, the Most High glory be to Him, ensures the sustenance of every living creature on earth. It also indicates that besides determining the sustenance on earth, Allah Almighty willed to connect these resources to creation and to make them available to them regardless of their ability to access them. We kept for a long time hearing from positivist economists that one of the axiomatic premises of modern economics is the scarcity of resources, against a high number of wants and desires. They told us that the essence of economics is how to reconcile 'scarcity' with 'plurality of wants and needs'. Hence, they define it as the science of managing finite resources to meet the needs of people outweighing the resources. From a faith perspective, this is not true. What led them to this misconception is that they dealt with the subject of resources, focusing on purely material considerations, while ignoring moral considerations such as the effect of piety represented in the acquisition of blessings, and the impact of the absence of piety reflected in the lack of blessings, as I will explain later. This is a consideration, inter alia, which led me to assert the need to reconsider the economics taught in universities.

However, it is only natural that certain nations need some resources unavailable to them in their countries, or may not be aware of the availability of such resources. The diversity of nations' needs reflects one of the great wisdoms of the Great Creator, which is the need of peoples to exchange benefits. However, that does not mean that resources are insufficient. He, Glory be to Him, wanted not to create a land where all the needs of its inhabitants would be fulfilled, but rather to provide a part of what they need in another land, thus strengthening relations and ties between peoples. This applies to all regions of the world, and does not mean that the resources that Allah has made available to people are limited.

Accordingly, we, as Arab and Muslim businessmen, must act as a medium of development integration at the level of our Arab world, and at the level of our Islamic community. Historically and geographically speaking, Arab countries are one country and one people, united in their faith, customs, and even their food and drinks. But colonialism and politics caused the fragmentation of this community. They divided them with the aim of breaking them, keeping in mind that together they stand but divided they fall. For centuries, history has presented a clear and unmistakable picture of the strength of this community when living in unity and synergy. The Romans, the Persians, the Mongols, the Tatars, and the Franks were the great powers in those worlds and times, while Arabs had no equipment nor tools. However, the ummah was victorious when Allah honored it with Islam. They prevailed over all those forces, defeated them, and torn them to shreds. I hope that the model of genuine Arab unity, with all its beautiful chapters, will be a story told to all young Arabs living abroad. This is particularly true at this time. It is no longer a secret to firmly realize that tearing the Arab countries apart and dividing Muslims is the weapon agreed upon to dismember Arab countries one after the other until the Arabs become strangers, migrants and displaced persons, even in their own countries, with no sign of hope, not knowing what to do with these disasters. If we take the relationship between Egypt and Saudi Arabia as an example, we will find labor, fertile soil and water in Egypt while Saudi Arabia has natural resources and advanced industries. Therefore, the focus on developing exports between them will be in the interest of both countries. With 100 million consumers, Egypt is the largest Arab market. There must be economic integration between the two countries. If we look at the proportionality between resources and production, we will find that the Arab world has many rivers, but it does not grow enough wheat nor rice. Does this make sense? In fact, we have all the natural and human conditions not only to be self-sufficient but also to be the world's food basket. We have fertile soil, water, labor and the right climate. That is why I say that nothing, but laziness and indolence will keep us in this state. On a personal level, and as I belong to this region, I did my best to embody this integrative view in my work at the level of the Arab region, and I also tried to instill it intellectually. I am from a generation that entertained the hope of realizing Arab unity. However, unfortunately, the same generation is now witnessing the Arab division instead. I hope that we will return to how we used to be, and to dream of Arab economic, not political, unity. The Arab common market is an aspiration that is easy to achieve if we spare ourselves our evil and that of foreign interventions. In short, Arab economic integration is a necessity and a matter of life or death for all our communities. We need to establish an effective, not superficial, integration that will bring the greatest benefit to all our communities. As for Islamic countries, there is a need to establish a common Islamic market and to bring about comprehensive economic integration in the Arab and Islamic region. We must all strive to achieve this goal, and do our best as investors, kings and presidents to realize this pursued dream as Arab countries and as an Islamic community.

We must be like a solid building whose different parts enforce each other. So, if we do not invest in our countries, and turn rather to the West, as it is easier to invest in, who else will do so?!

One of the most important means of achieving Arab and Islamic integration is to remove the obstacles facing the Arab and Muslim investor coming from another Arab or Muslim country, motivated by patriotism,

Arabism or Islam. This investor comes out of his own will. He could go to other countries that are more developed and easier to work in and that provide higher profitability. Therefore, we should offer him a business enabling environment, facilitating procedures for him. In fact, there are enormous administrative complexities and approvals always come after too late, suggesting that there are parties that have no real desire for real cooperation. For long, there have always been customs exemption agreements between the Arab countries, after which intra-Arab trade decreased instead of increasing, because the customs officer did not understand the importance of Arab integration. The decision was taken at leaders' level and did not reach the bottom. On a personal level, the purpose of the efforts I made at ICCIA and in the CIBAFI was to provide a cornerstone of Islamic integration.

While chairing the ICCIA, I have endeavored to table intra-Islamic integration consideration on a permanent basis. The ICCIA studied several relevant projects, including the project of cultivating rice on the Senegal River, which was expected to satisfy an estimated 70 percent of the need of Arab and Islamic countries for this basic commodity. I am fully confident that if this project is implemented, it will represent a qualitative leap.

However, our efforts as Arab and Muslim businessmen to achieve development integration should be "subordinate" to our efforts to develop our prime country, which, obviously, has priority. If the businessman gives priority to his homeland, he would be implementing the directives of the Messenger of Allah, may Allah's peace and blessings be on him, that spending and giving charity applies a fortiori to one's relatives. Abu Talha had the greatest wealth of date-palms amongst the Ansar in Medina, and he prized above all his wealth (his garden) Bairuha', which was situated opposite the Mosque (of the Prophet). The Prophet used to enter it and drink from its fresh water. When the following Ayat was revealed: "By no means shall you attain piety until you spend of what you love," (3.92)

(لن تنالوا البر حتى تنفقوا مما تحبون).

Abu Talha got up saying "O Allah's Apostle! Allah says in His Book, 'By no means shall you attain piety until you spend of what you love' and I prize above all my wealth, Bairuha', which I want to give in charity for Allah's sake, hoping for its reward from Allah. So, you can use it where you like." The Messenger of God, may Allah peace and blessings be on him, said: "Excellent!! It is a profitable property, it is a profitable property. I have heard what you have said, and I recommend that you distribute this amongst your relatives." So, Abu Talha distributed that garden amongst his relatives and cousins. Needless to say that the people living in one country are closer to each other than people living in several countries. In addition, the security that the home country provides to us is one of the considerations that obliges the businessman to give his country a priority for his investments. In fact, on a personal level I was amazed at the emphasis placed by the imams in the mosques on the supplication of "Oh Allah, grant us security in our lands." I did not feel the value of this supplication except after the first Gulf war when Saudi Arabia was under threat following the invasion of Kuwait by Iraq. Missiles were passing over my office in Riyadh. Not only that, indeed the fact that our children and grandchildren will live in this country is one of the considerations that obliges the businessman to give a priority to investing in his own country.

Exerting efforts in dealing with the global economy and establishing a fair and moderate global financial system would save the world from a real collapse and put the world on the threshold of wisely exploiting the harnessed resources. The world of today, as it is known, is interconnected. Indeed, it is highly interconnected. Therefore, we find, for example, that the destructive effect of greedy capitalism was not limited to the countries that fully implement it but extended to include all parts of the world. A minor economic damage to an influential country quickly inflicts the entire world, even if the severity of the impact is different. Everyone feels the harm. However, it should be clear that saving the economy needs a genuine international will.

There is a very large number of decisive measures that must be taken and several surgical processes that must be performed to reduce the terrible level of imbalance affecting the body of the current global economy at various levels, including resource management, and moving towards the establishment of a balanced global economy. The measures taken in this regard may be too numerous to mention here. Therefore, I will just mention a few of them.

One of the most critical measures to be taken is to stop the use of agricultural products as an alternative biofuel. The global economy has been harmed using agricultural products as a biofuel as an alternative to petroleum, as this has come at the expense of an important economic need for humans – and on the top of that a necessity –namely, food. Tampering with the environment is extremely dangerous and has irreversible reper-cussions. This is clarified by all the monotheistic religions, especially Islam. Islam is a religion which advocates development and the preservation of our ecology trailered by Allah. Even in the darkest hours, including wars, there are rules to preserve the environment that Islam requires to comply with. For example, the Prophet, may Allah's peace and blessings be on him, commands us in Shariah-compliant wars not to bury a well, cut down a tree, and not to kill a useful animal. This is the position of Islam in a time of war, which some people use as a pretext for the violation of the ecological system on the grounds that necessity dictates it. How can people then justify an unnecessary action in peacetime!

One of the major actions to be taken to reduce the level of the gross imbalance in the body of the current global economy is to address riba "usury" and its dire and countless effects, the most salient of which are the massive inflation waves. I firmly believe that *riba*, which led to making money a commodity, is one of the main causes of this inflation. One of the reasons why Islam prohibits riba is to prevent monetary inflation. As soon as prices became commodities, many disasters occurred in the world that we live in now. This is due to the violation of the Divine rules of economy. Islam does not allow money to be treated as a commodity per say. Money has been made a measure of value only, and Zakat has been imposed to absorb money if it is not operational. We have a holy Hadith that says {'Whoever sells a house or property and does not use the money for something similar, deserves not to be blessed therein.}, as selling your house and putting your money in a car constitutes a major corruption.

If you sell an asset or real estate, you must buy something similar to it that is beneficial, rather than purchasing a consumable good, thus undermining development. This Hadith is one of the major economic foundations the compliance with which puts nations - not only individuals - on the path to real development. All the world's communities feel the urgent need to significantly reduce the rate of inflation waves and minimize the rate of acceleration of inflation, especially that the income level of citizens in most countries of the world, no matter what increases they may register, can no longer keep pace with the price trends.

The third decisive action to be taken urgently is to stop the financial derivatives that started in 1990s. The essence of most of their applications lies in "selling what one does not own." These derivatives are devilish products. The real size of the world economy is 69 trillion USD, while the volume of such derivatives is 660 trillion USD, which is ten times the size of the real economy. This led to a huge bubble that exploded in the face of the entire world. The banks were risking people's money, running after profit. This was the first harbinger of ruin for the entire world economy. After the 1990s, in light of the infinite freedom they enjoyed in the West in manipulating the affairs of the economy, the investment companies and the commercial and investment banks, began to do whatever they wanted without oversight nor control. The banking sector and the financial market were at the origins of the financial disaster witnessed by the world. We are living its effects. In this regard, the primary responsibility in some states rests with the central banks.

"Selling what you do not possess" is a bridge to increase "hypotheticality" in the field of commerce and the instability of financial positions. The prohibition of selling what one does not own is one of the bases of the Islamic perspective of wealth. It also constitutes one of the foundations of the financial system in Islam. In many situations, Islam forbids a person to sell what he does not own. It has been reported that the Messenger of Allah, may Allah's peace and blessings be on him, said: "If you buy something, do not sell it until you have received it." Abu Dawood narrated from the Hadith of Abdullah bin Amr: The Messenger of Allah, may Allah's peace and blessings be on him, said: "The provision of a loan combined with a sale is not allowable, nor two conditions relating to one transaction, nor profit arising from something which is not in one's charge, nor selling what is not in your possession". Abu Dawood also narrated from the Hadith of Abdullah bin Amr: "I bought olive oil in the market. When I became its owner, a man met me and offered good profit for it. I intended to settle the bargain with him, but a man caught hold of my hand from behind. When I turned, I found that he was Zayd ibn Thabit. He said: Do not sell it on the spot where you have bought it until you take it to your house, for the Messenger of Allah, may Allah's peace and blessings be on him, forbade to sell the goods where they are bought until the tradesmen take them to their houses". Selling what you do not own opens the way to hypothetical and bogus deals. A contingency may arise that prevents delivery. I am most concerned today that selling what you do not possess started to leak to our markets. Its applications began to multiply. This comes within the context of an attempt to simulate forward contracts and non-Shariah compliant options, which spread in capital markets, constituting one of the causes of the financial crisis that hit the United States, Europe and the world in 2008. I am certain that the reason for the weakness of Islamic banks is due to their imitation of the West and their dealing with a hypothetical economy that relies on selling before taking possession of goods.

I learned the lesson that one should avoid selling what one does not own in real life. In the 1990s, our Group acquired the world's third largest tea company. It made a profit in the first year we bought it, but it lost in the second and third years. I went to New York and asked them to show me all the contracts they were using in in making purchases. I found that most of the losses, if not all, resulted from short selling contracts, that is, they sell the product before buying it. This is what the above-mentioned noble Hadith forbade. I prevented them from doing so despite their opposition.

Indeed, when they followed my instructions, the profits returned at the end of the year. In the second year, we made up for the losses of the previous two years. I believe that "for he who fears Allah, He prepares a way out, And He provides for him from (sources) he never could imagine." We should always have this Ayat in mind. I also recall that German Chancellor Merkel visited the Kingdom of Saudi Arabia, with a high-ranking ministerial delegation. I met her at the Jeddah Chamber of Commerce. She was aware of my work in Islamic banks. She asked me about the secret of the Islamic banks not being affected by the global financial crisis that crushed all the world's banks at that time! I answered her: We operate and believe in the real economy, not the hypothetical economy in which the world's banks operate. It is a matter that our religion has shown us and our Prophet Muhammad, may Allah's peace and blessings be upon him and the Prophets of Allah, guided us to. She said: Show me the way. I said: Here is the Hadith of the Prophet: "Do not sell what you do not own" If only this Hadith were applied, no bank would have gone bankrupt, no individual would be broken, nor would a nation lose. The Chancellor asked me to elaborate. So, before she left, I sent her three pages in this regard. Two months later, Chancellor Angela Merkel called me: "Do not sell what you do not own" is now the law in Germany.

The fourth decisive action to be taken is to redefine the role of the major financial institutions that control the global economy such as the World Bank and the role of the International Monetary Fund (IMF). First, these institutions need to be brave enough to embark on a real and daring study of the implications of ethics abuse in the finance. Moreover, they must stop politicizing the global financial system. It is the duty of the IMF, and any institution that assumes a role for itself in drawing monetary policies in the world, to set rules for the issuance of money in states and the circulation of currencies. One wonders about the IMF real role as an international authority and as the world central bank!

The fifth decisive measure that must be taken to reduce the horrific level of imbalance plaguing the body of the current global economy, and to move towards the establishment of a balanced global economy, is to combat policies of banks seeking to dump people in debt, especially through personal loans and credit cards. Banks in the current economy have over-encouraged the clients to consume more than they can afford to repay. This approach is literally destructive. Therefore, it is imperative to fight greed and stick only to what a person can repay.

Last but not least, the other surgical intervention that must be performed is to reduce the horrific level of imbalance in today's global economy, and to move towards the establishment of a balanced global economy, freeing the world from the monopolies and monopolistic practices of giant corporations. Economic activities monopolized and controlled by a few specific institutions, tightened their grip over the world. Therefore, we must put an end this situation. The first step that contributes to addressing monopolies is for small and medium-sized enterprises to merge, if they are established on bases other than those, which prevailed in recent years, so that they can compete with giant companies. There is no room in today's world for small enterprises; they have to merge into larger entities.

As I call for the world's economy to be saved. I think that the major surgical procedure to be taken is to root out the greedy capitalist approach that devours everything it sees. This is unquestionably the most important current obligation. Capitalism has caused extensive damage to the world economy and caused countless disasters over the past two centuries. These catastrophes included the above-mentioned inflation waves. They also include rising severe depression waves. They caused greed to go up to unprecedented levels. The world has turned today into a wild jungle where there is no place for the weak. Strikingly enough is that in this jungle the situation may flip overnight, even against the strong.

Justice and moderation come at the forefront of the features that should characterize the global economy we seek. Justice is the right of all humankind. We must all admit that the entire human heritage, in all regions, forms and religions, speaks of justice. If justice is not the basis of the economy, let us brace ourselves for inextinguishable disasters and crises. International organizations are primarily responsible for achieving economic justice in the world.

The world tried socialism, which failed. It tried greedy capitalism. It led to crises the effects of which we have experienced. Why do not we try moderation then? It suits all religions. It is our hope to see the ethical moderate school in economics assuming its responsibility and offering applications that combine the fulfillment of aspirations to achieve financial returns and the embodiment of morality. In this regard, I recall that at the General Council of Islamic Banks and Financial Institutions, we have prepared a document on the principles of economic moderation for a fair financial system. We did not issue the document as an "Islamic document", but rather as an easy way to implement and understand moderate document, in order to achieve justice and serve everyone. In this context, it is necessary to set global standards - not ceilings - that govern the new economy, which we want to be moderate and ethical.

229

One of the foundations of this fair and moderate global economy is its link to the element of development and not the element of time. By calculating production and profits, we can determine the real impact. Because the retention by a single party of huge profits and allocating a specific return to the bank, are wrong practices. The bank's domination, on the pretext that its money and its returns are guaranteed, and that it is the party that will bear the consequences, is also wrong. There is no solution for us, then, except in the "growth" of the work in which the money is used, not the period during which it is used. Among the prime duties of the ethical middle school in economics is seeking to restore commercial and financial prosperity in various parts of the world after this long-lasting depression. It must set the rules for central banks to contribute. The central banks should comply with such rules in order for the economy to recover and breathe.

I believe that one of the foundations of the desired global economy is the adoption of a moderate model for the relationship between the public and private sectors, especially with regard to privatization, in which I believe "management" rather than "ownership" is important, so it is not a defect if the government owns a property. The real defect lies with the government managing properties. I said previously that one of the negative symptoms that emerged in the general investment environment is the widening of the gap between the public sector and the private sector. In many countries of our Ummah, the state has insisted on adopting the model of a large, publicly owned and operated sector. On the other hand, the private sector insisted that the safest approach was to adopt the "lean state" model in which the state limits its interventions to basic functions. As for me, I saw the need to "taking a middle position" between these two parties. I deem that the vital issue in privatization is "management", not "ownership". It is not objectionable for the government to own property, but it is objectionable for it to manage it.

This view implies an important control not known to many people. The essence of this control is that the businessman should aim to build his business on his own. He should not count on quick enrichment by purchasing publicly owned companies at a cracked price. This is a dishonest way to get rich.

Rather, it is an enrichment at the expense of others. Indeed, I fear that the call by some for the state's expansion in privatization conceals a desire for easy and quick enrichment. Let the state keep its possession of the companies. The challenge for the private sector is to manage them efficiently. There is no harm in the private sector making a good return from such management.

One of the indications of the success of the businessman is that he does not look at what is in the hands of the government in order to seize, own and sell it and get rich quickly. The reason that led me to advocate privatization was my view that privatization would contribute to reducing "slack administrative structures" and minimize "administrative corruption".

I championed this type of privatization in view of the increased rates of slack administrative structure and administrative corruption, and the absence of a disciplined, ethical governmental system that would hold accountable, punish the abuser, and reward the benefactor. We need privatization in the economic aspects because the state's excessive expansion in the provision of services led to the deprivation of the poor and the disappearance of distinct services. It also led to a move to the private sector, which brings affliction to the poor class who cannot afford to seek such services. Privatization should mean improving management practices to promote services, not selling government property to the private sector. This will eliminate administrative corruption and increase development rates.

Another element that achieves the goal of *istikhlaf* and complements the element of "developing the country" is the revival of the instinct of love of work. In the first place, work is a means of survival. However, at the same time, man fulfills the sense of his humanity through work. Man is naturally inclined to the love of work. Work does not always signify need, but often, it is a demonstration of self-assertiveness and the personal value. All of Prophets of Allah used to work and eat from the work of their own hands. Wasn't Noah, peace be upon him, a carpenter? Wasn't Daoud a blacksmith and a maker of large baskets, palm leaves baskets, and shields? Was not Prophet Ibrahim, peace be upon him, a textile merchant? Wasn't Idrees, peace be upon him, a tailor? Was not the first man, Adam, peace be upon him, a farmer since the beginning when he sowed wheat and ate of it? Did not Prophet Muhammad, may Allah's peace and blessings be upon him, work for a while herding, then as a merchant? Look at the behavior of the Companions, may Allah be pleased with them. When the Muhajireen went with the Prophet, may Allah's peace and blessings be on him, to Madina the Ansar shared their property with them. However, when one of the Ansar wanted to give our master Abdur Rahman bin Auf half of his property, bin Auf thanked him and said: "No, show me the way to the market". Unemployment or the professional begging dispossess a person of part of his humanity. This is what the Noble Qur'an taught us by repeating the concept of good deeds and by linking faith with good deeds. The link between faith and good work was repeated 51 times in the Holy Qur'an including "Indeed, those who believe and do righteous deeds and establish prayer and give Zakat will have their reward with their

Lord, and there will be no fear concerning them, nor will they grieve."
(Al-Baqara 277).

﴿إِنَّ الَّذِينَ آمَنُوا وَعَمِلُوا الصَّالِحَاتِ وَأَقَامُوا الصَّلَا ةَ وَآتَوُ ا الزَّكَاةَ لَهَمْ
أَجْرُهُمْ عِنْدَ رَبِّهِمْ وَلَا خَوْفٌ عَلَيْهِمْ وَلَا هُمْ يَحْزَنُونَ﴾. (البقرة: ٢٧٧)

The Messenger of Allah, may Allah's peace and blessings be on him,
repeated his directives, urging people to desist from begging and to strive
and work even if the work was simple including. "No doubt, you had
better gather a bundle of wood and carry it on your back (and earn your
living thereby) rather than ask somebody who may give you or not."

Unemployment is one of the major reasons of decline of the individual
and the community. If it is said that intoxicating liquor (khamr) is the
"mother" of the gravest sins, I call unemployment the "grandmother" of
gravest sins." Unemployment is the cause of all misfortunes. If unemployment is addressed wisely, the economy will flourish. Unemployment is the
grandmother of major sins because it leads young people to terrorism and
drugs and brings about a sense of despair. It also pushes some to commit
suicide. One of the main reasons for the increase in crime rate among
the unemployed is the feeling of the unemployed that he has no sense of
humanity.

Reviving "the instinct of love of work" is complemented by refreshing
the "intuition of love for employing people" in the minds of businessmen
and financers. The importance of employing the servants of Allah can be
inferred from the noble Ayat. (...and raised some of them above others in
rank that some of them may take labor from others;...)

(...ورفعنا بعضهم فوق بعض درجات ليتخذ بعضهم بعضا سخريا...)

Allah elevates of the rank whomever He wills from among His servants in
order for them to be a reason for providing work for others. The moment
the businessman stops hiring people, the preference will cease to exist.
Once he has no concern other than money-making, he will be among
those whom Allah has promised in His saying: "Woe to every slanderer
and backbiter. Who has gathered wealth and counted it. He thinks that
his wealth will make him last forever! Nay! Verily, he will be thrown into
the crushing Fire. And what will make you know what the crushing Fire
is? The fire of Allah kindled. Which leaps up over the hearts. Verily, it shall
be closed upon them. In pillars stretched forth (i.e. they will be punished
in the Fire with pillars)".

﴿ويل لكل همزة لمزة. الذي جمع مالا وعدده. يحسب أن ماله أخلده. كلا لينبذن في الحطمة. وما أدراك ما الحطمة. نار الله الموقدة. التي تطلع على الأفئدة. إنها عليهم مؤصدة﴾.

The primary duty of businessmen is to employ people. Islam has set priorities in this matter, first with yourself, then with your dependents, your closest next of kin, then those who follow from other relatives, then your neighbor. If every employer, when working on the feasibility study for his business, allocates a number of jobs to citizens, the unemployment problem would be easily eliminated. Government money and businessmen's money is estimated at trillions, so why hadot we use them to create jobs for our children. The real success of every businessman is his ability to "create" projects that realize real development and move the largest number of people from unemployment and slackness to work and giving. Therefore, I mentioned in my speech that I measure my success as an entrepreneur according to the extent of my contribution to the development of the land and according to the magnitude of my contribution to employing people.

The first category worth of employment is that of people with special needs, as it is the most deserving, and the best in terms of the level of performance and results. Many statistics indicate that people with special needs give a perfect performance.

Often, they outperform those who do not sustain a disability. Care must be taken to treat the person with a disability the same way other co-workers are treated, and to avoid indulging in pretense that leads to adverse results. People with special needs have the right to have passages, accesses, etc. prepared for them by the society. However, unfortunately, very few people take care of training and employing people with special needs. Many buildings may be very luxurious, but regrettably, they are not disability friendly. It goes without saying the state must oblige businessmen to employ a specified number of people with special needs. However, from the perspective of the community and businessmen, each one should ask himself: Do I employ people with special needs in implementation of the law, or do I employ them for other considerations higher than the obligation to comply with the law?

However, Islam wants the employer and the jobseeker to understand that creating job opportunities is better and has higher priority than employing people. A job opportunity is different from the job itself.

The preference of independent work over a salaried job could be construed from the Hadith: The Prophet said, "Nobody has ever eaten a better meal than that which one has earned by working with one's own hands. The Prophet of Allah, Dawood used to eat from the earnings of his manual labor." Therefore, the jobseeker, must start by exhausting all available possibilities for a self-employment career before rushing to apply for salaried jobs. He must not give in to the temptations of salaried jobs. On their part the investor, and community mentors such as scholars, thinkers and university professors would do well to direct first the jobseeker to find a job opportunity during which he will be independent. This is taken from a collection of Ayat and Hadiths, including what the Most High said about Dawood peace be upon him "And We taught him the fashioning of coats of armor…"

(وعلمناه صنعة لبوس...).

A workmanship or a craft is an honor and a medal for the individual. I refer here to the Hadith of the Messenger of Allah, may Allah's peace and blessings be on him, in which he told a man to go logging. In this situation, the Messenger of Allah, may Allah's peace and blessings be on him, did not direct the man to join work for others, but rather directed him to undertake an independent job, even if it was simple. There are several applications of the principle of giving priority to job creation over employment.

One of the applications of this principle is to encourage handicrafts and crafts. Before the term "corporate social responsibility" (CSR) was known, Dallah was the first to establish a training institute. Dallah held a graduation ceremony for the first batch of carpenters and bakers, professions that were almost extinct.

Also among its applications is the encouragement of productive families and micro and small enterprises, to allow them to contribute to opening markets for them and enable them to develop their businesses.

Many of these projects are promising and offer really new inputs on a commercial level. The experience of the productive families market and small enterprises, proved o to be very successful in many countries which supported such experience to see the light. During my career, I saw many ideas presented in the form of creative small projects, in which there was a lot of creativity. Through my presidency of the Chamber of Commerce and Industry, I adopted a policy supporting productive families and owners of small and medium industries and providing them with expertise.

We endeavored to train the productive families on how to make their own "brand", how to produce with the same level of quality, and how to certify their methods of manufacture and work, to serve as guidelines for them and for those who succeed them.

Based on the argument that creating an independent job opportunity is more important than working for others, I claim that it is more appropriate for young people who aspire to enter the world of production to give priority to creating their own products, provided that they agree with a manufacturing company to license their product. Leadership is about adding something new. I encourage franchises to motivate young people to think of out of the box to add new franchises, not to get existing franchises especially if the franchise is for a non-local product. If some of the owners of well-known brands in the food and beverages industry encourage and begin to formulate regulations regulating the process of granting trade licenses, they would help create job opportunities for hundreds of unemployed young people who do not like to work as employees but to have their own businesses. This could create thousands of jobs in the Kingdom if we can have four or five such franchises. Throughout my working life I have never tried to franchise a foreign merchandise. Indeed, I have tried to do the opposite, namely making a brand name for a (local) product and try to make a success story. I have done so in the US where I thought our numerous popular foods, like "Muttabaq", which is similar, and even superior, to pizza, and "Mabshour", a popular dish in the Hejaz, which can become a fast-food product, could make international foods. The idea was ripe in my mind. I recruited a fast-food expert to write the recipes. I actually started with opening a restaurant in Los Angeles. Unfortunately, the partner to whom I assigned work and taught, fell ill several months later, so the idea died before I started, because he did not train anyone to work.

Among the applications of the principle of the priority of the opportunity for independent work on the job is that entrepreneurs give control to their children in a timely manner rather than waiting for the last moment. Unfortunately, many people do not give their children control, and treat them, no matter how old they are, as if they are still young children.

Confused after the death of the founding businessman, his children lose what he built for them throughout his life. One of the best things is to educate and train your children in your life. When you feel that they are qualified enough to take on the work, let them take the lead immediately. I retired and let my children run my business, and I let them make mistakes in my life to learn. I have to make it clear that I do not encourage the phenomenon of dividing money in a person's life, Allah has established rights of heirs, so we should not interfere in that.

On a personal level, from a young age I liked self-employment and did not like a salaried job. My father was a government employee with a limited revenue. However, our neighbors in Makkah were merchants and they were well-off. So, I decided not to work in the public sector like my father for fear that my income would be limited. By comparison, I found that self-employment is more rewarding. When I was nine years old, I used to play in Makkah's neighborhoods. One day I went to my mother, may Allah have mercy on her, and asked her to cook *balila* for me.

She wondered, "what are you going to do with *balilah* all alone?". "I will sell it to my friends", I replied. "Shame on you", she said. "No, it is not", I answered. I think that was the beginning, which inculcated in me the love of work and a feeling of pleasure in work and profit. Had I not taken that step that day, working would not have become a hobby for me. This early start was the beginning of my career in self-employment and the beginning of the good that Allah Almighty bestowed upon me. I was the head of the scouting team when I was a high school student in Jeddah. At the time the shops did not sell Scouting supplies and tools except for one in Beirut and another in Egypt. So, I borrowed 3000 riyals from my father, may Allah have mercy on him, and traveled to Beirut, bought the Scouts' supplies and brought them with me. Thereafter, I started putting them in our car's trunk. I would sell them at break times. Sometimes I would go to the other schools to sell them. I think that Scouting is one of the very important activities because of the role it plays in developing the youth with a spirit of seriousness and love of volunteering and helping others.

One of the turning points in my life was my transfer from Cairo University to the Faculty of Commerce at Riyadh University because of my family circumstances. I had to work in my father's profession, Tiwafa during Hajj. The University of Riyadh was a hub for the Riyadh community, so I came to know many government officials, which opened doors for me in my work. I became well known in the Riyadh community at that time. While I was a student at the preparatory, secondary and university levels, I built strong friendships with my professors who were high-ranking officials in several ministries. It was a good start not only for my studies, but also for paving the way for my business. When I was studying at the university, I established a commercial printing press that had a great financial value in my life.

While studying, I engaged in various activities and did not attend classes. I was exhausted at night when I would borrow notebooks from my class-mates to copy summaries of their classes. I wondered about establishing a small printing press and agreeing with the professors to print and publish their classes Thus, I would achieve academic and financial excellence at the same time. Indeed, the idea brewed in my mind, and I took the first steps forward. In those days, there was a wave of leaflets in Riyadh. So, I went to the then head of intelligence, Omar Shams, may Allah have mercy on him, to introduce my idea to him to avoid mixing my publications with the leaflets that were widely circulated at the time. I offered him to paid jobs for intelligence typists after office hours. Three of them were allowed to work with me on the printing of notes. I rented a small shop and began to work there in. Although my dress was stained with black ink every day, I succeeded in selling publications to colleagues, and I benefitted greatly from this experience as I succeeded in creating the first real capital in which I approached my first million. I remember that the cost of this project was 30,000 riyals, and I had more than that amount at the time. Out of the profits of the activity of this office, I bought the first car with my own money.

When we took over the Tawaf Post Project (a project for the transmission and distribution of internal mail), I got acquainted with the entire geography of the Kingdom because I went to all the places that the mail reached. I measured the distances, the gasoline consumption, and the number of driving hours, to keep an eye on the drivers. Afterwards. I entered into a cleaning project in Jeddah. It was the first time for companies to have a share in this matter, as it was always in the hands of the government. We worked in it for several years. I remember that on Eid-eves when people go to visit relatives and friends, my brothers and I would stand by the street, given that on the eve of Eid gift wastes multiply. They were estimated at several tons. We had to move them from the city center so that when people come the next day would find the place clean. Together with my brothers, Dr. Hassan Kamel and Dr. Omar Kamel, I used to oversee the work. When I had enough experience, I launched Dallah.

At the time, and as it is today, the government was the largest client of the private sector. Therefore, we focused on the services sector for a while. After we established ourselves in this area, we started to focus on industry and non-government matters. Later, we tried to work in everything that is halal in the world, and we left no stone unturned. The major breakthrough that Allah graced me with was the signing of a contract with the Ministry of Air Defense in the 1970s. After Allah, the All-Mighty, the credit goes to Prince Sultan, may Allah have mercy on him, and grant him peace in his vast gardens. These are some of the landmarks of my journey with self-employment and with starting a business.

I was so fed-up with salaried jobs, and my love of self-employment and establishing new businesses, to the extent that I could not tolerate the restrictions of the manager's job even in my own company.

I mooned over starting a new business, so it defined my life. As soon as the new business I have established ripens, I start longing for launching another business. I was not made to be a traditional manager. One of the motives of the love of self-employment and the love of establishing new businesses is the strong feeling that one must offer an added value to the world as long as one is alive. Whoever is given an insight, and the ability to explore and lead, has received abundant good. It is important for him to learn how to develop that insight and how to refine it. Insight is common among all young people, but it comes with self-knowledge, without hesitation or recklessness, in making a decision. Indeed, self-knowledge is one of the three keys to success. It is striking that many people reach forty or fifty years old without knowing themselves. The other two keys are Allah-fearing (And whosoever keepeth his duty to Allah, Allah will appoint a way out for him and provide for him from where he does not expect) and the parent's pleasure)

{ومن يتق الله يجعل له مخرجا ويرزقه من حيث لا يحتسب}.

At any rate, I think that the next stage, if Allah wills, will witness a shift from the limited salaried jobs to self-employment. With the help of Allah, creativity and promoting self-productive energies will dominate the market. Many employees will turn into entrepreneurs and professionals.

I took a job during my youth just to gain experience, not to stay in the career ladder forever. Following my graduation, I engaged in government work at the Ministry of Finance for ten years during which I worked in the office of financial representation as a financial representative. During those years, I passed through all the ministries of the Kingdom in Riyadh, and acted as delegate to the governmental departments in Makkah, Madinah, and Jeddah. So, I went through all the ministries and learned about the small details of government work. This experience allowed me to learn from inside. However, I was still determined not to continue in government work.

Proper qualification and training are conditions for a successful work system in society. When a poor man came to the Prophet, may Allah's peace and prayers be on him, asking (for assistance), the Prophet, may Allah's peace and prayers be on him, asked him to bring something from his house. He offered it for sale. Then, he sold it for two dirhams. He told him to use the money to buy food for his family, and an ax and go logging. He taught him how to cut wood. He also instructed him to go and sell the wood. In this shirt story, the Prophet, may Allah's peace and prayers be on him, gave a lesson on financing, education, training and follow-up. Proper training falls within the scope of social responsibility of companies and businessmen.

When the instinct of love of work and employment fades in a society, "mendicancy", which is discouraged by all divine religions, including the final one, spreads widely at the individual level, more than in other societies. Consequently, the state gets used to "begging" other states, falling in the abyss of debts. With the decline in the love of work and employment, work rates in the country recede. Accordingly, the unemployed start begging. The dire effects of the decline in the love of work and employment are not limited to the unemployed, but extend to some of those who have a job but have given in to laziness and become addicted to consumption, luxury and entertainment. Therefore, they exert pressure on the state or businessmen to grant them aid while they are not eligible for aid and able to work. This aid takes the form of grants and the cancellation of debts usually caused by borrowing for lavish consumption. It also takes the form of wage increases without a corresponding increase in production. This is one of the forbidden forms of begging included in the Hadiths of the Messenger of Allah, may Allah's peace and blessings be on him, in which he says: Allah has hated for you three things: -1. Vain talks, (useless talk) that you talk too much or about others. -2. Wasting of wealth (by extravagance) -3. And asking too many questions (in disputed religious matters) or asking others for something (except in great need). When all this happens frequently at the individual level, general productivity decreases, the state competitiveness declines, official spending on undue items increases and the currency weakens, so the state tends to borrow.

Consequently, I repeat in my statements that if we contemplate and understand well the Hadith of the Prophet, may Allah's peace and blessings be on him, in which he says, "Seeking earning is an obligation" (weak Hadith narrated by Tabarani), we would not need any aid from the wealthy states, but rather we would have counted among the rich states .

Responsibility for the decline in the love of work and employment and the spread of unemployment lies with all the stakeholders.

First, the responsibility lies with many young people. Every young man wants a car and high salary effortlessly. We must reduce the extravagant and wasteful habits in society. The social requirements of the young Saudi should not be exaggerated. I believe that contentment and ambition are two wings indispensable for a bird to fly.

Although contentment and ambitions seem to contradict each other, the opposite is true. Contentment is satisfaction. It represents a psychological state that leads gradually to reassurance. To be satisfied with my situation does not mean that I should not seek to improve it. This is what ambition is about! The wise Muslim moves forward with his ambition on his right and satisfaction on his left in two parallel but inseparable lines. He continues to exert efforts and persists in his endeavors. This is a source of peace and certainty to the soul. Big dreams should always be entertained, while delivery should be according to the ability. Trying to realize dreams in one fell swoop causes one to lose everything. On a personal level, I do not remember ever in my life complaining about the limited financial resources while growing up even though I aspired from an early age to be a merchant and a businessman. Indeed, I endeavored to improve my financial situation whenever I had the chance. As I mentioned above, I was brought up in a family that could not even be described as a middle-income family. Indeed, I was closer to poverty than to richness. However, thanks to Allah and then to my parents, contentment prevailed in our house. At the same time, satisfaction did not prevent us from dreaming of improving the reality in which we grew up. Whining and expressing grief represents a lack of acceptance of the Act of Allah. They do not befit a Muslim and lead only to a life marred by constant anxiety, desiring what others have, envy and greed that sicken the heart.

Second, pampering their children excessively, some parents also share the responsibility for the decline in love of work and employment and the spread of unemployment. Spoiling children produced an exaggerated tendency with the youth to indulge in luxury and entertainment, even if the time and place are no longer the same with their inability to do what used to.

Third, some businessmen share the responsibility for the decline in the love of work and employment and the spread of unemployment. Unfortunately, some businessmen do not give the citizen a priority and do not realize that their main duty is to employ people. Islam has set priorities in this regard, beginning with yourself, your dependents, your closest relatives then your neighbor.

Fourth, most banks, including Islamic banks, are responsible for the decline in the love of work and employment and the spread of unemployment. Instead of investing the huge liquidity available to them in labor-intensive projects, or even in projects with medium employment rates, most banks resort to trading in goods, buying and selling, just to achieve profits to increase their equity. The outcome of such investment solutions, in my opinion, is not in line with the purposes of Sharia, even if they are permissible. My experience in the world of banking allowed me to see banking practices that do not bring real developmental returns, especially at the level of employment, such as trading in international goods, which does not add any real value other than profits.

Islamic banks are investing $300 billion in western copper markets. What did the people reap from that? For Allah's sake, consider the number of workers for whom you can open up jobs if this amount is invested in labor-intensive projects or even projects with medium employment rates. I also hope that you would imagine the number of individuals for whom you can create "independent job opportunities" on the sidelines of these projects (transportation services - food services - industrial products, etc.). Therefore, I recommend you to think about the numbers of the dependents who will be paid for by those who are employed or given independent job opportunities (families and relatives). After estimating these numbers, please also guess the number of individuals that these workers will assist in establishing new businesses. Please also figure out the size and value of the innovations that some of these workers would come up with in their work in factories and laboratories. Can you perceive the volume of development being missed for failing to invest in a way that would raise employment rates? Do you imagine the amount of opportunity cost associated with it? After estimating this loss, please consider the number of crimes that some of these individuals would have committed if they remain in the quagmire of unemployment and idleness, which high rate of employment could prevent. Can you see the magnitude of the socio-economic impact of this investment option?

I believe that some investment options, even if not prohibited, may produce indirect damages that the perpetrators are responsible for at the individual and collective levels. Although some of those options do meet Shariah requirements, such as trading in copper, their outcome is not acceptable to Shariah.

Fifth, the community itself shares the responsibility. There is a wrong cultural norm in the Saudi society based on the conviction that if a Saudi young plumber with an up to 30,000 riyals income, and a 3000-riyal-salary university graduate, propose to my daughter, I will welcome the university graduate and reject the plumber. This is a shallow culture. A decent educated plumber is better in this case than a university graduate who is educated but cannot work with the knowledge he has acquired. There is nothing wrong with any honest profession. As I said, most of Allah's Prophets had professions. Among them were the carpenter, the blacksmith and the tailor, and our Prophet, may Allah's prayers and peace be upon him, was a shepherd and a trader. So why do we look down to honest professions? This wrong cultural norm puts pressure on the youth. It did not exist in our generation.

I remember from my early childhood up to my adolescence that most of the people we dealt with in various professions and fields were Saudis. The butcher was a Saudi, as were the beans vendor and the carpenter and the barber... Even donkeys and sheep shearers... The shoemaker and the maker of *mutabaq* and the pastry, all were countrymates with whom, we lived together. None of them felt ashamed from their profession. They used to teach their children their profession, not repulsing them from it as long as it obviated the need for begging. Today, however, we despised professions and professionals until they deserted their jobs. They abandoned their fathers' craftsmanship to the expatriates to multiply, while our affluent sons turned up their noses and did not even think about participating or taking the initiative.

Sixth, the decline in the love of work and employment and the spread of unemployment may also be attributed to planning policies and the way some of them are implemented. A case in point is the method of implementing the Saudization policy. I do not find fault with Saudization per se, but rather the way we handle it. It was treated emotionally. There was no sufficient preparation for young people to take interest in all works as long as they were honest. There are many professions that Saudis do not accept and refuse to practice, primarily manual labor. We must prepare the society culturally and psychologically for the Saudi youth to accept such professions and not to despise them. There are professions that Saudis do not accept, so how can we Saudize them If we do not prepare the society culturally to accept this issue? It is not logical to Saudize professions which we know will not be sought by Saudis. One of the defective policies encountered is the policy relating to the vocational education system. We have offered vocational education in institutes that are only accessible to those who failed to get good high school scores that qualify them to join other public universities or institutes.

Our youth have been negatively affected by this practice. Some of them refuse to work as a mechanic in a workshop for 4,000 riyals, preferring rather to be a typist for 1,000 riyals. Billions were spent on the vocational education system and the end-result has been a fiasco. There is no good in knowledge that is not beneficial. Unfortunately, education in our Saudi society has become a social status or a social pass. We value the certificate, not its holder and we no longer respect handicrafts.

Seventh, some of the unbalanced interpretations found in the discourse of some preachers, especially those spread in some Muslim countries, are partially responsible for the decline in the love of work and employment and the spread of unemployment. For example some interpretations of the Tradition of the Prophet, may Allah's peace and blessings be on him, do not reflect a comprehensive understanding of what was narrated about the Prophet, may Allah's peace and blessings be on him, praying to be gathered with the group of the needy (on the Day of Resurrection), without relating that to the fact that the Prophet, may Allah's peace and blessings be on him worked in trade, made profits, distributed dividends and worked for our Mother Khadija, may Allah be pleased with her, in her trade. He did not stay without work and was not without ambition. The consequence of not connecting the two matters is that some people stop cherishing ambitions and pursing the quest for sustenance.

This understanding is the fruit of a journey that spanned for more than forty years in trade and investment in about forty-two countries, and in Islamic banking, of which I was a pioneer, and in chambers of commerce, formulating policies and proposing legislations.

In this book, I present the overall principles that underpin this understanding, the most prominent findings of an evaluation of the Islamic banking experience, and the salient conclusions of evaluating the investment environment in our country. The presentation of these general principles is also followed by a very brief presentation of the new investment models that Allah guided me to formulate, which embody those principles, such as the mega investment bank, the participatory exchange for development and employment (MAQSF).

INDEX

INDEX:

INDEX: